Undesirable

Other Works by Laura Kalpakian

Fiction

The Great Pretenders
Three Strange Angels
The Music Room
A Christmas Cordial and Other Stories
American Cookery
The Memoir Club
Educating Waverley
Steps and Exes
The Delinquent Virgin and Other Stories
Caveat
Cosette: A Sequel to Les Misérables
Graced Land
Dark Continent and Other Stories
Fair Augusto and Other Stories
These Latter Days
Crescendo
Beggars and Choosers

Nonfiction

Memory into Memoir: A Handbook for Writers
The Unruly Past: Memoirs

UNDESIRABLE

The Vietnam War and a Father's Battle for Justice

LAURA KALPAKIAN

UNIVERSITY OF NEW MEXICO PRESS | ALBUQUERQUE

ISBN 978-0-8263-6979-6 (paper)
ISBN 978-0-8263-6980-2 (ePub)

Library of Congress Control Number: 2025054607

Founded in 1889, the University of New Mexico sits on the traditional homelands of the Pueblo of Sandia. The original peoples of New Mexico—Pueblo, Navajo, and Apache—since time immemorial have deep connections to the land and have made significant contributions to the broader community statewide. We honor the land itself and those who remain stewards of this land throughout the generations and also acknowledge our committed relationship to Indigenous peoples. We gratefully recognize our history.

Cover illustration: courtesy of *TIME* magazine
Designed by Felicia Cedillos
Composed in Adobe Caslon Pro

This book is for Paul Kleinwachter.

Captain Kleinwachter, if you will save my son from the fires of hell I will be eternally grateful. Perhaps someday the time will come somewhere, sometime, somehow, either thru me or mine, I will be able to repay you in some way.

Bill Johnson
July 19, 1970

It is a wise father that knows his own child. Well, old man, I
will tell you news of your son. Give me your blessing; truth
will come to light.

WILLIAM SHAKESPEARE, *The Merchant of Venice*,
ACT II, SCENE 2

Contents

PART I

<table>
<tr><td colspan="2">A Playlist B</td></tr>
<tr><td>Feel Like I'm Fixin' to Die Rag</td><td>COUNTRY JOE AND THE FISH</td></tr>
<tr><td>For What It's Worth</td><td>BUFFALO SPRINGFIELD</td></tr>
<tr><td>(Four Dead in) Ohio</td><td>CROSBY, STILLS, NASH & YOUNG</td></tr>
<tr><td>My Back Pages</td><td>BOB DYLAN, THE BYRDS</td></tr>
<tr><td>Draft Morning</td><td>THE BYRDS</td></tr>
<tr><td>Turn! Turn! Turn!</td><td>THE BYRDS (VIA PETE SEEGER AND ECCLESIASTES 3)</td></tr>
<tr><td>Where Have all the Flowers Gone?</td><td>PETER, PAUL AND MARY</td></tr>
</table>

1. The Sandal

<u>Late August 1970</u>

McChord Air Force Base, Washington, sprawls in the shadow of Mount Rainer, a distant, brooding volcano, snow-covered even in late summer. Bill Johnson, having passed through security protocols, stands on the tarmac, awaiting the plane that will bring his twenty-year-old son Douglas home. Doug should have rotated out of Vietnam on June 9, 1970, after serving there for a full year. Now it is almost September. These past three months have been an unending nightmare for Bill and his wife, Peggy. They have spent their nights in a sleepless cauldron of fear and their days writing and typing increasingly desperate letters, relentlessly importuning members of Congress, the White House, the Army brass—anyone who might listen or heed—seeking information about their son, who had seemingly vanished into a void of silence. In mid-June they learned that Doug had gone AWOL in Cambodia and that he had been caught and arrested. But for that entire summer, they did not know if he was in military prison (again), or possibly hospitalized with malaria and hepatitis (again), if the Army was going to court-martial him (again), and, if so, when. For a time they did not even know the exact charges against him. And, given Doug's heavy drug use, they did not know if he was completely strung out or hopped-up or otherwise crazed or comatose—in Bill's words, "turned into a vegetable."

The only reliable word they have had of their son comes from Captain

Paul Kleinwachter, Doug's randomly assigned defense lawyer for his second court-martial, which is pending. After a summer of grueling uncertainty, Captain Kleinwachter has informed Doug's parents that their son will take an Undesirable discharge "for the good of the service" so that he need not face this second court-martial. It means, thank God, that Doug can be out of the Army altogether. He can come home. *At last*, Bill Johnson tells himself as he sees the plane approach. *He's home. My boy is home. The nightmare is at an end.* The plane circles, lands, taxies, and comes slowly to a halt.

Bill Johnson is a trim fifty-two-year-old man with a broad forehead, a round face, green eyes, and a shock of gray hair. Mindful of appearances, he is carefully attired in a suit and tie. Ordinarily, and as part of his job as a pharmaceutical salesman, Bill exudes reflexive bonhomie, but not here, not now. His every nerve is fraught with relief and fear: relief that his son is coming home at last, fear of what fourteen months in Vietnam have done to his boy, who is returning like a criminal, under guard. Bill watches the metal stairs being wheeled up to the door of the plane. The door swings open and uniformed men disembark one after the other. Finally a ravaged figure wobbles down the steps. Doug Johnson is skinny and stooped. His dark eyes are empty whorls; his hair is longish, unkempt; his chin is stubbled, his skin pale, almost gray.

Bill bolts forward and enfolds his son in his arms, both men crying as they hold one another. When at last they step slightly back, Bill sees that Doug is holding a dirty sandal. The young man gives a wan smile. His teeth are a mess. Little over a year ago Doug Johnson was a piano prodigy, an Eagle Scout, a good Mormon boy, a kid with charisma to spare. Now, clutching the sandal, he moves with an uncertain tread, as though, Bill thinks, he might at any moment step on a booby trap, as if he might be blown to bits.

From McChord Air Force Base Bill accompanies Doug and his guard to Fort Lewis, only a few miles away. There, in a utilitarian building, Doug is granted formal leave to go to the Rodeway Inn in Tacoma with his father. His leave will extend to 0800 hours the following day, August 24.

At the hotel, as best Bill can make out from Doug's erratic speech, he learns that the sandal belonged to a dead Viet Cong, a man his son had killed. Doug will not be parted from the sandal. Bill pleads with him: *Please. Please. Please. Don't let your mother see this.* At last Doug yields up the sandal.

He won't be carrying it when he sees his mother, and she won't have to see the tracks up and down his arms from shooting heroin and mainlining speed, at least not then. Bill has thought ahead and brought a long-sleeved shirt. It hangs oddly off Doug's frame; he weighs fifty pounds less than when he joined the Army the previous year. His toes are black with fungus. His body is peppered with sores from jungle rot. The nightmare of the last fourteen months may be over, but Bill knows that another is just beginning.

At 0800 the following day father and son return to Fort Lewis for Doug to begin the processing that will release him from military service. This includes a brief physical in which the Army takes his weight and does a serology and a urinalysis. They might have added these results to his medical records, except that the soldier who guarded Doug from Vietnam to McChord has somehow lost them. This health and financial paperwork is nowhere to be found.

The following day, August 25, Doug signs the last official papers that will release him from the Army. One of them cautions of his "Expulsion from United States Military Reservation" and provides a long list of dire consequences should he ever again step foot in Fort Lewis. No need to worry: Doug Johnson has no wish to go anywhere near the Army again. N. H. Carter, Acting Assistant Adjutant General, also signs it. The release papers note that Doug is leaving the Army "Under other than honorable circumstances" and bear the printed admonition *Save This Paper. It's Important.* And then N. H. Carter hands Doug Johnson his official discharge.

To see oneself declared UNDESIRABLE would undermine the psyche of the strongest person. Whatever its effects on Doug Johnson's interior life in August 1970, this document means that in future he will not have access to any veterans benefits: not medical, not educational, not a path to home ownership. Indeed, it means that he will be barred from many professions, even from many jobs. It means, in short, that his military service was for naught: that from his twenty months serving his country no recognition will accrue, no regard, no respect, no medals, *nada*, unless you count the sandal he brought back and the jungle rot crawling across his body.

"My son enlisted and has served his year in VN. He deserves an Honorable Discharge," Bill Johnson had written in July to George Romney, Secretary of Housing and Urban Development, "but at this point I cannot and do

UNDESIRABLE
DISCHARGE

FROM THE ARMED FORCES OF THE
UNITED STATES OF AMERICA

THIS IS TO CERTIFY THAT

DOUGLAS SCOTT JOHNSON   PRIVATE E-1   REGULAR ARMY

WAS DISCHARGED FROM THE

UNITED STATES ARMY

ON THE __25TH__ DAY OF __August 1970__

AS UNDESIRABLE

N. H. CARTER
CPT   ADA

DD FORM 258A

GPO 917708

not really care as long as he comes home now. I will pay his medical and psychiatric costs. I want my boy home and exonerated." So now, at the end of summer, 1970, Doug is home. But exonerated? No.

Exoneration will test Bill Johnson's courage and endurance. Exoneration will oblige Bill Johnson to fight the slow, grinding bureaucratic machinery of the United States Army for three years. Exoneration will mean that the burden of proof rests repeatedly on Bill who will indomitably insist that the

Undesirable was undeserved—more than that, unjust: that his son is due an Honorable discharge.

William J. Johnson was my father. He used his pen like a weapon in his battle against the Army, three years of unrelenting activism on behalf of my brother, Douglas.

• • •

Father and son return home to San Bernardino, California, where Doug's mother, Peggy, his younger sister, Helen, his little brother, Brian, and his fiancée await him. Thirty-six hours later, the Johnsons have Doug admitted to Loma Linda University Medical Center, about fifteen miles away. He will be a patient there for ten days. His father visits him daily; they sit on the hospital lawn and talk. Doug sobs, recounting what he saw, what he did, what was done to him, what his father will later call "acts incompatible with his conscience." Loma Linda medical staff find Doug to be suffering from malnutrition, an enlarged liver and spleen, anemia, rotting gums, jungle rot on extensive swaths of his body, and the remnants of ringworm. Repeated bouts of malaria and hepatitis have shattered his constitution, to say nothing of what drugs have done to him. So physically compromised is Doug Johnson's health that the presiding doctor writes he could not have lived another six months in those conditions. At Loma Linda Doug is also put under psychiatric care. Following his release, his parents engage a private psychiatrist for him. This professional's description reads in part that Doug is "psychiatrically extremely disturbed. His diagnosis at the present time must be considered psychotic depressive reaction chronic, very severe."

Doug's medical care, both in the hospital and after his release, puts staggering financial burdens on my parents, expenses that must somehow be paid from the wages of a salesman and a secretary. But other burdens accrue from the Undesirable beyond the financial: burdens not as easily measured, burdens that will take a terrible toll on this family—my family—that will mire my father in a years-long fight and mire all of us in the unforgiving slough of Doug's drug addiction for decades.

For thirty years Doug remained a drug addict, beset as well with post-traumatic stress disorder (PTSD) and bouts of mental illness. No one whose life touches that of a drug addict is immune or indemnified. He caused pain to his family and the people who cared about him. He was in and out of hospitals and rehab clinics, returning to drug abuse again and again. Arrested and jailed on drug charges, judicial ineptitude or sheer luck meant those charges were dropped. He was unstable. His rages and breakdowns were unpredictable and terrible to behold. He made frequent raucous, drunken phone calls, blathering rants about his sex life. He was high, buzzing, drunk, destructive, uncaring, and without scruples. My parents' house was burgled more than once, possibly with Doug's connivance. He was pursued by violent drug dealers to whom he owed money. On one occasion these men threatened Doug through people in his family. He wrecked cars and lives, including his own. He could not hold any kind of job for more than a few months. He was sometimes homeless. He sometimes stood on street corners, rattling a can with loose change in it. He hit up assorted family friends and associates, sometimes going to their homes and outright asking for cash, a smiling, smarmy, unsettling presence at the front door or in the waiting room of the family dentist. *Oh, yes, just a loan. I'll wait.* Although he retained—when he wished to exert it—the ability to be affable and occasionally charming, his time in Vietnam left Doug Johnson brutally scarred, his life blighted and his gifts wasted.

At the heart of this book lies a tragedy: not a death memorialized on a granite wall, but the loss of a life that might have been. Before Vietnam, Doug Johnson was a young man of promise, musically gifted, endowed with charm and personality, attractive to women and admired by many. After Vietnam, Doug floundered for thirty years. He became truly undesirable to many people who loved him or who wanted to love him but finally had to distance themselves. His lies, his rages, his bullshit, his return to the needle strewed sorrow, disbelief, fear, and anger among all those whose lives touched his.

And yet there was one person, his mother, who never ceased to excuse his relapses or to applaud his short-lived milestones. He broke her heart more than once, but she never wavered. Time and again she wrapped him in a mantle of love and unblinking forgiveness. One evening at dusk in 1972, from the kitchen window Mom and twenty-year old Helen watched Doug get out of a strange car and start up the driveway toward the house, waving a gun, ranting wildly, rabid with rage. (Mercifully, Dad wasn't home.) Helen wanted to call the police, but Mom forbade it. "He won't hurt me," Mom promised her. "You hide in the hall." Helen did, sitting on the floor, knees pressed to her chest, terrified, while Mom opened the door, stepped onto the porch, and barred Doug's entrance. Helen was too terrified to remember what was said between them, but Mom kept him on the porch, talked him down, and Doug finally left without shooting Mom or anyone else. That doesn't mean she wasn't hurt.

. . .

The underlying irony—or whatever it is that makes one look back and marvel that so much could have hinged upon so little—is that all this stemmed from what amounted to a spasm of adolescent swagger following a fight with his parents.

Doug Johnson, like all the young men of his generation, faced the prospect of being drafted after he graduated from San Bernardino High School in 1967. To be drafted in the late 1960s almost surely meant being sent to Vietnam. To evade the draft a young man had choices. He could hotfoot it north to Canada where, the word was, there was work available near Upper Slave Lake. Or he could drink a half bottle of Jack Daniels, prop his foot up on a chair, and aim a loaded gun at his big toe and shoot. Or confess he was a homosexual. Or get a shrink to swear he was too mentally ill to kill people. (I knew or knew of men who used these and even weirder tactics.) More simply, he could be a full-time college student. Doug was enrolled at Valley College, the local two-year school. All he had to do to avoid the draft was to carry sixteen units.

Then he dropped a class.

When his parents found out, a huge row ensued. Bill raged at his son for stupidity while Peggy sat by tearfully. As the fight escalated, Doug declared he was going to enlist. At that, Bill urged him to try the Navy, in which he had served in World War II. Doug refused. Bill wanted to go with Doug to the recruitment center, to steer him toward some branch of the service that would offer him training, skills he could use later. Doug refused.

Two days before his nineteenth birthday in January 1969, Doug strode into the Army Recruitment Center on Union Street and enlisted in the 4th Infantry under the auspices of a Sergeant Lopez, who no doubt saluted him and said, "Welcome, soldier." When I picture this scene, I hear the bleakly whimsical lyrics of the popular song, "It Looks Like I'm Fixin' to Die Rag" by Country Joe and the Fish, about the half-assed kid who's off to Vietnam. Whoopee!

January 1969 was the first month of President Richard Nixon's first term in office. By January 1970, another ten thousand Americans had died in Vietnam. Opposition to the war intensified, gathering momentum as casualty lists mounted and as newspaper coverage and footage on the network news showed appalling close-ups of the fighting. A Vietnamese soldier executed point-blank, a bullet to the head. Bombs dropping on villages and villagers. Great swaths of landscape defoliated by Agent Orange. Revulsion against the war on the home front took the form of noisy political unrest: well-planned, large-scale antiwar marches, what one of my history professors called, "a petition in boots." In autumn 1969 a vast coalition of peace activists planned a nationwide Moratorium, a day of strikes and marches where the cry everywhere was *No More Business As Usual!* In one concerted moment, people across the country were exhorted to walk off their jobs and bring their feet and voices to antiwar demonstrations. People who feared they would lose their jobs if they walked out in protest were asked to wear black armbands to work. Peggy Johnson was secretary to a pompous, portly insurance agent and his self-important son-in-law, vocal supporters of Nixon and the Vietnam War. My mother wore a black armband that day. The office was tense.

The fact that my brother was a soldier in Vietnam heightened the stakes for my own participation in these marches. I was a graduate student in history living on the East Coast. At the Moratorium in Washington, DC, I joined a large, vocal, mostly but not wholly youthful throng, a quarter million strong. We chanted, *What do we want? Peace! When do we want it? Now!* Nixon had called out the National Guard and tensions were high. Armed soldiers stood three and four deep before sandbagged government offices, facing us, their expressions stoic. Military vehicles swarmed everywhere, and National Guardsmen patrolled the streets and intersections.

Six months later, May 4, 1970, the National Guard, called to an antiwar protest at Kent State University in Ohio, opened fire on a group of protesters, killing four. Soon after, the doleful anthem "(Four Dead in) Ohio" by Crosby, Stills, Nash & Young blared from radios nationwide. On May 15 at Jackson State College in Mississippi, a predominately Black school, city police and state highway patrolmen opened fire on students, blasting a dormitory with gunfire, killing two men, wounding twelve others. Outrage at these campus killings engulfed the American public as photographs captured the unthinkable sights of a girl kneeling beside a body in a pool of blood at Kent State and the bullet-blasted dorm at Jackson State. The May 25, 1970, issue of *Time* magazine carried the photo of that dorm, labeling it "Kent State II."

My parents were longtime subscribers to *Time*, and my mom even subscribed for me, living far away. This May 25 issue will figure—both directly and obliquely—in my brother's story. In its pages there is a long, laudatory review of the book *My Lai* by Seymour Hersh, based on his Pulitzer Prize–winning journalism. Through Hersh's dispatches the public had learned the unthinkable particulars of the massacre two years before, 1968, when hundreds of women, children, and old men were slaughtered by American GIs in the Vietnamese village of My Lai. This issue also ran a five-page spread detailing the Nixon Administration's announcement—or, more correctly, their belated admission—that US troops were invading Cambodia, chasing the Viet Cong under "Operation Pacify West One." However grandiose that title, the actual headline reads: "Cambodia: Now It's 'Operation Buy Time.'" *Time* quotes President Nixon himself in their opening paragraph. In speaking to a conference of governors, Nixon remarked that the invasion of Cambodia "ought to be called 'Operation Buy Time.'" This is a demeaning description of an undertaking that would cost lives, young men who would never be coming home. *Time*'s coverage included map inserts and photographs. Spread across pages 30 and 31, a color photo taken by Italian photographer Ennio Iacobucci shows eleven anonymous soldiers of the 4th Infantry. These young men shamble side by side, awaiting a helicopter to take them to fight in Cambodia. A portion of this vintage photograph graces the cover of this book: Doug Johnson is second from the left, the one with the head covering, flashing the peace sign and a smile.

When Mom opened this magazine and saw this photo, she started to scream. Doug was within twenty days of DEROS [Date of Estimated Return from Overseas], when he ought to have rotated out of Vietnam and come home. Instead, his parents now knew he had been sent to Cambodia. They were desperate for news. They had heard nothing from him, no letters for months. And now Doug fell into an unfathomable void.

In mid-June, through the Red Cross, his parents found out he did not fight in Cambodia. He went AWOL. He had been arrested and sent to the notorious Long Binh jail, where he had been a prisoner before. In July 1970 he was released from LBJ and returned to his unit at Camp Radcliff, where he faced a court-martial, his second. He went AWOL again. Bill Johnson spent that whole summer of 1970 writing increasingly frenzied letters, sending telegrams, making phone calls, cage-rattling, demanding, pleading with the Army, with Congressmen, senators, White House aides, the US Vice President, Cabinet officers, Mormon chaplains for information about Doug, scrambling to learn what the charges were against him and when the trial would be held. He implored these people to take action to save his son from "the pangs of hell," from "becoming a vegetable." He literally begged for mercy at the same time that he accused the Army of injustice and "premeditated murder of my son."

In mid-July 1970 Captain Paul Kleinwachter, Doug's assigned defense counsel, opened communication with Bill Johnson. Even though what Captain Kleinwachter told the parents was appalling, his letters were a ray of light amid the darkness, giving Bill and Peggy information about their son and his situation from someone who actually knew him, saw him frequently—someone who was clearly on Doug's side. Dad barraged Captain Kleinwachter with letters and, when he could, phone calls. Many of his letters audaciously instructed that "confinement must be suspended. I repeat, confinement must be suspended." He wrote this even though he knew from Captain Kleinwachter that this second court-martial would likely result in a prison sentence, returning Doug to Long Binh Jail, a hell he had already visited.

But that second court-martial never took place. In lieu of it, Private Doug Johnson opted to take the Undesirable discharge "for the good of the service." This meant he could leave the Army in late August of 1970: that he could be on a plane, under guard, flying out of what he would later term "that wretched country" to McChord Air Force Base, where he would stagger into his father's arms clutching a dead man's sandal.

2. The Safe

Someone smarter than I once observed that, historically speaking, the end of one era is the beginning of another, but the people living through it are only aware of the end. It seems to me that politically the end of the tumultuous 1960s took place in series of events that has come to be known simply as Watergate. Watergate began with an attempted break-in at the Democratic National Headquarters on June 17, 1972, and spiraled out in a long swirl of unthinkable venality and corruption and a cover-up by men in the top rungs of government, men who were later convicted of conspiracy, including John Mitchell, once the face of the Justice Department—indeed, the Attorney General of the United States—who was sent to prison for his role. Another man convicted of conspiracy in the Watergate scandal, Assistant Attorney General of the United States Robert C. Mardian, would be essential to my father's battle with the Army. In the summer of 1972—the most crucial and convoluted, even the most tragic of Mardian's long, eventful life—he would aid Bill Johnson in his fight to exonerate Doug. My parents, indeed our whole family, believe that without Mardian's influence Dad's efforts to get the Undesirable changed, however strenuous, would have failed.

After Doug came home his father learned of circumstances that convinced him that the Undesirable was undeserved, unjust, unfairly foisted upon a young soldier who was mentally and physically shattered. Bill Johnson began a furious campaign to see that Doug was given an Honorable or a Medical discharge. From the autumn of 1970 until spring 1972, he battled unsuccessfully with three different military tribunals. After those defeats, in

June 1972—driven by some fateful combination of delusion and desperation—he cold-called Robert Mardian's Washington, DC, home and asked him to act as Doug's attorney. Bill approached Mardian on the basis of the ethnic heritage he shared with Doug's mother, Peggy, an Armenian born as Pakradouhi Kalpakian in Constantinople, Turkey, in 1922 and just a toddler when her family emigrated to Los Angeles in 1923.

Robert Mardian's Armenian father had fled Turkey in 1912 and established himself in Pasadena, California, founding the Mardian Construction Company. He had four sons and one daughter. Robert, the youngest, was born in 1923. He served in the Navy during World War II and graduated from the University of Southern California Law School in 1949. He practiced corporate law. His brothers had a prosperous construction business in Phoenix, and the Mardians were active in high circles of Republican politics. A conservative, rock-ribbed Republican, Robert Mardian acted as Richard Nixon's 1968 campaign manager for the western states. When Nixon came to power, Mardian moved to DC and served the administration in various important posts, including in the Justice Department as Assistant Attorney General of the United States. In May 1972 he left the Justice Department to become counsel to the Committee for the Re-Election of the President (CREEP). There, Robert Mardian joined all the President's men, including former Attorney General of the United States John Mitchell, CREEP's director.

The five men arrested for the actual, abortive Watergate break-in on June 17, 1972, were allied with CREEP; in fact, they had ties to the White House itself. A vast conspiracy unfolded to conceal this connection from the public. Slowly the allegations and extent of the conspiracy came to light through the journalistic feats of Bob Woodward and Carl Bernstein of the *Washington Post*, followed in summer 1973 by long televised sessions of Senate testimony that held the nation horrified and spellbound. On March 1, 1974, a grand jury brought indictments against those involved in the criminal cover-up. Robert Mardian was one of those charged, and in January 1975 he was convicted of conspiracy. He was given a prison sentence but served no time while he appealed. The appeal was eventually successful, and in 1976 the Special Prosecutor declined to retry his case. But the damage to his reputation remained as a Watergate conspirator.

I do not know how my father found Mardian's home number, and I can't even imagine what that conversation was like. I also cannot imagine why Robert Mardian did not tell Bill Johnson to butt out and go to hell. But he didn't. He intervened, gently, subtly guiding Doug Johnson's case and the copious materials my father had assembled into competent hands. In December 1972, the Army Board for Correction of Military Records amended Doug's Undesirable—not to the wished-for Honorable, but to a General Discharge Under Honorable Conditions. The Johnsons were jubilant and grateful, though my father was not yet done. In April 1973 he petitioned for an unambiguous Honorable discharge, but the Army denied it, firmly and finally and forever.

After receiving that letter, the parents packed up the vast reams of paper that testified to their long struggle, documents my mother kept in individual manila envelopes, and stuffed the whole on the bottom shelf of a large safe. They closed the door, turned the lock, and walked away from what had been a life-consuming ordeal. They seldom spoke of it to any of us, and never to their grandchildren.

• • •

In 1987 my parents sold their San Bernardino home and moved to Washington State to live near me and my sons, Bear and Brendan. I had just bought a big house, and that safe came to rest in our basement. There it remained undisturbed. In 2023, looking for documents allied to my widowed mother's care, I opened it. I saw on the top shelf a bound notebook with carbon copies of the letters my father had written beginning in 1969. Since his handwriting was a sometimes-illegible scrawl, every letter had been painstakingly typed by my mother (an artist at that keyboard). Thus each went out with the equivalent of white gloves, polished shoes, and business attire. Even glancing at these carbons I could see that my parents' struggle was far more profound, complex, and intense than I had guessed. At that time, a glance was all I could give them. My mother absorbed all my energies: At 101 years old, she was living in a nursing home, wheelchair bound, deaf, nearly blind. Her organs were failing and her fears escalating. Dementia had totally altered her sunny personality. She could swiftly spiral into irrational rages, so there was no way I would mention anything I had found in the safe or remind her of those terrible ordeals.

My mom died just before Christmas 2023. In February 2024, I returned to the basement and opened the safe. On the bottom shelf I found materials I had never seen and knew nothing of. Stuffed in haphazardly were perhaps forty big manila envelopes, pounds of paper relating to my father's battle on Doug's behalf more than a half-century before. I put the whole in boxes and hauled them upstairs, laid the envelopes out across the dining room table. Everything smelled of damp, disuse, and darkness; the staples were rusted and the paper clips crumbled when I removed them. To pull the actual UNDESIRABLE Discharge paper from its envelope—to stare at its shocking, ALL-CAPS one-word indictment—brought visceral shame. I had always been told—or at least led or allowed to believe—that Doug had been given a General discharge in the first place and that Dad had gotten it upgraded to Honorable. This was not so. Holding this document, I understood why the Undesirable was unspeakable. I understood why the parents would have let the rest of us think what we did. I began to understand the extent of their despair and marveled at their sheer, unflagging perseverance. I recycled the envelopes and put the contents into new folders marked for my own recognition. As I sifted through this sea of paper, reading and rereading, a chorus of voices rose up, most of them from the grave.

I have asked questions of the past unearthed from the safe. Many of those questions do not have answers. *Undesirable: The Vietnam War and a Father's Battle for Justice* does not aspire to be a scholarly tome with footnotes, nor is it a historical reconstruction of the Vietnam War, nor is it a Watergate chronicle. It is a tale fashioned from letters and other documents detailing a father's long, gallant fight to exonerate a beloved son who would prove sadly prodigal and destructive, the story of one family's ordeal, a memoir marbled with conjecture and imperfect recollection. Writing this book redeems a promise I gave my mother in October 2020 when I went to her house to tell her that Doug had been diagnosed with terminal liver cancer. I promised that one day I would write about Dad's fight for the Honorable discharge. She nodded and got misty, but she did not correct me about the Honorable, and she said not one word about what was in the safe, what I would find if I looked there. I had no idea what these letters and documents would reveal, no idea, then, that they even existed.

• • •

From the time he set foot in Vietnam, Doug Johnson found trouble. My father's letters on his behalf begin in the autumn of 1969, before my brother's first court-martial, and continue until April 1973. Over the years Bill Johnson tried every imaginable avenue, approached every conceivable person to whom he could appeal. He called on both sides of the family backgrounds, reaching out to the Armenian Robert Mardian in 1972 and, before that, cage-rattling chaplains and high-placed Mormons, the faith in which he had been raised. Among these pages are letters and documents to and from senators and congressmen, Cabinet secretaries, lawyers, doctors, shrinks, chaplains, Army brass of every stripe and variety, the Red Cross, President Nixon and Vice President Agnew. If these men (and they were all men) did not reply to Bill Johnson's initial entreaties, they got more letters in rapid succession, telegrams, long-distance telephone calls, sometimes to their homes. Among these papers are the transcript of Doug's November 1969 court-martial and the whole May 25, 1970, issue of *Time* magazine. Doug's service records noting a sorry assortment of underachievement, screw-ups, and hospitalizations are here. (A timeline from these records and other sources can be found at the end of this book.) There are doctors' and psychiatrists' evaluations in excruciating detail. There are newspaper clippings about obscure plane crashes in Vietnam in December 1969. One yellowed newspaper clipping from May 12, 1972, details that Secretary of Defense Melvin Laird was offering for the first time a program of forgiveness to GIs who had been given bad conduct discharges for drug charges. There are five fearful, anguished letters dated in the summer of 1970 from a mother in Wisconsin whose son, Ed, was a prisoner in LBJ with Doug. In one letter she writes that she is afraid to approach her congressman for fear of making trouble. Her timid tone breaks my heart, especially compared to my father's Atticus Finch–like, hard-hitting, nonstop eloquence, his vaulted, vaunted language that sometimes strains to excess, many of his letters closing with the declaration "I stand before you without shame or trepidation," as if he actually addressed some unseen tribunal.

Particularly vivid is the transcript of Doug's testimony at a hearing held by the Inspector General's office at Fort McArthur in San Pedro (Los Angeles County) on Friday, December 4, 1970. The IG hearing was my father's first attempt to get the Undesirable reversed. It had been initiated at the request of Congressman Jerry Pettis, Bill's stalwart ally.

The hearing was led by Colonel Robert R. Duddy. Doug's voice in this transcript is clear-spoken as he describes detailed combat experiences, as when "late at night you have to hang on to the guy in front of you because you can't see. If you let go, you have to stop because of the intensity of the dark." He relates candidly his persistent and abundant drug use, shooting up speed and heroin before going "on point" into the bush as the lead soldier to flush out and kill the Viet Cong: "I was walking forward leading some people through an area where you don't know if you are going to live or die before sunset." Asked by Colonel Duddy if the soldiers he was leading knew he was shooting up, Doug replies that they did. Probably they were high, too. Norman Camp, MD's *The U.S. Army Psychiatry in the Vietnam War* (Borden Institute, 2014, available online) supports my assumption that the men following Doug were probably equally stoned, certainly equally "scared shitless," in Doug's phrase, though in the Duddy hearing he does not use these words.

Also in this archive are eight letters Doug wrote to Dad and to the family from Vietnam. The first is from October 29, 1969, when he knew he was about to face serious court-martial consequences for his AWOLs and for drug possession. The last is from January 2, 1970, when he was still in solitary confinement at Long Binh. What happened to all the other letters he wrote home? Surely they would have been saved. They're not here and they were not among my parents' effects after they died. Perhaps those letters were read and reread, creased and carried in my mother's purse, clutched in her hand, held to her heart. When my mom was one hundred years old she wrote of the years that Doug was in Vietnam, "After going to bed at night, I would wake up in three or four hours, lie awake wondering if I had awakened because something awful was happening to my son." Perhaps she pulled those letters from under her pillow and held them until the paper dissolved from her tears.

I have reprinted here the eight letters I found including, intact, the heartbreaker from December 26, 1969, fourteen legal-sized pages of scrawled shriek that Doug wrote from a psychic abyss. The handwriting starts out big and loopy but diminishes into small and cramped and the paragraphing is all smashed to the right margin. His pain, his groping in the darkness, his "reaching for a hand to guide me" are palpable and horrifying. Read it and weep.

3. Righting Wrongs

Bill Johnson was part of what has been called the Greatest Generation. He served in the Navy, in the Pacific Theater in World War II. But very likely there were other Greatest Generations. Maybe the young men who fought the Punic Wars were a Greatest Generation who came home carrying the pain they had inflicted and the pain they had suffered, as did the soldiers who fought in Iraq and Afghanistan and at Austerlitz and Waterloo, who survived Normandy and Shiloh and Gettysburg and Yorktown, the Somme and Culloden. Peace treaties agreed upon by old men had nothing to do with the grief, the burden of what these soldiers saw and heard and did.

Fifty years have passed since Vietnam. The once-young men who fought there until the chaotic US retreat in 1975 are old now. All except the fifty-eight-thousand-plus dead, whose names are engraved on the Vietnam War Memorial in Washington, DC. They are not old. No doubt there are still American homes where their young faces gaze out of framed military photographs set on mantels beside carefully folded, now faded flags. Those soldiers who survived, many of them, banded, bonded together to form the Vietnam Veterans of America, a proud, active group offering services and solidarity to their members. Vietnam vets have also created a vast informal network of remembrance on social media, different groups offering daily Facebook posts and photographs, often commemorating the fallen, the KIA as the acronym has it. Each photo has a tale to go with it: some of these young soldiers died mere days after setting foot in Vietnam, some in a few months; some deaths were accidental; some lives were lost in "friendly fire"; others died heroically so that others might live. Seeing these youthful faces in the photographs, reading the stories of their unthinkable perils and hardships, I keep hearing the wistful questions posed in the song "Where Have All the Flowers Gone?" with its melodic cycle of sadness. Sometimes there are posts seeking information about the long ago comrades of deceased or ailing husbands or fathers or brothers or uncles. Particularly poignant for me is reading social media posts of deaths or wounds suffered on dates that align with what I know of my brother's time in Vietnam. On November 14, 1969, for instance, a young soldier had his leg blown off. On November 14, 1969, Doug Johnson was sitting in front of a court-martial, tried for going AWOL. I have to wonder if Doug survived *because* he was a fuck-up with a lousy service record, persistent AWOLs, jailed twice, hospitalized time and again. I marvel that he lived at all.

But he did. He came home to his parents in Southern California. His fellow prisoner Ed came home to his parents in Wisconsin. That bedraggled dude you see at the freeway interchange with his scrawny dog, his dirty backpack, his sign *Vietnam Vet, Anything Helps*, he came back. Or at least their bodies returned intact. How many were in thrall to addictions, tormented by nightmares, unable to find fulfilling lives? How many of them were clutching sandals, metaphorically or otherwise?

Bill Johnson wrested the actual sandal away from Doug, but it seems to me to represent the burden of those "acts incompatible with his conscience." This is the formal phrase my father would later use persistently, without ever being specific. It shrouded stories Doug told him as they sat together on the lawn of Loma Linda Hospital, including, no doubt, the one about "a chain of human ears" that Doug once mentioned, almost idly, standing around with a group of us in my mother's kitchen one Thanksgiving. I felt sick, as if I were in the presence of something truly cruel and hideous, as though a foul miasma oozed off my brother.

In thinking about my brother, I still struggle with conflicted, complicated, unsettled emotions that veer from the depths of pity to the shoals of contempt. But in writing this book I have found new compassion for Doug, who described himself to Colonel Duddy as "a scared, cautious and unsure young man. Scared to die, cautious not to die and becoming at that time, an opium addict." In Vietnam he was engulfed in events, endured ordeals, and made choices that changed his life forever. The average age of soldiers in Vietnam was nineteen, just like Doug. The official wording—that Doug accepted the Undesirable for "the good of the service"—strikes me as humbug. Really, was the service any better for tarring twenty-year-old Doug Johnson with this label for the rest of his life? For choices he made when he was not old enough to vote? When he was not old enough to buy beer in California? I am angry on Doug's behalf, and on behalf of my mother and father and my sister Helen and my remaining brother, Brian, and on behalf of Doug's second wife who genuinely loved him, on behalf of friends who helped him or tried to help him, on behalf of friends he lost. And for this anger there is no palliative, even though while I have worked on this book there have been historic instances of the American military making up for past mistakes.

In June 2024 President Joe Biden announced that he was "righting an historic wrong" by, according to National Public Radio, "granting clemency to all troops expelled during the 60 years that the military explicitly banned consensual gay sex." In the past, the article continues,

> Commanders often used other ways to push gay troops out of the military, like issuing violations or offering a less-than-honorable discharge in lieu of court martial, the formal legal proceeding of the military. . . . An other-than-honorable discharge is more than a brand of shame; it strips veterans of automatic VA benefits and health care. It can be difficult to then procure a civilian job because employers often ask about military service and character of discharge when hiring.

In July 2024 an even older wrong was reversed, a wrong from 1944, eighty years before, when fifty men defied the Army and were court-martialed for refusing to return to work after an explosion at the Port Chicago Naval Magazine, citing safety fears. "With the stroke of a pen on July 17, Navy Secretary Carlos Del Toro fully exonerated the sailors charged in the incident," wrote the *Washington Post*. What did exoneration mean to the descendants of those men who "all bore the stain of court-martial convictions for the rest of their lives"?

• • •

What if my brother had not been cursed with the Undesirable? First—and this is no small consideration—an Honorable or a Medical discharge or even a General would have offered him an exit unclouded by shame, disgrace, and failure. Any of these would have meant VA benefits, a partial sharing of those burdens that my parents bore alone (hospitalizations, medical, dental, psychiatric). Certainly the financial toll could have been considerably diminished. And the time! An Honorable or Medical or General discharge would have spared my parents years of ceaseless pen-wielding activism. Days, probably weeks Dad spent coaching Doug, prepping for the Duddy hearing. Days that Dad rose before dawn to make telephone calls to Washington, DC. Days he surreptitiously slipped away from work to go to the public library for research. Days he went home early to write letters, passing his scrawled pages to my mother who sat up nights, clacking away at the Underwood manual typewriter. In the morning she drove to the post office before going to her job at the insurance office where she sometimes stayed late to use their electric typewriter. What if my parents had not been shackled to these obsessive, unremitting endeavors? Where and to whom might all that time and energy and emotion and expense have otherwise gone? Could it have been lavished on Brian, a boy still in middle school? On Helen, a teenage girl blighted with fragile health and multiple major surgeries complicated by slow, unsteady recovery periods? Might all that energy have been better concentrated on healing the hollowed-out shell of a human being, the psychotic mess that was Doug Johnson? Even had Doug had an Honorable discharge—had there been a brass band and pom-pom girls to meet him at Fort Lewis, and never mind the dead man's sandal— integrating a drug addict back into the Johnson family would have taken a toll no matter what. The fight to reverse the Undesirable, compounded daily with the pain and fear and uncertainty of a traumatized veteran in the house, sapped every ounce of energy and time and thought and care and emotion that my parents had.

• • •

Doug Johnson was certainly not alone carrying scars seen and unseen. One of his high-school classmates whose little sister was friends with Helen returned from Vietnam so troubled that a few years later he died in a shoot-out during an attempted bank heist. The Johnsons' house on Turrill Court was not the only one torn by trauma.

That house was a modest four-bedroom, two-bath rambler in a cul-de-sac, a neighborhood of postwar tract homes. The neighbors were all middle-class white families like ours. We moved there in 1958 when Dad was transferred to San Bernardino, originally a railroad town, some sixty miles east of Los Angeles. I was twelve, Doug was eight, Helen was six, and Brian was a babe in arms. Unlike our previous house in the San Fernando Valley, where Dad had built a redwood fence, a roofed patio, bookshelves, and kitchen cabinets and landscaped the property with fruit trees, at Turrill Court the parents made no changes or improvements, not even air conditioning. In the merciless heat of a high desert summer they affixed a big swamp-cooler to a window; fed by a hose, it sluggishly churned out cool, damp air until about October. The narrow kitchen faced the street. Beside the kitchen table the back door opened to an unshaded brick patio that concentrated and radiated heat. From the front door a T-shaped hall led to the bedrooms, two facing the front, two the back. On his return Doug got the quietest bedroom at the back of the house. He slept continually. Sometimes, even when he was awake, his eyes would roll back in his head, a bizarre sight. In Nam he had learned to sleep with his eyes open. Dreaming, he would twitch and shudder and wake suddenly startled, momentarily confused.

In a 1972 letter to his ally Congressman Jerry Pettis, Bill confessed, "Frankly it was extremely difficult for our family those first six months after our son was at home. We are very close family. We all suffered with him."

I did not suffer with them. I did not endure the immediate shock, the turmoil of living with Doug's shattered mental and physical health, with the weight of the sandal he metaphorically still carried. I did not live there during the parents' long campaign to exonerate him. I was on the East Coast, a graduate student in history at the University of Delaware and later teaching at Lincoln University in Pennsylvania. Not until 2024 when I began to read through this salvaged archive did I fathom the toll of those fourteen months in Vietnam on Doug's life, and the cost of the fight to free him of the

Undesirable—which, it turned out, was not the same as freeing him of that shame or that past.

Scrutinized, these exhumed documents reveal evidence that renders that shame, that past all the more tragic: an injustice and a cover-up by the US Army concealing punitive vindictiveness meted out to a vulnerable twenty-year-old soldier. A wrong. What if the Army were now to right that wrong? What if the Army were to exonerate my brother and give him a posthumous Honorable discharge? Would it matter to Helen or Brian or me? My father is dead. My mother is dead. Doug is dead. Certainly, it's too late to change the sad trajectory of his life or undo the pain his addictions wrought for decades.

PART II

<table>
<tr><td>A</td><td>Playlist</td><td>B</td></tr>
</table>

Can't Find My Way Home	BLIND FAITH
We Gotta Get Out of This Place	THE ANIMALS, BLUE ÖYSTER CULT
Nowhere to Run, Nowhere to Hide	MARTHA AND THE VANDELLAS
Fortunate Son	CREEDENCE CLEARWATER REVIVAL
Bumble Boogie	JACK FINA ON PIANO
Rhapsody in Blue	GEORGE GERSHWIN ON PIANO
Polonaise in A Flat Major	FRÉDÉRIC CHOPIN
Polonaise Militaire	FRÉDÉRIC CHOPIN
Andante in E Sharp Major	LUDWIG VAN BEETHOVEN

Johnson Family, 1967.

4. Before

1969

As a boy, Doug Johnson was certainly one of those on whom fortune seemed to shine. He was the Johnsons' second child, and eldest son, some four and a half years younger than I. All four of us had piano lessons, but Doug early on demonstrated real musical talent, and while the rest of us played scales and learned "The Spinning Song" with matronly, uninspired teachers, our parents found for Doug the demanding Mr. Hulburt. No-nonsense, crew-cut, steely blue eyes, clad always in a suit and tie, Mr. Hulburt was an exacting mentor. Doug could play "Rhapsody in Blue," "Malagueña," "Bumble Boogie," and difficult classical pieces at a very young age. In addition to the piano, he effortlessly picked up other instruments. My mother always liked to tell the story of how Doug wanted to learn to play guitar. Mom enrolled herself in a cheap night-school guitar class, and when she came home she showed Doug what she had learned. Within two or three weeks, she quit going. He had absorbed enough to set him up practicing and playing well. He was an instinctively charismatic performer.

Even cast into solitary confinement in the notorious Long Binh Jail, Doug wrote on December 31, 1969, or possibly January 1, 1970:

Could I put in a few requests for items to be sent? I would like the music (my copy) of Beethoven's Andante in F sharp Minor [*sic*], Chopin's

Polonaise in A flat Major and Polonaise Militaire. This is for three reasons. 1. I can find comfort in reading the music to myself. 2. I can keep my memory of the music from dissipating altogether and 3 possibly get a "job" playing for the officers or something which would also keep my mind sharp and my fingers limber. I'd appreciate it. Only send those 3 pieces until I see if I can get this job. If I do get it, I'll write for the music I want that they don't have here. . . . The Andante with the chocolate stain on the first page has quite a lot of sentimental value and I'd hate to lose it. It's been there since I've been playing and it's part of the music to me.

In 1963 the parents had sold the little spinet that had served us for a decade and bought a baby grand piano befitting their son's gifts. With its high, impressive wing, it dominated the living room at Turrill Court. In that same letter, Doug writes, musing about himself and his fiancée:

I think when I get married which won't be for a while yet after I settle down and get a home of my own (when we're tired of apts etc) I think I'll take the piano with me. I bet you forgot didn't you that piano was "incentive" for playing Chopin's Polonaise in A flat major from memory in front of some type of audience which I did while in the 8th grade at my Eagle Court of Honor. I remember I hated the piano they had there. On the part about the horse's hooves getting louder and louder (the part where the left hand goes over the other) either mom's or dad's favorite part. I can remember who exactly, one key was dead and I kept hitting it harder and harder to make it sound and no sound ever came out of it. It made me <u>so mad</u>!

I am astonished that, amid the rats and manifold miseries of Long Binh Jail, his memory returned to Chopin's "Polonaise in A Flat Major" and a malfunctioning piano at Arrowview Junior High School where he became an Eagle Scout.

Bill Johnson was committed to the Scouting program; he helmed the local Boy Scout troop, and he had prodded Doug toward achieving the Eagle

News item: Douglas Scott Johnson, Eagle Scout, 1963, age thirteen.

Scout honor at the early age of thirteen. Dad was always very proud of Doug's achievement. A photo of this occasion—Doug in Eagle regalia standing beside his mother and father—was pinned above the workbench where Dad spent countless hours in his old age making fanciful wooden flower boxes.

Doug was a chubby youngster, but once in high school he outgrew that. He was not tall, but he had a good physique, thick, curly dark hair, and "the most beautiful eyes and eyelashes," a female classmate recalled. He was charming, socially adept in that teenage world, something of a show-off, popular especially with the girls, judging from his San Bernardino High School senior yearbook (which ended up at my house). The yearbook abounds with the usual teenage high spirits, hijinks, and in-jokes; its pages are slathered with "luv ya" and "bestest buddies," with high praise and good wishes from friends and teachers and many references to his excellent musicianship, including playing guitar and performing folk music. He graduated in 1967, the so-called Summer of Love, with its catchphrase, "Tune

(Sun-Telegram photo)

EAGLE SCOUT — Douglas Scott Johnson, 13, son of Mr. and Mrs. William J. Johnson, 3246 Turrill Court, San Bernardino, will be raised to the rank of Eagle Scout during a Boy Scout Court of Honor to be held at 7:30 p.m., April 30 at Arrowview Junior High School. He will perform two piano numbers at the Court of Honor. He has been a Boy Scout Troop 36 scribe, assistant patrol leader and patrol leader. He is a student at Arrowview Junior High School.

In, Turn On, Drop Out," and also the summer of *Sgt. Pepper's Lonely Hearts Club Band*, with the Beatles celebrating "Lucy in the Sky with Diamonds." (And if you can't remember or fathom that moment, suffice it to say that young people could all but hear the world turning on a hitherto unknown axis. We shared the conviction that we were part of some sort of Brave

New World where peace and love and brotherhood would expand along with our hearts and minds.) More to the immediate point for Doug, like a lot of 1967 high school students, he had probably puffed a few illegal joints with his friends while drinking beer that they were too young to buy.

Even before Doug stormed off to the Army Recruiting Center in January 1969, he had many adolescent clashes with Dad. In high school and when he was a student at Valley Junior College they fought frequently about Doug's mediocre grades, partying, and reckless driving. (Pretending that he was driving a stick shift, Doug wrecked the transmission of my mom's enormous 1960 Ford station wagon, after which the car was sold for scrap.) Dad imposed restrictions and insisted on standards of conduct that Doug continued to defy.

In the letters Doug wrote home from Vietnam, he makes persistent regretful references to not having heeded the guidance that Dad tried to invoke or instill in him. He expresses contrition that he failed to follow or had outright rejected Dad's advice. In October 1969 he writes:

Dad, you are a man among men and the greatest person there is and the best father a person can have. How you can go on under all the pressures you're under and have add to your worries and still go on is beyond my imagination. I can see now everything you've been telling me as though it were a rainy day and you're telling me that the sun is still in the sky and I would believe you until the sky cleared up. Well the sky has cleared or is beginning to and I'm beginning to see the sun. Beginning to see that you were right and I was wrong. How does one go about attaining wisdom and determination as you have? Please tell me. I want to be able to make the right decisions like you can. I get the guts you have to hang on when there's seemingly nothing to hang on to and come out on top in the end. I'd like to say now thank you for not just telling me to get lost when I was causing you so much trouble. I think I was lost then, I really WAS lost. I have a very very strong feeling that from now on it's going to be okay. I'm only sorry it took so long to come about. I can see now that I was wrong. So DEAD WRONG. Dad to me you're the greatest man that ever lived. I couldn't even begin to list all the things that make you what you are. Mom, well all I can say is that there is no other mom quite like my mom in the whole world. I love you both SO much.

I want to stop there. I'm getting a little too strong on my thoughts and they tend to keep me depressed.

. . .

When Paul Kleinwachter, Doug's assigned attorney for his second court-martial, opened communications with the Johnsons, my father besieged him with character references from Doug's teachers and our neighbors, testimonials to be delivered to the court through Paul. These, too, were in the basement safe. Just beneath their unanimous praise there lurks in these letters the bewildered, unspoken *How could this kid have ended up in military prison facing a court-martial?*

My dad asked me to write as well, to send a personal note to Paul Kleinwachter on behalf of my brother. Below is my hand-corrected letter that went out on the University of Delaware History Department's impressive stationary even though I was only a teaching assistant/graduate student. (The secretary there was always very kind to me.) When I came upon this letter in the files, I got misty. Here were contemporary incidents of Doug's teen years that I had entirely forgotten, incidents that decades of anger had effaced, erased from my memory, and that rose up afresh. My brother wasn't always a destructive addict. Doug really, truly was the person described here.

July 25 1970

Dear Capt. K—

While I do not wish to make incursions on your busy day, I still feel compelled to write this letter regarding my young brother, Douglas Scott Johnson—currently your client—(so to speak). I realize this is a civilian term, but then I am a civilian. My comments can hardly be admitted as evidence in a court-martial, as I am related to Douglas and therefore prejudiced in his favor, but I do think that whatever the nature of the court may be—that you as Doug's defense should know certain things about him—perhaps I can provide you with a kind of insight that Douglas himself may not be able to give. In view of the gravity of the situation I think it imperative that you know these things.

Douglas and I are the eldest of four children. We are five years apart. Douglas is 20, I am 25. What is Douglas like? I have no doubt but that you have formed your own impressions, but let me add to your impressions a few of mine. Douglas, as I'm sure Father has told you, was an Eagle Scout at 13. He has always been particularly proficient in swimming and water sports. He is an endurance swimmer rather than speed swimmer. (Having made the mile swim at age 13 also). Douglas is a first rate surfer and can cut thru a wave like a knife through water. He has a talent, even a brilliance with music and can play the piano so that you think even the piano will get up and dance. He taught himself the guitar, the drums, the banjo, the mandolin and plays each with amazing spirit and beauty.

Doug worked at various jobs around San Bernardino. He was always best at jobs where there was contact with people as Douglas has disarming charm and a warm, interested approach to people. At one grocery store where he worked, people who are perfect strangers to me will come up and inquire after Douglas. They still remember him well two or three years [later]. There is a warm generous impulse about Douglas. People respond to him and enjoy him. His friendships I think are very telling. Rather than having a great many friends that changed with each season, Douglas has sustained successful relationships with three or four close friends since grammar school and junior high. This is remarkable, I think considering the mortality rate on friendship during adolescence. As for girls, Douglas is now engaged to a lovely girl whom he has been going with for two years now. Once again, a sustained successful relationship.

I guess one of my most vivid memories of Doug is one day, summer

1967. He had been working as an aquatics instructor at a Boy Scout Camp in the mountains above San Bernardino. The parents and my other brother and sister were away on vacation. I was at home at the time, getting ready to leave for the East. Douglas came home for the day and in the late afternoon I started to drive him back up the Hill. The Hill (as we call it) is very steep and it was very hot. My car—old and rickety—overheated. Douglas opened the hood and the radiator exploded in his face and eye. For a while he lost sight in one eye and the pain must have been intense. We had to hitchhike back down the Hill to a hospital. Douglas never cried or complained, he just held a rag over his eye and was very quiet.

Once at the hospital the doctor told us that his eye, while not seriously burned would require complete dark for three or so days and that he would be OK. So for three days Douglas stayed in the house with all the blinds drawn and dark—he could not do anything that would require any use of his eyes, no TV, no reading. We had no air conditioning, and the heat just blared away outside. (San Bernardino, I might remind you, is on the edge of the desert.) But before those three days were up, every kid (young and old) in the neighborhood was over at our house as Douglas brought out all his instruments and they brought some of theirs and formed a band. So you see, there is something magnetic and special about Douglas. Even through his pain and discomfort he took time to show some of the younger ones how to play various instruments and filled the whole, hot, baking house with music and laughter. He could not go out—they all flocked to him. Douglas has, I believe a unique gift for living, that needs to be cultivated, freed from his present unhappy circumstances and cultivated, not crushed.

So how is it then that this boy that I have described comes to be your client. How is it that the person I described came to be the person that you know with his multiple problems—of every variety and shape? Captain K, I would not presume to inform you of the horrors of war, but the difference between the individual I have just described to you and the PFC Johnson of your acquaintance can be summed up in two words. Viet Nam. The kinds of charges now leveled against Douglas would have been literally <u>unthinkable</u> a year and a half ago. We would not have thought them, and certainly Douglas would not have thought them [possible]. War, whatever its purpose or its merits, is not meant for everyone. I'm sure that your daily practice must demonstrate this. Not everyone is cut from the same fabric as General Patton or Sgt. York. There are other kinds of heroes, Captain K. Not to be facetious, but let me remind you that General Patton could not play the piano. Had the Army assigned Douglas to any capacity, any other place but a battle zone in Viet Nam, he would not, most assuredly would not be in his present circumstances.

Douglas has a bright, a beautiful talent. He has a sensitivity and a warmth that should not be crushed, since it is a rare commodity and few people are so gifted. He has an intelligence that seems to express itself through his creative hands on any instrument he so much as touches. Captain K, I have just introduced you to Douglas Johnson <u>BEFORE</u> Viet Nam. What is he going to be <u>After?</u>

. . .

As I read through all the hundreds of letters my father wrote between autumn 1969 and April 1973, one theme is unchanging. Dad insists upon Doug's fundamental worth, his many fine attributes and accomplishments: an Eagle Scout with thirty-five merit badges, a good Mormon boy, a piano prodigy, never any trouble with the law, a fine young man before Vietnam. Dad is a one-man Mormon Tabernacle Choir singing Doug's praises, often describing him in Emersonian hyperbole. He insists that anyone aiding Doug will one day be proud to say they "helped fulfill the greatness that is Douglas Johnson," that Doug will be counted as "a man among men." Reading these letters, one after the other (the same letter often going out to many recipients) the constant affirmations grow repetitive; they are a monotonous litany of virtues that can and shall and must be redeemed if only the undeserved Undesirable is changed. Clearly, and throughout this struggle, my father remained acutely aware of the psychic stain that would result, indeed, remain if Doug suffered this shame, disgrace, and failure so early in life. Bill Johnson fought the Army not only to amend the Undesirable to an Honorable—that is, to amend Doug's past—but to ensure his future.

5. "Scared Shitless"

<u>1969</u>

Nineteen-year-old enlistee Douglas Scott Johnson reported to Fort Ord in Northern California for Basic Training. In January and March of 1969 his service records note that "Conduct" and "Efficiency" were "Excellent." His Army photograph following Basic Training looks suitably serious. The parents went up to see his graduation from Basic. They stayed in a hotel. They took pictures in the hotel room. In these snapshots my mom smiles with teeth so gritted you can all but hear them grinding; her eyes look glazed with terror. Doug, in his spiffy uniform, has an arm draped over her shoulders and he looks youthful and confident. Dad has a close-lipped, stoic smile. From Fort Ord, they all three drove home to San Bernardino, where Doug spent his fifteen-day leave. This was the only leave granted him in all his twenty months of military service.

E-3 Douglas Johnson arrived in Vietnam on June, 10, 1969. Twelve days later, on June 22, he went AWOL. After twenty-three days, on July 14, Private Johnson returned to his unit, but he only stayed for about two weeks. From July 31 to August 7, 1969, he was AWOL again. Returning to his

Doug during Basic Training, US Army, May 1969.

41

unit on August 8, he emerged from the bush (or wherever he was) so visibly, wretchedly sick that he went directly into the hospital to be treated for hepatitis and malaria. He remained hospitalized for fifty-three days.

Doug was court-martialed for these AWOL offenses and possession of marijuana on November 14, 1969. The record of the trial is among the documents I found in the safe. In it, Doug, as the accused, offered this mitigating statement:

> [The accused] was on a fifteen day leave and asked for an extension so that he could be home when his younger sister came out of the hospital after serious surgery. He had applied for a fifteen day extension and the extension was denied. The other AWOLs were to make phone calls home to find out what the outcome of further surgery performed on his sister was. He stated that he sent $120 per month home to help his family defray the medical bills. He stated that he sends this money home every month. The witness was excused.

My father would later write regretful letters to his Congressional ally, Jerry Pettis, to Doug's battalion commander, and to Dr. Shirasu in the military hospital in Japan detailing the life-threatening surgeries seventeen-year-old Helen had undergone. Bill expressed formal remorse, even shouldering blame for Doug's bad behavior because in telling the young soldier just how sick his sister was, Dad had unthinkingly added to Doug's mental stress.

But even if the above statement to the court-martial tells us *why* Doug went AWOL, it tells us nothing about where he went or where he lived or who he was with or what he did. Where does a nineteen-year-old American go in a strange, war-torn country where he has no idea of the language or the terrain, the customs or the people? How does he live, survive on the lam in what Doug later termed, "that wretched country"? Food? Shelter? Water? The heat? The rain? The jungles? The villages? Who among the villagers were armed VC and who were not? Was Doug armed? In uniform? How crazed or fearful was he? Surely crazed and fearful were emotions he lived with daily. How sick was he? He suffered almost nonstop from hepatitis, malaria, jungle rot, dysentery, and other maladies. Malaria, no doubt was a condition of life in Vietnam. The hepatitis probably resulted from the use of dirty needles.

These AWOLs were, in all likelihood, related to drugs. At the Inspector General hearing conducted in December 1970 Doug admitted to Colonel Duddy that by August 1969 he was mainlining speed and opium "seven or eight times a day. My arms had become literal pin cushions." Thus, in a matter of some seven weeks in 1969 (three in June, four in July) Doug Johnson—Eagle Scout, piano prodigy, folk singer, and good Mormon boy—went from a kid who might have passed around a joint and a beer among his high-school friends to a soldier shooting up repeatedly, tripping, popping multiple daily doses of amphetamines and narcotics.

Immediately upon his release from the hospital on September 30, 1969, Doug went AWOL again until October 6. Where did he go? With whom? Why? We do not know. By this time, his state of mind can be described as "scared shitless," as he wrote in a letter to me in autumn 1969. Because the letter has long since vanished, I don't know if "scared shitless" referred to why he went AWOL, why he was doing hard drugs, his reaction to combat and death, all of these and, likely, things that I can't even imagine. The psychiatrist who treated him after his return wrote that Doug's madness was the result of "living in combat experiences during his 16 months in Viet Nam. Most of which was spent on patrol with his platoon in situations of very great hazard and terror." This description seems to me an apt definition of "scared shitless." Doug told Colonel Duddy at the hearing:

> I used opium for several reasons. One, being it relaxed extreme nervousness and tensions that build while walking forward leading some people through an area where you don't know if you are going to live or die before sunset. Secondly, I used opium because I didn't care at that point whether or not the opium killed me. My reasoning at that time was if the opium didn't kill me the VC would.

By October 1969 he knew he would be court-martialed. The prospect of jail, too, could have left him scared shitless. Conditions at Long Binh Jail were notorious and the year before there had been brutal riots among the prisoners. At Doug's November 14, 1969, court-martial, an additional drug charge, possession of marijuana, was dropped due to a technical error. After about a thirty-minute trial, the court's sentence was a pay cut of two-thirds and a demotion to the rank of E-1, but an additional five months' hard labor was suspended, so he was spared Long Binh. Some twelve days later, November 26, he again developed malaria and hepatitis and was sent to Nha Trang Hospital.

Following his release from Nha Trang on December 18, Doug was unable to return to his unit because two plane crashes in the vicinity had disrupted travel and communications. He disappeared and was gone for eight days. This incident would become the most contested of Doug's time in the Army. (I cannot bring myself to use the phrase "his Army career.") The Inspector General's office who conducted the Duddy hearing would later maintain that there were no such crashes to impede his return and that he was simply AWOL. Bill Johnson's rebuttals to the Inspector General's interim and final reports included wire service news clippings to prove that the two plane crashes occurred on December 19, 1969, when Doug said they did. Bill added:

> Applicant, under oath, swore he made every attempt to return to unit,
> but was unable to do so on account of the plane crash. In addition, he
> knew he had limited duty for one month [after hospitalization] after
> which time he was to report back to the hospital for re-examination on
> 15 January 1970, and he was fully aware of the suspended sentence.

All of this is true. But it is nonetheless misleading. Two of Doug's letters to his father reveal that he knowingly went AWOL in December. These letters also indicate that in going AWOL he knew he had forfeited the suspended sentence from the court-martial.

In the massive case he presented to secure an Honorable discharge in 1972, Bill finishes that paragraph with this: "During the 8 days the Army considered him AWOL, applicant remained at the Nha Trang Hospital where he ate his meals and slept until he was able to get a flight back to Pleiku." My father's bland invocation of Doug eating and sleeping at the hospital was also misleading. If, in fact, Doug was back at that hospital, it wasn't so that he could play solitaire among the potted palms in some mythical common room. It's because drugs were an epidemic among enlisted men, available everywhere, including hospitals. Moreover, at the Duddy hearing, Doug revealed it was *at the Nha Trang hospital* where he "was introduced to two more drugs to which I had not been exposed before. These were LSD and speed. I began using speed to alleviate the necessity for opium and found myself using the two together to provide a different result than that to which I was accustomed." If Doug did return to Nha Trang Hospital, drugs were the allure.

These eight days in late 1969 resulted in a psychic breakdown described in fourteen pages Doug wrote on December 26 (chapter 8). This ranting letter, roiling with pain, describes the soul-searing maelstrom he endured over those eight days AWOL. But we learn nothing of his physical circumstances. Writing to his father on December 29, Doug underscores, "I needed desperately those few days." But where he spent them, and how, he does not say. In those eight days—wherever his body was—Doug's mind was cast into hell.

At the Duddy hearing he described when finally, on December 26, he had fetched up where he was supposed to be. "I was asked if I had anything to say, to which I replied, 'Yes.' He [the personnel staff officer] answered me with, 'I don't want to hear it, get out.' Confinement orders were typed out the same evening and the next morning I was on a plane with two armed guards bound for Long Binh Jail." Doug did not serve out his five months at Long Binh because he fell dangerously ill with hepatitis and in mid-January had to be airlifted from the prison hospital to the military hospital in Japan, where he came under the care of Dr. Shirasu.

All of this—drug addiction, multiple AWOLs for weeks at a time, being scared shitless, long hospitalizations, court-martial, prison—took place in the first six months, June to January.

Doug's sorry service record is peppered with many AWOLs, some a few days, some a few weeks, so many, in fact, that they can be confusing. In the Inspector General's report of 1971, Major General William Enemark writes:

Records of subsequent AWOL's and periods of confinement for disciplinary reasons indicated that during the period 21 June 1969 until July 1970 a period of 374 days Private Johnson could possibly have performed his duties as a rifleman only for 115 days. The remainder of the time, 259 days, he was not present in his unit.

At the Duddy hearing Doug talked freely about his abundant drug use, about combat, about his time in military prison. But he did not mention any of his AWOLs. No doubt Dad coached him on this, told him *not* to mention them unless asked directly. After all, the point of the hearing was to get the Undesirable changed to an Honorable, not to remind the Inspector General's office of his many infractions.

In the sixty-eighth of the ninety-six questions Colonel Duddy put to Doug, he inquired after Doug's whereabouts when he was AWOL in May and early June 1970. Doug said that he stayed at the place of some unnamed ARVN (Army of the Republic of [South] Vietnam) translators who he says "were friends of mine." They were "division interpreters and they had a place on base and also in downtown An Khe." Doug said that he stayed in both places. Here he picks up the story after his return to his unit:

I informed my CO that I had not slept in six days and that I was pending court martial and that there was no possible way I could stay awake all night. He completely ignored me and placed me guard duty anyhow and then came out and caught me asleep on guard. He notified me that this charge would be added on to my previous cm [court-martial] charges and at this I panicked and again went AWOL. I returned to the ARVNs' house where I was living before and stayed there with them.

I became increasingly dependent on the use of drugs to maintain my sanity. I was losing weight at a rapid rate and the use of these drugs became my only concern. I began staying awake 24 hours a day and seven days a week and continued this until I was caught . . . When the MPs caught us I weighed 128 pounds.

He does not say how he was caught, or where, or what might have brought the military police to the door, or indeed if he was caught at the ARVNs' house on base at Camp Radcliff or in the town of An Khe or somewhere else. Other than this particular reference to the MPs, we have absolutely no indication of what might have brought Doug back to his unit after his many AWOLs. Hunger? Fatigue? Fear? Sickness? The need, the search for drugs? When Colonel Duddy questioned him, "How was it possible that you obtained the amount and varying types of drugs while under combat conditions?" Doug replied that they were available everywhere, from the Vietnamese or other GIs. Other sources I will cite later, Army sources, corroborate this testimony: GIs could smoke or shoot or pop, drop, get high any place, any time. Drugs were omnipresent, essential to life, and, the implication is, forgiving in death.

Did Doug spend those AWOL days mainlining himself into an opium coma? Dropping acid? Speeding frantically, awake for days on end? Some unholy combo of all of these? His second defense attorney, Captain Paul Kleinwachter, spent a good deal of time with Doug in July and August of 1970 and assessed him thus:

> I have seen Douglas Johnson on several occasions while he was "speeding" and frankly it was frightening and pathetic to see such a sight . . . From all indications Private Johnson was a conscientious, hard working young man with high aspirations prior to coming to Vietnam. Whatever his reasons were, he is now a drug addict . . . The offenses with which he is charged are all directly or indirectly related to his drug problem. His periods of AWOL were precipitated by his desire to obtain and use speed. In fact, while he was gone he mainlined to the extent that he hardly slept, and upon returning he fell asleep on guard. His total involvement with drugs does not excuse his offenses, but perhaps a sick, sick individual who is badly in need of treatment.

Paul's introductory letter to my father, dated July 12, 1970, has an especially poignant paragraph: "At Doug's insistence, I have not mentioned his use or misuse of drugs. Suffice it to say that I feel he has a problem in this area and I am determining the extent of the medical and/or psychiatric help which is available to him." "At Doug's insistence" implies that Doug was ashamed of his addictions, that he didn't want his father to know what he had come to.

Doug Johnson was a drug addict. At the dictates of his addictions he willingly and knowingly went AWOL, alone or in the company of others—except that Doug never mentions a single name of anyone who might have accompanied him. Of his May and June 1970 AWOL, he says, "When the MPs caught us I weighed 128 pounds." But there is no indication of who "us" might be.

Doug Johnson was no loner; he was a sociable creature who flourished best in the company of others, people who would admire him and applaud. I cannot imagine him popping off into the jungle solo. But in all his testimony and in his few contemporary letters still extant, he never mentions another soldier by name. Despite the dangers, the testosterone-charged tensions, the rigors of military life in Vietnam, he seems never to have had the proverbial "Army buddy." Vietnam veterans, in their recollections, their social media posts, often refer to the intense bonds forged in combat, a profound sense of brotherhood. Doug claimed to have "climbed down a 90 foot ladder from a chopper to rescue a wounded soldier while machine gun fire was going on," but this comrade has no name. Doug was told he would receive "two Bronze Stars for risking my life to save those of my buddies." But these buddies are nameless. My father wrote of Doug that "his friend standing by his side was hit in the head and killed. While under fire Doug picked up his body and carried him back to the chopper on his shoulder." The friend whose head was blown off remains anonymous.

In a harrowing incident he related at the Duddy hearing, Doug stated, "I was on a short mission with some tall grass surrounding the area and my buddies and I were within 5 or 10 feet at times from a group of NVA soldiers doing a sweep of this area." Doug and his companions radioed for the protection of a helicopter gunship:

> We were told by the gun ship that they refused to come in due to the close proximity between our position and that of the enemy. Rather than take another chance on being killed, we lied to the gun ship and told them that we had moved our position to another location and asked them once again to come in and sweep the area, thus bringing the gun ship right in on top of us, taking the chance on being shot by our own men. When the barrage was finished my friend and I both look at the ruck sack lying between us . . . this ruck sack had several holes and the [canteen] had two holes from our own mini guns.

The buddies who shared this awful moment in the tall grass, the friend who was with him, mere inches from death, none of them have names.

Responding to Colonel Duddy's question about gang beatings he endured in Long Binh Jail, Doug says that some friends came to his rescue, but he doesn't have names for them either. Nicknames, nothing more, and he does not offer those.

Questioned by Colonel Duddy, Doug cannot remember the names of any of his sergeants or captains or any such person or officer with whom he dealt, save for a very brief, oblique reference: "I only recall one person's name, but he wasn't there when I transferred. He came later. His name is Capt. Hughes." But a week later on December 10, 1970, Doug and Bill returned to Fort MacArthur for Doug to declare under oath before Colonel Duddy that "Captain Hughes" was not an officer under whom he served. Leaving out this one, only three names emerge from the entire twenty-one single-spaced pages of testimony from the Duddy hearing: Dr. Shirasu, the doctor at the military hospital in Japan, Captain Paul Kleinwachter, Doug's assigned attorney, and Dr. Frank L. Cantrell, who, as we shall see, is crucial to this story. Doug's letters home offer no names at all.

Even in the company of others, was Doug Johnson truly, existentially alone? The lack, the loss, the vacuum of any specific names, of any specifics whatever about Doug's AWOLs in all these reams of paper makes me wonder if his whole fourteen months in Vietnam passed in a nameless, faceless, drugged-up, hepatitis-inflected blur, his body quaking with malaria, his liver shot, his mind a rocky atlas of psychedelic peaks and bleak, blackened valleys.

Sometimes when I look back over Doug's life, I wonder if he ever did come down from being high, or find his way back, not simply to his unit, but to his essential humanity. Every time I hear the 1969 Blind Faith song "Can't Find My Way Home"—from the moment the phonograph needle first hissed as I lowered it on to the original record, and now, a half century later—at the sound of those wailing lyrics, I think of my brother, lost, alone, wasted, wandering, seeking some ephemeral path home. Then the song ends, and when the music stops, the jungle closes over my brother and he vanishes.

6. "Dad Will Do Something, Dad Will Do Something"

Autumn 1969

I can only guess at the timing of my parents' dawning awareness of Doug's drug use. I suspect I knew of it before they did. I remember the letters Doug wrote to me in Delaware as plaintive, except for the parts where he would describe how great the drugs were and how high he could get. I remember writing back that he should stay off that shit. Sadly, those letters have vanished. But by October 20, 1969, my dad clearly knew something about Doug's habit, though not the extent of the problem—that is to say, Doug's own later admission that by August 1969 he was mainlining daily and that his arms were "like pincushions." That autumn Doug faced court-martial charges for being AWOL and also for marijuana possession. Dad had a medical background, and if he knew of Doug's repeated bouts of hepatitis, he would have guessed at the equation of dirty needles and drugs. But when did he know or guess? Not before October 1969, that's what I think. Such a descent into addiction would have been unthinkable for my parents; the very words *drug charge, AWOL, court-martial, hard labor, confinement in a military stockade* tolled with unspeakable foreboding and menace. Doug's eight poignant surviving letters suggest that he was deeply ashamed of his freefall into mainlining and addiction and that he wished to keep that knowledge from his parents for as long as he could. Paul Kleinwachter's note to my dad, "At

Doug's insistence, I have not mentioned his use or misuse of drugs" further substantiates that shame.

Doug's earliest letter is dated October 29, 1969, and the last January 2, 1970. They nearly all include requests for Dad to act, to do something, to intercede in some way on his behalf. Douglas turned to Dad, believing, as we all did, that Bill Johnson was a sort of force of nature, that Bill Johnson could stride into any situation and accomplish what other people could not. He might have been a mere sales rep for Lederle Laboratories, but to us he seemed powerful, even heroic.

Experience bore out this belief. For instance, my sister was supposed to graduate from high school in 1970, but her health was so frail that, even though she had had a home tutor and completed the coursework, she had hardly ever been on campus, not in three years. Thus, the school said she had too many absences to qualify for graduation. Helen was devastated. My father paid a little visit to the counselor and the principal and worked out an arrangement so that for the rest of the school year Helen could show up for the first two periods and then leave if she needed to and still be counted as present for the whole day. He bought her a car, and this is exactly what she did. Helen Johnson graduated with the class of 1970.

That same year, I was living in Newark, Delaware, and became very ill with a rampant inflammation of the inner ear. The student infirmary was useless. I went to a doctor in town. Whatever he did, I don't remember because I passed out from the pain. Someone told me of a famous ear specialist doctor in Wilmington, a city about half an hour away. I feared that this doctor would not see me; after all, I had no insurance, and as a grad student, of course, no money. I was awash with pain and fear and tearfully called my father in California. The following day this Wilmington doctor's office called me and set up an immediate appointment. I needed surgery, which he performed in his office. They allowed me to pay for treatment, including the surgery, at something like twenty dollars a month, no interest.

Doug, too, called on Dad, continually as these few letters attest. The first page of the letter below has been lost, but Doug's health situation can be inferred. The closing line, "Well I'll write again [pencil too faded to read] adios amigos and happy neuvos anos" suggests it was written on January first or second, 1970. Doug was still in solitary confinement in Long Binh Jail.

If I have got hep [hepatitis] again I think my bod is in for some bad days ahead. Is there anyone who you could talk to and get some action I'm OBVIOUSLY not going to get any from this end. I feel badly about having to put you thru all the hassle, but I know at least you care enough to get something done.

As I understand hepatitis can be fatal and to say the least I'm becoming a little concerned. Since I have no power except to ask (which is completely forgotten) at least YOU have some kind of power, connections to help me out. I'd appreciate it immensely if you could see somebody about getting something done as quickly as possible. Please hurry. I think letters would be too slow. Either wire or better yet, phone, commercial is better there's no time limit and no "over" at the end of each sentence. I'll cover costs of all calls as I know you're having enough problems already. I feel so badly about causing you MORE. Sorry. I've been the cause of too much already but I should least have the right to decent medical care.

Doug was correct that somehow and even from a great distance, Bill Johnson could help him. On January 18 he was airlifted from Long Binh Jail to a military hospital in Japan to be treated for hepatitis. He stayed there for a month.

My father would later confide to his unwavering supporter, Congressman Jerry Pettis:

The Army would have you believe they magnanimously transferred Douglas from the Long Binh Stockade Hospital in January of 1970 to Japan. He was dying of hepatitis there. In desperation I called the home in Wash. DC of Secretary [of Housing and Urban Development George] Romney (who is of my faith) with a desperate appeal for help. He in turn advised me that he called Secretary [of Defense Melvin] Laird and the next day Doug was transferred to a hospital in Japan.

This, again, in the strictest confidence.

. . .

Our dad seemed to us a powerhouse figure, but William Jess Johnson had humble beginnings. Born in 1918 in a rural hamlet, St. Anthony, Idaho, an area supported by sugar beet fields and a sugar beet processing plant, he was the eldest of five living children of William Andrew and Mae Johnson. Bill's was essentially a frontier childhood, surrounded by homes without electricity or indoor plumbing, living amid pioneering Saints who carved dry farms out of wilderness and fought off plagues of locusts, beating tin pans to save their crops. They broke the ice in rivers in January so they could go under the waters for baptism, total immersion. As a boy Bill was sent to work on an uncle's farm for board and lodging. At thirteen he harvested sugar beets in the field for thirty-five cents an hour.

His father, William Andrew Johnson, the eldest of eleven children, was born in 1887 in an Idaho dugout. At age nineteen, and leaving his younger brothers behind to help on the dry farm, Will Johnson enrolled in Ricks Academy in Rexburg (now the campus of Brigham Young University Idaho). He graduated from the eighth grade in 1908. He was twenty-one when he accomplished what he ought to have done by fourteen, but his pride in having graduated beams out of a studio photograph where he holds his diploma beside a vase of wilting flowers.

In 1914 Will married Mae Henderson, the daughter of English Mormon converts. The couple had a temple wedding, an honor granted only to the most upstanding of Saints. Over the years Will homesteaded, he taught in one-room schoolhouses and worked in the sugar beet factory and as a carpenter, house painter, mechanic, and assorted other callings. However meager his earnings, he gave 10 percent tithing to the church. A devout practitioner of the faith, he also led the young people's groups and the choir and played the violin. In 1936 Will, his wife, and their five children loaded up their car and drove to Coeur d'Alene in northwestern Idaho, where they lived first in a log cabin uphill from Coeur d'Alene Lake. My dad hauled water in buckets daily for cooking and washing. Eventually the Johnsons moved into town, renting a house at the corner of Lost and Dollar. (I am not making this up.) By the late 1930s Will was teaching naturalization classes for immigrants.

Alone of his siblings, Bill inherited his father's reverence for education. After graduating from Coeur d'Alene high school in 1937, he joined the

Civilian Conservation Corps for a while and with his wages bought a radio, a couch, and an overstuffed chair that were delivered to his mother, the first new furniture Mae Johnson had ever had. He enrolled in Ricks College in Rexburg, living in his car for a time, then renting a room in the basement of a laundry. Around the time of Pearl Harbor, he transferred to Utah State University, where he earned a BA in physiology. At Utah State he was part of the Marine Reserves, and he trained with them for a while in South Carolina, but transferred to the Navy. They sent him to Long Beach, California, where he served as a pharmacist's mate on the USS *Bairoko* in the Pacific Theater.

My father never spoke of his wartime service. The one anecdote to come out of it was told to me by mother. She said his hair had turned gray while a Japanese sub prowled beneath the USS *Bairoko*, The ship turned everything off and instructed all sailors not to stir, to not so much as light a match. How long that terrible moment lasted, I've no idea, but it's true his college pictures show brown wavy hair, and I can't remember him with anything but gray hair.

World War II pulled Bill from the enclaves and assumptions of his youth. He forsook the Saints and took up cigarettes, coffee, and alcohol; he made friends he would otherwise never have met. He met Peggy Kalpakian at a USO dance in Los Angeles. She was a USC student in business administration, an urban Angeleno, an Armenian born in Turkey, and a naturalized American citizen. After a six-month courtship, Bill and Peggy were married by a Navy chaplain in September 1944. They had very little time together. I was born in June 1945 while my dad was still at sea and my mom and I lived with her parents and her three sisters.

In 1948, using the GI Bill, Bill earned a Masters in Public Health from Cal Berkeley. He went to work for the Red Cross and was transferred in 1949 to Great Falls, Montana, where Doug was born in January 1950. (And where he almost died, requiring emergency surgery for an infant hernia.) After eighteen months in Montana we returned to Southern California. Dad got a job as a pharmaceutical rep with Lederle Laboratories, and using the GI Bill he and Mom bought a new tract house in the San Fernando Valley. We lived there for seven years.

Every Sunday, after attending the Methodist church, we drove into Los

Angeles for lunch with the Kalpakian grandparents, joined by our aunts, and cousins. In these years my father expressed no interest whatever in religion. We had almost no contact with the Mormons, save for a visit by Dad's lively old widowed Aunt Kitty, who was addicted to Coca Cola, and later, a visit from Will and Mae, who were less lively and did not drink Coca Cola.

Then, in January 1956, not yet seventy years old, Will Johnson suffered a stroke. Dad immediately went to Utah, but his father died before he arrived. When he returned home to Southern California, perhaps ten days or two weeks later, Dad was like a stranger to us. Doug was only six and Helen only four, but I was ten and old enough to register that something profound had changed. (I describe these unsettling events and my dad's background at length in my book of memoirs, *The Unruly Past*.) In the spasm of intense grief and guilt following his father's death, Bill Johnson returned to the Latter-day Saints with what can only be called a vengeance. My mother was very upset, but she either couldn't or didn't fight him. That said, Mom never converted, politely resisting all pressures on her. But from then on we children were all raised Mormon, went under the waters of baptism, total immersion. Though my father embraced the Saints and for a time participated in the obligations of the priesthood (a title bestowed only upon males) he did not give up cigarettes or coffee or alcohol, so it's not as if we were raised in an abstentious home. After about ten years Bill's grief and guilt abated. He lapsed from actively practicing the faith, but he was certainly sufficiently steeped in Mormon culture to know how to approach the various Latter-day Saint worthies from whom he sought help for my brother. And he could and constantly did assert that Doug was a good Mormon boy raised in a good Mormon home.

• • •

The earliest letter from Doug that I found in the basement, dated October 29, 1969, is written to the family. He writes that he knows he will be court-martialed and that, in addition to the AWOLs, there is charge of marijuana possession from an arrest on October 10. Apparently these crimes were sufficient to get him considered for a "212" release from the Army. The 212 was a release for the generally unfit, often given to alcoholics. This designation indicated that the individual was not soldier material, but it had not the stain or disgrace of Undesirable. (At that time no such possible exit was available for drugs.) Doug's letter sounds jubilant about the possibility of his getting a 212; he is confident he'll be home by Thanksgiving or Christmas. (The nameless lawyer he mentions is emphatically not Paul Kleinwachter.)

Dear Fam

Well I'll fill you in as to what's happening. I slid out to talk to the col [colonel] yesterday and he said its his policy to just give me my 212 so I'll be home and out of the Army very soon, probably a month or so. Groovy, huh? I may or may not be home for Thanksgiving, but I should be home for Christmas. Groovy, huh? I spoke to my lawyer and he said its 4th Div policy not to send first offenders to jail unless it's murder or rape or something like that. So that's good to know. I have this stupid Captain who is trying to get me in jail and a Bad Conduct Discharge. I don't think I'll go to jail tho I must admit it scares me quite a bit to say the least. So if I get my 212 I won't be able to go to school for 6 months at which time I can be taking it easy and later on get a job and save some money to buy a car with and support myself with (apt, gas etc.) All I care about is getting that discharge. I've been screwed over so damn much lately, I don't care how I get it or what I get as long as I get out. I'm going insane with everybody hassling but spose I can hack it as long as I keep the thought that I'm coming home soon I can hack just about anything.

I want to tell you that I really love everybody very much and I'm really sorry for what's happening. I know it's hurting everybody but I've got to make my own decisions now and I don't have anyone to talk it over with so I've got to screw the Army and get the hell out. I wrote when I first got in country I would screw the army just like they have screwed me. Now's my chance. I'm gonna take it and go all the way with it.

I sure wish I could get you to change your INNER feelings about [girlfriend]. I know you think she's groovy and all but I don't feel as tho that feeling is a solid one. I'm not sure (I'm not sure of ANYTHING anymore) however [girlfriend] and I, it seems at this point as though it's gonna be a long time for us. She's the most wonderful person. I think it's groovy that she and mom are rapping together on the phone. I don't what it is but there's a definite feeling I get . . . telling me it's good, telling me it's okay. Hard to explain.

I want to thank you for standing behind me on this little crisis. I'm not really worth it but it's such a good feeling to you're always there. I wish I were ¼ or ½ as you build me up to be. If I were I'd be a grateful person. I really feel alone over here, all this damn sickness and hospitals, trouble, lifers trying to screw me to the wall, officers trying to get me in jail, it's quite depressing and deflating my own image of myself. I'm actually beginning to feel like some sort of criminal.

Dad, you are a man among men and the greatest person there is and the best father a person can have. How you can go on under all the pressures you're under and have add to your worries and still go on is beyond my imagination. I can see now everything you've been telling me as though it were a rainy day and you're telling me that the sun is still in the sky and I would believe you until the sky cleared up Well the sky has cleared or is beginning to and I'm beginning to see the sun. Beginning to see that you were right and I was wrong. How does one go about attaining wisdom and determination as you have. Please tell me. I want to be able to make the right decisions like you can. I get the guts you have to hang on when there's seemingly nothing to hang on to and come on top in the end.

I'd like to say now thank you for not just telling me to get lost when I was causing you so much trouble. I think I was lost then. I really WAS lost. I have a very very strong feeling that from now it's going to be okay. I'm only sorry it took so long to come about. I can see now that I was wrong. So DEAD WRONG. Dad to me you're the greatest man that ever lived. I couldn't even begin to list all the things that make you what you are. Mom, well all I can say is that there is no other mom quite like my mom in the whole world. I love you both SO much.

Don't send any Christmas presents please save them till I get home. Send lotsa food though. Dig that "back in the world food!"

Well I'll be home soon. Mom, next time you talk to [girlfriend] tell her everything. Keep her posted. She worries a lot too. I love everybody. See you soon and don't stop writing. That's my only high point in the day,

Love and God Bless
Doug

His next letter, just the day following, is even more wistful, thinking he'll be home soon:

October 30th 1969

Dear fam, Well tomorrow is Halloween! Wonder what I should dress up as? As [neighbor kid] always says "on Halloween Doug dresses up as a human." Wonder if he's right?

Rec'd the two pics of H and BJ and Chief [the dog]. I really dig getting flicks. Dad I haven't seen a greenback since I left. It's good to see one again. Well all I will disclose at this point is that I will be home before Christmas. I hesitate to say more. I may be delayed in my out-processing and I'd hate to have everybody waiting for days on end for me—so when I get home I'll just pop in—So between the middle of November and December 25th I'll be home. Don't send any Christmas packages. Tho I could use a wallet. Only a wallet please save the rest. I'll open them at home. I figure that's better. Besides, I'll have enough junk to haul around as it is. So if you would send a wallet for Christmas I'd really appreciate it—oh, put a pic of the fam inside if you would please. Thanx. ([girlfriend] too if you can get one)

I'm so anxious and excited to see everybody. I can hardly wait.

Tried to call last night. Didn't get through. Will try again tonight. With crossed fingers.

Mom, would you please fill [girlfriend] in as to the latest developments.

Well gonna jet. Gotta go. Be home soon. Ho HO HO (Bad bad poetry)

Love, Doug

PS will let you know when to stop writing till then don't even slow down. Keep it coming. It's the best part of my day.

It will remain one of the saddest ironies of this sad story that these two letters—where Doug expected, hoped, looked gloriously forward to a 212, to being out of the Army, to "popping in" at Turrill Court by Christmas—did not reach his father sooner. At this time Dad was heavily under the influence of an unnamed former sergeant major, a lifer in the Marines. This dude convinced my father that Doug was a sniveling crybaby who simply needed his butt kicked, that whatever Doug had written that was upsetting to his family was just slop and there only to "elicit sympathy." My father initially and, I think, reflexively endorsed this no-nonsense approach; it echoed the frontier mentality he'd been raised with, something on the order of: "Shut up, show up, get out there and do your duty."

I have no idea who this Sgt.-Major-Kick-His-Butt was or how my father knew him, but in phone conversations with me, Dad shared and endorsed his opinions. In protest I wrote to Dad on October 20, 1969, four single-spaced typed pages of redundant lamenting and pleading (edited here, though I have left spelling and punctuation errors as they were). I begged Dad to reconsider, to reject this kind of mindset, to recognize that Doug was cracking under the strain of Vietnam. The contents of this letter make clear that I already knew about Doug's woes, including the drug charge. It also sounds as though Doug specifically asked, wanted me to give this news to Dad so that he (Doug) would not have to do it. And I had already written to assure Doug that "Dad will do something," believing, as we all did, that Bill Johnson could achieve what others could not.

Dear Dad—

Even tho I perhaps ought to call, I guess writing will do for this letter since we are all universally hurting for coins. I have thought all weekend about your Friday nite call, and this is primarily what I want to discuss. I think that the action that you took (i e. writing to Doug's commanding officer) was a good one and that probably this is the best thing you could do given the circumstances and our total lack of any kind of <u>objective</u> knowledge about Doug and where he is etc. But I think that "advice" or point of view that you seem so intent on, at least the opinions offered to you by your friend the retired sgt major are wrong. Firstly you have to consider the source. I am not knocking your friend, I just think that you ought to see, if you don't already that being a retired lifer from the Marines gives him a point of view that is not necessarily valid, What else, let me ask you, what else is there for a lifer to say? Yes, Mr. Johnson, your son is right, the whole thing is a crappy mess over there and he's getting the worst of it? No way is a man who has dedicated his whole life (voluntarily) to the service going to say that. The military as I see it has to defend themselves in certain ways, that is by making all people who are for peace (be they civilians or servicemen) seem like idiots who do not realize the complexity of the situation (killing etc can be very complex particularly when you endow it w/ all sorts of fine phrases, that and make an organization, a profession if you want, out of killing . . .) What else <u>would</u> a lifer say? Nothing. That is exactly the lifer point of view, that everyone who bitches about Viet Nam is simply trying to elicit sympathy etc. However marve, your bud may be this is still his bias . . . and just because he has been a Sgt. Major in the marines does not necessarily make him some kind of oracle for the truth of what is going on in <u>your</u> son's head.

On the phone you said you were going to "kick Doug's rear end, and tell him to get up off his butt and do something and etc, etc etc." This is <u>not</u> a kind of "put-up-your-dukes-and have-at-them" kind of problem.

This is not the kind of problem that can be solved or even mitigated by that kind of advice. This is a HEAD, problem, dad. Tho I know you hate this kind of terminology, it is in some ways, a psychological, or even a moral problem. The old Protestant ethic of give 'em hell, do your bit etc. will not work w/ this kind of problem. I have always admired your guts, dad, and always thought of you as being very tough, in the best sense of the word. I maybe have not always gotten along w/ you in certain respects, but I nonetheless have never lost my admiration for your toughness and your courage in the face of adversity. What I am saying is that the kind of answers you've been able to employ in the past is not what this situation requires. When Doug was in Boy Scouts you urged him on w/ kind of encouragement—do your best, don't let anybody get on top you, "work" and "sweat" (so to speak.) That was groovy then, and it was just what he needed. Douglas I'm sure is well aware now that all the similar stuff you told him when he was screwing around Valley College was similarly true. But it's not true now. Doug is <u>not</u> in a competitive situation where one can "triumph" by putting up the dukes and fighting it out w/ the locals, and getting off one's ass, so to speak. This is a head, or a mind, or a psychological or a moral kind of problem, that he has to face. You cannot put up your dukes and get off your ass, because your mind is the thing that is being torn up, destroyed, kicked around, or whatever. That kind of advice is nothing but hot air, or wind, or at best, meaningless.

It is true that Doug is the kind of person who needs an occasional kick in the pants (who doesn't) but it can't be ministered at this time the same way it was ministered when he was living at home. Douglas is up against the wall and the crap is descending on him from all directions whether it really is or not (as your lifer friend would believe) is beside the point. Doug <u>thinks</u> it is. For him it really is. The last thing he needs to think is that his family is similarly shitting on him and has no comprehension of the situation. He <u>can't</u> put up his dukes, he can't at this point, get off his ass, because that's not the kind of problem he is facing. Your friend notwithstanding, I find it very hard to believe that the military will administer a tap on the wrist (like the "office hours" you mentioned and the cut in pay) and let it go at that. Doug has been busted, dad, in the vernacular that means a dope charge. The military I'm sure is well aware that an awful lot of smoking (marijuana) goes on but when they catch someone, they are most certainly not going to excuse him on the basis that everyone does it. . . . Maybe they will just give him an extension of working time and a cut in pay. Marve, if they do. Maybe Doug will learn to lay off that crap, but I don't think so. When I wrote to him I told him that a drug induced euphoria was no escape from his problems, but rather it compounded them, particularly if one already <u>has</u> problems. I told him if he did not have any problems and was forced to make them up, then groovy—but such is not the case. He has got plenty of problems and does not need to add to them. The best thing he can do for himself is to keep his mind clear and his head as calm as possible. Easier said than done.

Doug wrote to me, I think in the hopes that I would tell you because he was scared to death to tell you [about the AWOL and the drug charge] Dad will have to know sometime, he wrote, but I don't know what or how to tell him. He [Doug] didn't feel that he could just whip all this junk on you. . . . In a lot of ways he is still terrifically immature and juvenile. All that serves to make his current situation all the worse, psychically. Even a mature person has probs hacking out VN, but for an immature person, I'm sure it is pure hell. If you want, I suppose you can construe his having gone AWOL as immature response to a situation, but immature or not, it was done.

But as Douglas says, he was "scared shitless." What do you do when you're scared shitless, dad, do you swallow it down and venture on? If you are mature and can at least physically cope w/ the situation at hand, think about your fear later—but if you are immature, your first response is to run. As Charlie Brown would say, there is no problem so big that you cannot run away from it. Alas, Charlie Brown was wrong. There are some that you cannot run away from and Douglas is facing such a problem. right now, He cannot physically run any more and he is rapidly discovering that all forms of psychially running have gotten him nothing but trouble, So being immature, his usual basis of response to trouble is gone from him, and he is left w/o anything. And he is suffering for it.

If you had gotten your info from anyone but a retired lifer in the Marines, I maybe wouldn't be so critical, but you seem to have adopted his opinions, w/o qualifications, and they <u>need</u> qualification. Your friend I think told you what is essentially the easiest response for <u>you</u> in this matter, but putting up your dukes and getting off your ass and doing your bit are meaningless phrases when your problems are in your head and in your mind and there seems to be no outlet, no way to turn, nowhere to go, and you are hemmed in by fear and confusion on all sides. This cannot be met with the old hard line of frontier virtues. I can almost hear you scoffing. I can almost see the look you get around your mouth when you heartily disapprove of something

I think that we (Doug's fam) can provide a kind of mental bulwark for him, because if we can't then no one else can, because no one else, and certainly not the army gives a shit about him. I think that <u>you</u> could be that one person for Doug who can help him. I can't really be it, nor can mother, but you Dad, can. He has more respect for you than I think he would care to admit. Begrudging respect, perhaps, but respect nonetheless. If <u>you</u> don't take some effort to Understand, if you simply hand out Protestant panaceas then what is he to think except that you totally do not want to help him in any way that is meaningful. And I'm sorry, I just can't see telling him to get off his butt as meaningful. When I got that letter from Doug I wrote to him and I told him over and over, Doug, I'm going to tell the parentos—DAD WILL DO SOMETHING. Dad will do something. I'm not saying that you must request a personal interview w/ Tricky Dick himself, or throw your bod before the Joint Chiefs of Staff, but I think he has to feel like you will do something, even if that something is only to understand what he is going thru.

I must close. I hope you at least get the gist of what I've been trying to say. I think that you can provide a moral guideline for Doug. I think he needs to feel, that you moreso than mother or me, that you understand and if you don't sympathize (if you actually do believe that he would write such a letter simply to elicit sympathy) if you <u>don't</u> sympathize, then at least let him know that you're not w/ the officers and investigators and lifers in general who are at this point heaping shit upon his head. I told him, Doug, don't you break down, you let someone else break down, but don't you do it. As far as whatever punishment he may receive, if your bud [Sgt.-Major-Kick-His-Butt] is right, then groovy. If he's not, well [a friend of mine] could tell you a few stories about the old military prisons that you wouldn't believe come out of the 20th century. (He was jailed in the brig on his ship for a week I believe on a rather trumped up charge, but [my friend] is tough too, and he didn't break, tho I honestly can't see how he did anything but break.)

I can't agree w/ you dad, that is not a serious situation. And I couldn't agree <u>less</u> w/ your lifer friend. So you do whatever you want, but please don't whip that get off your butt line on Doug at this point. Wait. He'll need it in a bit. But he doesn't need it now, A dope charge is not like stealing potatoes from the KP, Viet Nam is not WWII. The military is a law unto themselves . . . They don't choose MP's for the fine education and comprehension of the human animal. So I do worry about Doug. If it was a not a mind problem, then I too would write to him get off your butt and get to work. But work and sweat are not the answers for everything, Dad, they just are not. And I don't believe them to be the answers here. I don't believe Doug would write such a letter for sympathy alone, particularly when, as you pointed out, he gets letters and packages all the time from the fam. He needs you, more than he needs anyone write now. I don't want to see you fail him, for your sake and for his. I realize that the advice promulgated by your lifer friend is a lot more "comfortable" for everyone than what I have just said, but we cannot always live in moral comfort and the answers for one problem are not always the answers for other problems. There aren't any absolutes, Dad, not here, and not, for god's sake in Viet Nam. What is comfortable is not always what is right.

Well, I will close. If you don't get what I'm trying to say, then you won't. I know you have a lot on your mind, money, Helen's health, etc. But that shouldn't blind you to the fact that Doug's prob is not just trouble in school or a traffic ticket. It's a dope charge. Think on that one.

Tell Helen, I love her letters and I particularly love the sticks of gum she encloses with her letters. Will write to her soon, Also give that little boy Brian a big kiss from his sister and she will have a birthday present off to him shortly. (It may not get there on his birthday) Also love to mother. I am doing my work, and I am not losing sleep or crying incessantly over this thing w/ Doug, for that does him no good either. All I can do is keep writing, and hoping and praying. I will close. I miss you all at home.

I estimate my letter arrived at Turrill Court on or about Saturday, October 25. Doug's letters of October 29 and October 30 reached there sometime after November 3. How do I know this? Because on November 3—still in the thrall of Sgt.-Major-Kick-His-Butt and despite my long, impassioned entreaty— Dad wrote to Doug's commanding officer requesting that Doug *not* be given a 212.

November 3 1969
Subject: pfc Douglas S. Johnson
RA 1887491
Company D 2/35th Inf.
4th Infantry Division
APO SF 96355

Dear Sir,

Your reply to my letter of October 17th has not yet been received as of this date; however, due to the urgency of this situation I feel I must instigate a call for help. I am writing to you sir, in humbleness, gratitude and in earnestness. May I petition you to take time to save my boy from the pangs of repulsive antipathy. Your decision will be honored.

My son has stated in a letter that there is a possibility that he will be given a 212 discharge. This is the easy way out for my boy and perhaps an easy way out for the army. Generally speaking, and this no exception, both lose. The army loses a good soldier. My boy loses himself—his courage, his usefulness, his aims, his judgment, his identity, his desire to succeed, his ability to cope with difficult situations, his feeling of adequacy, his ability to fight, to study, to learn, to accept and be accepted, to stand up against decay, to maintain moral standards and be honest with himself.

My boy, with provocation, buckled, I feel, through fear, and broke the rules and regulations set down by the US Army. Because of this, corrective measures must be taken and discipline measured out to the offender. I give you 100% cooperation. May I, however, state my reasons why he is not a "212" material

Douglas is an Eagle Scout with 35 merit badges. He has been in the Explorer post. At age 17 he spent one summer as aquatic director at Scout Camp; was assistant scoutmaster for the church troop.

Douglas was a talented piano student for nine years, and many times played extremely difficult pieces before various groups.

I plead for your indulgence sir, to refrain from giving Douglas a "212." I plead that you will see fit to transfer or request a transfer to another area. I plead that this boy be given a second chance to prove himself a proud soldier of the US Army. It would be my impression that the unit he belongs to now would present too many innate and refractory problems associated with these same men, officers and conditions.

Sir, you and your colleagues have spent years in overseas assignments. I would venture to say that you have fought communism on many fronts and today you are fighting communism. You are stationed in Viet Nam to help save Southeast Asia from the ills and sickness of communists.

Would you sir allow a portion of an hour of your time to save one American boy who may sometime bring honor and integrity to himself as well as to the Army of the United States of America?

Sincerely yours,
William J. Johnson
CC LDS Chaplain
CC company Commander.

When I read this November 3 appeal, I am filled with sadness. I have no doubt that later my father bitterly regretted writing it. There was no 212 for

Doug. Doug was not out of the Army and home for Christmas, 1969. The returning soldier, would not "pop in" at Turrill Court, throw open the front door and thrill the home folks as they rushed to embrace him. A 212 would have been a mercy, a godsend. A 212 might have spared Doug the unthinkable pain that lay ahead and spared the family years of anguish.

And my own long, noisy letter of October 20 would prove sadly prophetic. The months and years ahead would show that "The army doesn't give a shit about him." Doug Johnson was just another hapless grunt stoking the war machine, as no doubt were many others, young men whose names are on the granite wall in Washington, DC, and many others who, like Doug, came back alive, but shattered. And my father would in fact spend years requesting the personal intervention of Tricky Dick, as well as throwing himself at the Army. And I was certainly, absolutely correct that "DAD WILL DO SOMETHING. Dad will do something."

7. "Light Still Shining upon My Lost Soul"

<u>November 1969</u>

Perhaps the pivot point for my father was Doug's rosy, imagined Christmas reunion, or the pathos of, "I really feel alone over here, all this damn sickness and hospitals, trouble, lifers trying to screw me to the wall, officers trying to get me in jail," but once Bill received Doug's letters of October 29 and October 30, he would never again pick up Sgt-Major-Kick-His-Butt's refrain. Henceforth Bill Johnson would conduct his own sort of war. Dad would indeed "Do Something." And this was not just wielding the pen on Doug's behalf, but writing to him often, extolling Doug's own worth and potential, applauding his great moral strength.

Doug's letter to Dad and Mom of November 8, 1969, responds to this inspiration.

Dear Dad & Mom—

> Dad your letters have brought to light what I was actually doing to myself. If I had any idea of how much I was getting into trouble wise, believe me I never would have done it. I was new and scared and found running easier than facing my problem squarely. So now I must face an even bigger problem.

I do appreciate everything you're doing for me. I'm not worth all the trouble and worry I'm putting everybody thru. Dad, I only differ on one stand you seem to have. I am <u>not</u> Mr. Great. Not yet. I must earn that title before I'll accept it. There's a saying over here—I just heard recently and since I am an Armenian I feel it very applicable to me—it goes—"when the going gets tough, the tough say _____ it."

I am <u>so</u> ashamed and I <u>want</u> to get back on the right track. I just don't think I'll ever be able to look anybody in the eye unless I stand up to this whole mess and face it like a man—otherwise I wouldn't be much of a man, would I? When I get home in June, I'll be able to say I did my job and I did it [four words scratched out] and now I'm home ready to continue my life and enjoy it.

Tho it may seems a lesser problem rite now it does play an important part of what my attitude is over here. I'm sure you know now what I'm speaking about [girlfriend]. She really means a lot to me, more than anybody (outside our family) I have ever known. I would <u>never</u> do anything to hurt her. Between you and me and the fencepost I <u>do</u> have a feeling I may be married to her not until I receive my degree. I'll play that situation by ear. I have discussed it with her and she feels the same way as I do however we're very excited at just the thought of [two words scratched out] sharing our lives together. I don't want to make <u>another</u> mistake and jump into anything where I don't know <u>exactly</u> what I'm getting into. Believe me before I <u>ever</u> make another move. It won't be made without my knowledge of pros, cons, consequences, loopholes, pitfalls and situation in general from <u>top</u> to <u>bottom</u>.

I just spoke with my squad leader and he says he wants me back with my squad. They want me back <u>anyway</u>! Some light is still shining upon my lost soul from the heavens of hope.

I have learned a great deal from this whole ugly thing. It has left a scar in the canyons of my memory—reminding me of what happens when a man shirks his responsibility. I only hope to be ¼ or maybe ½ the man you are, dad. If I can ever achieve that I will have succeeded. It will take many hours, years, decades to even come close. However my time has come—my moment of truth—I must face squarely and firmly and prove to myself, if to no one else, that I am a man and on the right road. If I am not a man myself, how can I show my son through my actions what it is to be a man. Enough talk—it has come now to the time for me to show through action I have tried to express to you in this letter.

I'm seeing the 4th Div chaplain tomorrow. I'm going to wait until I can see how this is going to turn out before I tell [girlfriend]. No use worrying her with uncertainly also besides, I'm ashamed—when I leave here I will be able to hold my head high and say I did right I am proud. I am at my unit and well (Pleiku)

I love everybody dearly (including [girlfriend]) as part of the family from here on out. <u>I do love her very much</u>)

You're the most wonderful parents in the whole world. I love you dearly.

Love,
Doug

Doug had met this girlfriend in high school, where she was a year behind him. In 1969 they had been together for perhaps two years. She was a very pretty, quiet girl: long brown hair, big blue eyes, content to let him shine in the spotlight, and thus perfect for Doug. She helped to sustain him, and for that alone my family would have been grateful to her and supportive of their young love. On December 12 while he was in the Nha Trang hospital, Doug probably managed to call her and ask her to marry him. She said yes. My sister remembers Dad taking the girlfriend downtown to a jewelry store where she picked out a beautiful engagement ring and he paid for it. Helen remembers the ring vividly: a tiny cherub holding a flower and in the center an orange citron gemstone cut like a diamond with facets.

• • •

On November 3 Bill wrote a flurry of identical letters to the two senators from California, Alan Cranston and George Murphy. Each asked:

Did he [Doug] go AWOL?

Was he apprehended with marijuana in his possession?
What is the maximum penalty?
Was he hospitalized for shrapnel and malaria?

Each letter pleads for Congressional intervention. To Cranston, he wrote:

> Senator, we need your help now. From the tone of my son's correspondence this company C.O. is pushing for a bad conduct discharge. An enlisted man, and especially under these circumstances, has very little, if any possibility of fighting this case alone. If he remains under this C. O., his life will become unbearable. This is the root of the problem as it is . . . Douglas is 19 years old and this is his first offense. He will make a good soldier and a good citizen if given medical attention and placed or transferred to an area that he can handle. This will give him a new lease on life and confidence in his capabilities. . . .
>
> We are spending millions of dollars to save Southeast Asia. Please open the way for new horizons for this boy, and save a citizen.
>
> I seek your aid sir with personal attention and with the speed of wire and sound and I am grateful for your assistance. Will you make this #1 priority?
>
> Sincerely yours,
> William J. Johnson

Cranston seems to have replied, but the envelope with the appropriate postmark is empty.

To Jerry L. Pettis, congressman from San Bernardino, Bill wrote:

> From correspondence it is my judgment that Douglas may now feel so dejected and tormented that it is affecting his attitude and sense of values. He is 19 years old. He may need medical attention. What is the possibility of his remaining in the service and being transferred to another duty station or to a training school to give him a new lease on life and confidence in his capabilities. This would undoubtedly be the best therapy and form of medication this boy could receive.

Even amid these pleas for a transfer, my father must surely have known that the court-martial would go forward on November 14 and indeed it did. I have the whole thirty-four-page official record of this 1969 trial. Many of these official forms are blank because Doug had pled guilty to the episodes of AWOL in June. The record includes Doug's brief mitigating statement, already quoted in chapter 5, about wanting a fifteen-day leave to be home when Helen came out of surgery (in June 1969) and looking for a phone to find out how her surgery went. The record of the trial also shows that Doug's so-called defense counsel made but one statement—and that cannot be construed as being on behalf of his client. "For two weeks prior to the trial the accused was restricted to the battalion area under armed guard." Yes. Eighteen half-assed words. That's all this dude said. In an act of unwarranted generosity, I am withholding his name.

Doug wrote to Dad immediately after the thirty-minute trial, a letter more defiant than defeated, more redolent of resolve than despair:

November 14th

Dear Dad,

> Well it's all over now—I just came out of court. I rec'd a 5 month suspended sentence, 2/3 forfeiture of pay and reduced to an E1 also getting a transfer to a different unit. They dropped the [marijuana] charge—they had illegal search procedure.
>
> I'm starting all over again now I have paid my debt to the army now I must show <u>myself</u> that I can do it like I <u>should</u> have to begin with. It was your letter to the battalion CO that saved me. There's only one way that I know of for me to say thank you that is thru my actions and deeds. I really love both of you so very much and as far as I'm concerned my parents are the greatest people alive and I thank God each time I pray that I was fortunate enough to have them help me thru my life. My only ambition now is to be a success in whatever field I choose and show you that your efforts have not been in vain—as it seems to you right now, I'm sure. I've profited quite a bit from this little episode, gained some wisdom and learned a lot.

I'm starting all over now. I'm going to make the best of it and put out 110% and be the true Armenian I really am inside. You'll see, let me show you I AM tough. I'll show this goddamn Army just how much guts I have got. I will write again tonight.

Love,
Doug

PS Thank you again for everything you've done and for standing by me when I needed it most. You're TRULY a wonderful person both mom and dad and the whole family too.

Drug use had already taken a toll on Doug. Even if he had been straight as a Methodist deacon at this trial, he was not in good health. Twelve days later he would be hospitalized for hepatitis and malaria for three weeks in Nha Trang where, as he later testified, he was introduced to LSD and speed, grim, ghoulish specters that would cast their miasma over the rest of my brother's time in Vietnam and, indeed, over the rest of his life.

8. "I Keep Reaching for a Hand to Guide Me"

Having made the baleful acquaintance of LSD and speed, Doug left Nha Trang Hospital to return to his unit on December 19 but did not show up for eight days. At the Duddy hearing he testified that no arrangements had been made to return him to his unit, that he could not get back or even let his CO know that he could not return because two plane crashes disrupted travel and communication:

> Upon discharge from the hospital at Nha Trang in December 1969 I tried to get a flight back to Pleiku. This proved to be rather difficult as an F-4 Phantom Jet had crashed on the military air strip and a civilian Vietnamese aircraft crashed into a school house extremely close to the air strip, the same day. As a result of this situation and many of the planes being used for military purposes, I was told my flight would be delayed indefinitely. I immediately got on the phone and tried to contact Pleiku in order to inform my commanding officer of the incident and why I would be late. Many of the lines were down, in addition to the usual difficulty trying to get a phone call through in Vietnam. I finally got a ride back to Pleiku and arrived there several days late.
>
> Upon walking into the S1 [personnel staff officer's] office, I was greeted

with a statement of Article 31, I was asked if I had anything to say, to which I replied, "Yes." He answered me with, "I don't want to hear it, get out." Confinement orders were typed out the same evening and the next morning I was on a plane with two armed guards bound for Long Binh Jail.

However, at this *actual* moment—December 26, when Doug "finally got a ride back to Pleiku"—his state of mind was not at all as lucid as this later measured, sober testimony implies. On the contrary, wherever he was and whatever he was doing in this time, something had cracked wide open in Doug Johnson. After the hospital released him on December 18, Doug spent some eight days—God knows where—before he returned to his unit, where he was promptly arrested on December 26. That night, between his arrest and being sent to Long Binh in the morning, Doug put pen to paper in a letter to his father. In these fourteen terrifying pages there are only two fairly straightforward paragraphs. The first, early on:

> First of all, to inform you the <u>vast vast</u> almost unreal changes that have taken place in my head since I was discharged from the hosp until now so you realize everything that I'm trying to convey has only taken place since the 18th of Dec 1969.

The second is toward the end:

> Well, in these last 8 days I have been in transit from the hospital to my unit. I am fully aware of the dangers I was putting myself into—as for the Army in command and tonight the <u>final</u> axe fell. I have been AWOL in that it took some 8 days to come back to my unit and when I returned tonite I was informed that I would be going to Long Binh because I supposedly was doing wrong going AWOL before suspended sentence was up. I am supposed to be leaving tomorrow.

These two paragraphs tell us that the mental changes Doug will record in the fourteen pages actually took place over an eight-day period. To me, this suggests that however calm his later recollection of his return on December 26 ("Upon walking into the S1 office . . .") *at the time*, how could he have been anything but utterly unhinged with all this roiling through his head? His reference to the "mars station" is the Military Auxiliary Radio System (MARS), a network of ham radio operators who relayed signals from military men to their families' telephone lines. Perhaps it was a mercy for Doug's parents that he could not get through, that they did not have to hear what's below, to listen and be helpless before the onslaught.

26 December '69

To a wise man and a fine father. Well, Dad I have much to tell you.

I suppose first I must apologize for not writing directly home sooner, but the rest of the letter, what you are about to read is explanation enough if I can make myself clear. I tried to contact you via mars, however I tried and tried and couldn't even contact the mars station. It will be difficult to explain on paper but very deep. VERY deep within my heart and mind. I somehow know that <u>you</u> will understand more than anybody and more completely than any other person in the world. I hope <u>I pray to god</u> that you will understand the series of events that have transpired since I last wrote home. I have <u>so much to say</u> and I just can't seem to write them down (my thoughts) fast enough. I've got to complete this letter before tomorrow because of the reasons made clear by the actual letter (gist) itself.

First of all, to inform you the <u>vast vast</u> almost unreal changes that have taken place in my head since I was discharged from the hosp until now so you realize everything that I'm trying to convey has only taken place since the 18th of Dec 1969.

My God, <u>my dear dear god</u> I only hope that I have changed enough to last me the rest of my life for if I have it will be worth everything that has taken place since I became aware of my [own?] being. As you can probably guess I am extremely desperate Oh God I just keep reaching for a hand to guide me and it just <u>isn't there.</u> I have a very strong feeling it's <u>your</u> hand I'm reaching for [Labor?] that going no further.

All I can really say is that I have <u>FINALLY</u> come to the full realization of everything you've been trying to tell me since I was old enough to understand language.

I cannot I simply <u>cannot</u> explain my feeling that I have inside, all I can explain is my conclusion and let you decide if you know what I mean. To the beginning. On the day I was discharged from the hosp I start on a series of thoughts about myself that will ultimately change my <u>entire life</u>. I find a desire to learn just for the sake of learning <u>KNOWLEDGE KNOWLEDGE</u> oh my <u>God</u> I all of a sudden want to <u>learn anything</u> just so learned and along with those feelings I experienced a good, clean uninhibited feeling as though I were being released from a cage and <u>totally</u> free a feeling of understanding understanding about everything an <u>unexplainable</u> feeling of knowing what is good in this world, what is bad where I was going how I was going get there. <u>I found the</u> (trite but true) <u>real Doug Johnson</u>.

I get so frustrated when I try to explain a very very <u>deep frustration</u>. Oh my dear dear God I hope you understand. I get frustrated to the point of tears, <u>Literal tears</u> when I try to explain my emancipation from a very very confused life and nobody but you and maybe mom possibly [can?] will ever really <u>double</u> understand. Trying to keep something of this magnitude is like having an atomic bomb blow inside your head, blowing away all traces of the cobwebs and screwy adolescent ideas, values and morals and you need <u>so</u> desperately to tell someone who will understand yet there is no one that knows and understands like I hope you will. I have become so frustrated inside that it has actually brought on vomiting and <u>physical discomfort</u>. I feel as tho I am going to break, crack in some way. I know that crying would help—altho—it is still not accomplishing what I'm trying to do and that is having somehow understand how I feel. Can you see? I could cry all nite and all day and it mite release tension temporarily but <u>still</u> nobody understands how <u>I feel</u>. Never in my entire life have I <u>ever ever</u> altered my thinking enough to warrant <u>total</u> bewilderment from [scribbled out] <u>everybody</u>. It tends to make one feel as an outcast, a weirdo, an abnormal human being. Have I changed so greatly that I have lost communication with my own species of animal? Oh God. I am <u>so lost</u>. As the small child must feel when separated from its mother in a busy place—where do you start looking? You ask people where your mother is, but they don't really care <u>totally lost</u>. Well now that I've explained or tried to scratch the surface barely of how I feel may I move try to scratch the surface of my realization of what was actually the cause of my "lost, empty feeling" I shall now try to explain to you what I have explained to others Well it is very difficult and I am becoming even more frustrated even as I write this letter. It's difficult. Please bear with me and try to understand <u>Oh my God</u> please try to understand.

I shall start with a very basic human need, love (I'm trying to slow down and relax a little, it's just that I've tried so hard, so many times before and failed)

Love, as I see it now after my little transformation, is something so much deeper than just physical attraction and even more than caring about someone beyond a normal relationship, love as I see it now in an (groping for words has been common lately) intense deep feeling that cannot really be explained—your love, Dad <u>YOUR LOVE FOR MOTHER AND YOUR CHILDREN</u> as you have so many times tried to explain to me is as intense as my love for [girlfriend] and my family. I know now how you feel. I don't know how or why or how I know that I'll prob never know but believe me, Dad, I "stand" before you now, I know that my love for [girlfriend] and my brother and my sisters and most of all my parents <u>you Dad</u> YOU DAD, and mom But mostly you Dad is intense as yours for your wife and children. I don't think <u>anybody could ever anybody</u> as much as you love your wife and children. And I can only hope to God that I can give [girlfriend] and my children <u>half</u> even <u>half</u> the love you've given your family. I will consider myself a successful father and husband. Oh Dear God. Oh my <u>Dear Dear</u> God if you only knew how I feel

If I tried to explain on paper every emotion, everything that I have realized in the last 8 days I could only <u>begin</u> to try to explain in 10 thousand <u>volumes</u> I would try to give you a small insight into the drastically and complex I've changed but even as I am writing this I am becoming even more frustrated at my <u>own inability</u> my ignorance to explain how I feel. I'm ASHAMED to admit that I don't have the ability the vocabulary to even explain my own feelings. Well what it [scribbled out] boils down to is what you have being trying to "instill" into me (as you would say) [scribbled out] all these years, decades as somehow, someway sank deep into my mind for me to <u>really really</u> understand what you have been trying so desperately to get me to understand for so long. Oh my God, oh my God has finally hit whatever spot you've been aiming for [scribbled out]I don't know of any other way to explain it [three scribbled-out attempts] without actually being there and without filling 10,000 volumes

What I did basically was look [scribbled out] into my brain and find all my faults but part of my faults is that my major faults and I came out of it <u>grossly grossly immensely</u> disappointed with myself. And I think part of my frustrations lie in the fact that I found <u>so many</u> things wrong with me that correcting them seems so futile and so distant that I get the "lost" feeling a child gets when it is separated from its mother. Oh my God, Dad, <u>OH MY GOD DAD</u> <u>please please understand</u> what my mind is going through. I'm going to go insane if someone doesn't understand soon. So much pressure on my mind for so long has taken me to the brink of insanity. Why doesn't <u>anyone</u> understand even basic things like <u>love</u> or <u>compassion</u>. God, Dear God, oh my Dear God I'm going to crack very very soon. My brain cannot take the pressure real <u>pressure</u> that this is forcing upon me.

Well, as you can possibly hopefully see my head has gone thru some drastic changes in the last eight days and will continue to go through changes with what I have at least corrected the faults I found, unfortunately they will probably take my entire lifetime to do it. I have only one real question left to answer <u>why why</u>, if these changes I'm going through are making me a better person, <u>why</u> are they bringing such terrible <u>terrible</u> horrible <u>horrible</u> frustrations and doubts as to even something as basic as simple as my own <u>sanity</u>.

Well, if I haven't reached you by now I have a strange feeling that I never ever will <u>really</u> reach <u>anybody</u>. I have a strange secure feeling that you <u>will</u> understand and you will reach out your hand to me and pull me up over the ledge that you have been trying all these years to help me over

Well, in these last 8 days I have been in transit from the hospital to my unit. I am fully aware of the dangers I was putting myself into—as for the Army in command [scribbled out] and tonight the <u>final</u> axe fell.

I have been AWOL in that it took some 8 days to come back to my unit and when I returned tonite I was informed that I would be going to Long Binh because I supposedly was doing wrong going AWOL before suspended sentence was up. I am supposed to be leaving tomorrow.

I am so upset and frustrated so near insanity—<u>literal insanity</u>—that I don't even care what they do to me because I feel very very deep within myself that in these 8 days, 184 hours I became a more mature person, I have actually found the Doug Johnson that I was meant to be. I found that [scribbled out] unexplainable quality that makes us tough <u>tough</u> Tougher than anything anybody can ever hurl at me to break me down. I'm tougher than <u>anybody</u> ANYBODY else in the <u>world</u>. God Damn! Let them throw me in jail, goddamnit let them try as they may to break my mind, but I think no matter what happens that that 8 days was the last time I ever [even?] invested in my entire life.

Somehow I even seem to have instilled into myself a confidence that I can do <u>anything</u> <u>anything</u> once I decide to do it and [illegible] confidence that when I make a decision, be it big or small, important or unimportant, I know within my and soul it will be the right one and <u>nobody</u> NOBODY will ever change my mind.

So I say <u>FUCK THE ARMY FUCK THEIR JAILS</u> and fuck their close-minded, stupid, never-be-anybody people I am <u>tough</u> and I can come out on top of <u>anything they try</u> to do to me.

Somehow I feel better, now, not quite as frustrated, a little more toward sane mind and somehow comforted in the fact that I know you'll understand me, maybe not to the degree that you may not realize how deeply I understand what <u>I know</u> you feel (the confidence, the love, everything) but I know you'll at least understand what has taken place in my head.

Oh my <u>dear dear God</u> DEAR DEAR GOD please help me help me reach the hand I've been groping for <u>so</u> long.

It's funny but even as troubled as my mind has been I find that can even <u>sleep better</u> it's a very relaxing sleep like I never really had before

I just know that however this whole bad dream is going to end, that I will be the better person for it in the long run. Being in jail <u>might</u>

just prove my point because there I'll have to show myself I'm as tough as I know I am. It's more or less of a real ultimate test of my ability to tougher than anybody else in the world—it is awful soon I mean haven't really straightened my out all the way but I've finally unscrambled my brain enough see what might I've done the biggest part of the transition into my "new life" and my frustration is really just my inability to cope with such a drastic sudden change. It will eventually work itself out and I will slowly become adjust to my new life

My new life.

I'm very proud of my newfound life and very proud I discovered it all by myself

I think I realize now the frustration you just have felt for so many years when you tried and tried to help me see and I just didn't—you are a very very remarkable man I can only hope that turn out to have half as much wisdom and knowledge and patience and understand as you have. If I turn out to be ½ just half of the man that you are dad, I will consider myself very very lucky and successful man. If I can even possible raise my family ½ just plain old ½ (one half) as finely and good and clean as you have raised your family I will be a very happy and contented man.

You have given something that will stay with me the rest of my life and insure that when death finds me, I will be a very very happy satisfied person

I just can't thank you enough for what you've done for me. But I'd like to take this opportunity to say

Thank you as simple and unelaborated as it may seem for sticking with me for all these years through thick and thin until I found myself, found what you've been teaching me for so long your efforts have not been in vain

Oh my God Thank you

I feel so grateful I think maybe you have slight inkling as to how grateful and indeed thankful I am for your efforts

And before I close I just want to say that I love you and will always be held in my mind as the greatest, wisest person in the entire world. I know I love [fiancée] and will have a prosperous and rich life together this I know. If can treat her half as good as you've treated me [my girl-friend] will be a very happy mother and wife as long as she lives.

Wither grace of God I am lucky enough to be Your Son,
Douglas Johnson
PS Tell everybody everything is OK & that I said "merry Christmas and happy new year"

• • •

At the Duddy hearing a year later, Doug described, calmly, coherently, what happened to him following his arrest and arrival at Long Binh Jail on December 27, 1969.

Upon arrival at LBJ I was immediately placed in solitary confinement, maximum security, a place they nicknamed "the box." Solitary confinement in this military stockade was to me one of the more horrifying excruciatingly painful encounters with which I have ever come into contact.

The only thing we had to look forward to was watching the rats three times a day as they ate the food off our plates. These rats ranged from 10½ inches to 2½ to 3 feet long. I was in a physical state at that time of being "strung out," that being completely without any drugs I was unable to carry on a normal conversation with another human being.

When I try to align this cogent testimony with the contents of the December 26 soul-shriek-psyche-dissolving letter, I have to wonder: When he arrived at LBJ was Doug Johnson put into solitary confinement, maximum security, because he had gone AWOL and failed to return to his unit for eight days, or because the prisoner was raving, flailing, crazed, possibly violent, a nineteen-year-old mind at the end of its tether?

9. "I Will Have Completely Emerged into a Totally New Person"

<u>December 1969 – January 1970</u>

As a parent I can hardly bear even to imagine my mother and dad's thoughts on reading Doug's awful screed, his cry for "a hand to guide me." They showed the letter to a doctor whose verdict was that "this boy is on the verge of a complete breakdown." Doug himself, however, does not seem to think of this letter as scary or demented. Quite the contrary; he describes it as a sort of monumental discovery, cosmic understanding bestowed upon him, "my new philosophy as I have come to term it."

Just days later, December 29, Doug wrote to his father twice in one day. What I believe to be the first letter starts off calmly enough, but the handwriting deteriorates as the intensity and velocity deepen as he begins to unravel, worrying about his fiancée's reaction if and when she finds out he is in jail. The responsibility of telling her this information, Doug puts on his father:

December 29th 1969

Dear Dad,

Well by now you should have rec'd my long (yellow paper) letter. Please write back and <u>BE SURE TO LET ME KNOW IF YOU REC'D IT</u>. It was a very important letter. I can only hope you <u>HAVE</u> because if you haven't this is probably going to come as quite a shock to say the <u>least</u>.

Well, thanks to a few people (one in particular) I have been sent to the infamous LBJ (Long Binh Jail).

I was well aware of what I was doing and I STILL believe that this is the only price I have to pay for finding myself, really consider myself rather lucky. Some people pay all their lives and still never found what I found. 19—almost 20 years—was a pretty long search but really nothing compared with <u>70</u> or <u>75</u> years.

So far it's not really as bad as imagined it might be except I had to shave off my beloved beautiful moustache—my new one.

Don't ask me (I don't know) why. I don't seem to be depressed or pissed off. It REALLY wouldn't do me any good anyway, I guess

They told me as they tell everybody that if I'm good I can get out in about 30 days. I am not here to hassle anybody—just to get my sweet ass out as soon as possible. I'm sure you are disappointed at the latest turn of events, but <u>I</u> know these people will never even come close to touching my mind. I'm tougher emotionally, mentally and spiritually than these people will <u>ever</u> know or be.

As far as my unit is concerned mail wise, don't send any packages NONE I can't receive any packages at all. I don't know what to tell [fiancée] what my new "job" is and my new address is

Douglas Johnson
[SSN]
Bldg 10 Hall Row
APO SF 9 6491

For letters I guess it sounds better written as Hall Row rather than Long Binh Jail.

It really does sadden me that I am here but I suppose being a natural optimist I should be glad I've got what I've got—it could really be much worse. For instance I could be here and never have made my transition into my new philosophy as I have come to term it. THAT would be BAD.

Being here is bad in itself but not "discovered" yourself would have been the real tragedy

I REALLY WANT TO RECIVE MAIL FROM EVERYBODY AT HOME TO INCLUDE [FIANCÉE] BUT NOT BEING AWARE OF THE PAST EVENTS IT MIGHT REALLY SCARE AND/OR SHOCK HER. IT JUST MIGHT scare her enough to say Ciao to old Doug After all this I think if that happened (ever) I would TOTALLY blow my mind as they say. I'm leaving this up to you dad to notice if she's becoming SUSPICIOUS in any way. . . . I'm not there to see the changes. I'd appreciate it if you would share with me this responsibly. Obviously a change of address is going to bring up the question. An answer like "somewhere in the Delta region" just doesn't seem to be enough of an answer. PLEASE RUSH ME AN ANSWER AS TO HER REACTION AND EXACTLY WHAT SHE NOW KNOWS. Also how she seems to feel about it. Has it changed any feelings of hers toward me or toward our engagement . . . It could not and that scares me. You've got to keep her head straight for me, Dad. . . . and if it IS changed for goodness sake not forget to say which way its changed good or bad.

That anything less than 100% truth so I won't "worry" I'll worry more if I get two different stories, or have any other reason to doubt the TOTAL VALIDITY of your answer. [Urges Dad to wire with news of the girlfriend.] I'm going to hold off telling [her] in a letter until I get your wire. Somebody's got to be there to tell her in person not I repeat not over the phone. I am depending on you dad to do your best which I know you will to keep her head from doing any drastic things. Please keep all the furniture in her head neatly arranged the way I hope it is now. Please Dad Please help me. Am anxiously awaiting wire then

details later in the letters. Please hurry that wire or call Yes DO CALL
Please don't be disappointed and

Your proud son,
Doug

Please don't be disappointed too long.
PS Please don't feel too badly about this predicament. I'll come out of the
whole thing a wiser and better man. I WILL you'll see
PS It's a learning experience not a totally detrimental situation. If I learn
something from it it's been worth it.
I'm the one going thru the bullshit at LBJ and I'm keeping my chin up.
Please help me by keeping yours up too.

I feel certain that my father carried out this responsibility, and that, as
requested, in person, he told the fiancée some version of this news. Did he
lie outright, or tiptoe around the truth about Doug being in jail? Maybe. A
few days later Doug blithely suggested that Dad show her "my 'long letter'
(yellow paper)." It's safe to say he sure as hell did not do that.

Doug's second letter dated December 29 is more plaintive, more uncertain.

December 29 #2

Dear Dad—

How are things going at home? I hope everybody is healthy and
happy.

I'm in a little lonelier mood today than I was yesterday just a little
more homesick.

I wrote a letter to [fiancée] that I said nothing about where I am just
a "hang on—I miss you & love you" type letter.

Until I hear some type of word from you—about who in the family
knows what—and how much [fiancée] knows and how she feels (ie. if
her feelings have changed) etc. I'm going to continue to write to you
not the whole family. So please hurry your reply. Also I'm doing pretty
well [and I] keep writing [fiancée] general-type letters. I should think
that if Norton AFB [Air Force Base in San Bernardino] can get the

hospital numbers they should surely be able to contact here. It would be so good to hear your voice. It always gives me a real lift to get mail and esp a call. <u>Do try please</u>. I know you're embarrassed as I know I am but what I learned, discovered, I feel was worth it for my discoveries will help me to lead a more prospers, healthy, happy life—and <u>I needed desperately those few days</u>. I hope you understand. What I'm trying to say. I don't know how anybody (except me) feels about anything that's happened and I haven't rec'd ANY mail since the 19th or 20th at the hospital. <u>Please write fast</u>. Not having one word from anyone has got me scared that everyone has maybe just given up hope on me. I guess this place maybe does weird things to one's head. Please write, call wire <u>anything</u> just so it's soon. Tell [fiancée] I love her and miss her very much I miss <u>everyone</u> & I hope to hear from you soon,

Love,
Doug

The following day Doug wrote again, and though there is no mention of drugs, I think that drugs or drug withdrawal played a role here.

Dec 30th 1969

Dear Dad,

Well here it is the day before New Year's Eve and another day closer to coming home.

I was going to wait before telling you this but since they're <u>obviously</u> not going to do anything about it here maybe you can talk to someone at Norton you know to get some action at that end. Maybe [a neighbor who worked at Norton Air Force Base] knows someone. I was told that if I got sick I would go to 24th Evac hospital here in Long Binh. Well my urine has been very dark for almost a week. I've thrown up 3 times today and I've been having cramps almost constantly. When I first got here I told them this and they took some blood—that was 3 days ago. I've requested an infinite number of times to see a doctor with no luck whatever. My eyes are turning yellow and my skin is too. I put my name in for sick call with NO results whatsoever every single day. I ask permission to go to the latrine because I'm going to vomit and the usual reply is something like throwing up never hurt anybody or something along those lines. The blood test takes all of 10 minutes to complete and I've waited three days now for the results and it doesn't look like there's a change in the near future. I haven't seen any officers except 2 both of which I told about my sickness and they said, in effect, yeah yeah OK. They said something would be done but there has been no word from either of them and it doesn't look like they remember <u>at all</u>. The only people I've seen who "run" this place SP/4's (one step above PFC) and their attitude is <u>clearly</u> "I don't give a ___ about you." Next page

But there is no next page.

By New Year's Day 1970, however, Doug seemed not only to have regained a measure of sanity and balance, but to have put into practice actual activities that could help him cope. The letter below is written in pencil; parts, especially the third paragraph, seem so full of hope, resolution, and conviction as to be downright buoyant:

Dear Dad

Well it's now 1970 the year of many changes. I'll be home in 1970. <u>Maybe</u> I'll be married in 1970 too, who knows, but I do know that 70 is going to be a much better year than '69. There's only two good things that happened in '69. On Dec 12 [girlfriend] and I became engaged and a few days later I "found myself." I sure wish I'd get some mail from everybody. I am fighting loneliness every day and WINNING. I've sort of set up a few programs for myself. I'm keeping a "diary" and writing all my dreams. I've instigated an isometric exercise program including some sit ups so as to try and get some muscles back on my skinny bod. I'm doing OK and doing many things to benefit myself while I'm here.

Have you told anyone about the change, not only me being here but my "mental change?" If [girlfriend] can't understand what has taken place in my head show her my "long letter" (yellow paper). I think I've found the reason for my frustrated feeling and the only solution to that is get home and where people care about me. I think the reason for the frustrated feeling was that even tho people would listen to me I knew somewhere deep inside of me that they didn't really care so I don't even want to talk to them. I'll just wait. I know <u>you</u> care and my family and [girlfriend] cares but nobody else really gives a damn.

I think by the time I leave here I will have completely emerged into a totally new person. I've straightened out my mixed up thoughts and aimed myself at the "road up" the tough one but I have a little help going up that road. I can make a decision from my heart and be it right or wrong I'm going to stick to that decision no matter what ANYBODY says or does. The going is slow right now but slowly I'll gain momentum and pick up speed until I am in high gear and sailing smoothly. I know I've said things before and not really meant them just to make you happy or because I knew that's what I was supposed to say but I think you know that I am sincere in what I say, that it comes from my heart. I think <u>you'll</u> know this. I know now the feeling <u>you</u> have, the feeling you've been trying to get me to know for so long. If there's any doubt you'll see when I get home. Until then be cool.

I love everybody and have everybody write me often.

Love
Your son
Doug

Doug's last few upbeat letters in the archive are the more remarkable to me because he wrote them while he remained in solitary. While he was there this "new philosophy" does seem to have informed a clear-headed notion of how he might best cope with the world. On January 2 he seemed to have achieved actual equilibrium:

Dear Dad, (¼ through here 7 days today)
How is everybody at home? Good I hope. Well I rec'd two packages today. Apparently had been sent earlier but they just now got to me The small one from the fam with the clam cocktail thing and two

cookies and two boxes of really nice candies. Well I asked to keep the Aristocort [antibacterial ointment made by Lederle Labs, the company Dad worked for] I do have a case of athletes foot and I'll know soon if I can keep it. My results for hepatitis came back negative after six days. I could have told them after six days. I hope I get some letter mail. Could you send a plastic pen (the kind Helen sent before) in a letter and a pencil with an eraser. I'd surely appreciate it. Don't send them in a box just tape them in a letter Just a pen and pencil kicking around the house. Just as long as they look like they'll last a couple of weeks. If everything works out right I won't be here more than 30 or so days. They say that's because you've been good but really it's because they are so full. I'm doing what I'm supposed to do, not causing any kind of hassle and I'll be out in no time. Only 3 weeks to go.

It's overcast but humid here. The days seem to be getting a little slower now. It's hard to occupy my mind for long periods of time and I still haven't got any mail yet (letters) and that may have some bearing on it also.

I'm doing as best I can and I know it's nobody's fault but my own (technically, legally) but nevertheless I am here so I must make the best of it from what I've got to work with. Could you enclose some sheets of blank paper for me to write back on and 2 or three envelopes? Thanks! I'm going to be running out in not too long and I have a funny feeling I'm gonna have a hard time getting more. Also my pencil is getting short. But no packages, OK? I sure miss everybody and I can hardly wait till I can see everyone again. As far as my R&R I've decided on the Hawaii trip. So now that's settled the next question is when? It'll be in the next few months sometime. [The next sentence is too light to read: something about Christmas presents he wants to send.] I couldn't cash that $50 at the hospital. No ID card (lost with my wallet, stolen) So I still have it.

Well, gotta write to [the fiancée]

Ciao
Douglas
I'm so sorry dad
Will write again tomorrow

After January 2 there are no more letters from him in this file. This is a great pity because we will never know how long these bright new convictions—"I think by the time I leave here I will have completely emerged into a totally new person"—endured. How long he held on to the belief in "my new philosophy." How long the soaring belief that "I'll gain momentum and pick up speed until I am in high gear and sailing smoothly" sustained him. Sadly, I think it was not long.

From later documents I learned that Doug was "transferred to the medium Security Compound on 3 January 1970, a total of seven days in solitary confinement." Once out of solitary, living among the general prison population where drugs were abundant, he was no doubt back to using. Five days later, on January 8, he was in the prison hospital for hepatitis. By January 18 so severe was the hepatitis that he was airlifted to a military hospital in Japan. If Doug wrote letters to the family after January 1970 they were not among the papers in the basement.

• • •

There remains some confusion about when Doug quit writing to the family, and when he quit reading the letters he received. Throughout these documents there are fleeting, random references to letters that Dad or the family had from him. At the Duddy hearing, Doug says of May 1970, just before he was ordered into Cambodia, "As a result of the letter I wrote home and action upon my father's part, I received a Congressional Inquiry as to my general state of health and whereabouts." Bill writes in July 1970 that Doug's fiancée received a letter from him dated June 16 stating that he would be out of the Army in one month. When my father wrote his long letter to the military court in late July, he said,

> [In February 1970] Douglas was returned to a fire base after hospitalization in Japan. Apparently this fire base duty was tolerable and here he was able to cope with existing conditions. He wrote quite regularly, wanted film and food and awaited anxiously his rotation home date, 9 June 1970 with plans and parties arranged on this end. Then came Cambodia.

At the Duddy hearing Doug testified about May 1970, "I was relying upon drugs heavily during this time. I had not written home in approximately three to four months." This would place his last letter in about March. Doug continues:

> I had gotten to the point where I was not even reading the mail I was receiving from home. Any thoughts that occurred to me concerning my mother or father, my sisters and brother, and especially my fiancée were excruciating. So much so that the very inkling that I was going to be thinking about home threw me into an uncontrollable and very horrible depression. Thus the reason for my using amphetamines to erase my mind from the agony I was experiencing.

He added, "I found out through my lawyer that my father had begun making inquiries as to my whereabouts, my state of mind and my state of health, due to the fact that I was long past my rotation date and yet not returned." Paul Kleinwachter became Doug's lawyer in July. This means that Doug was not only no longer writing home, but no longer reading letters that came to him. And they would have come. The family and the fiancée would have written often, regularly, sending love, support, affection. It's fair to assume that for months, possibly since March of 1970, Doug was in too much pain, too lost or stoned or wasted, too ill or psychically adrift to read their letters. By the time he returned home in late August the only thing he had to cling to was a dead man's sandal.

10. "My Boy Must Be Saved"

January–February 1970

Doug's screeching fourteen-page December 26 letter probably reached his parents by Friday, January 2, 1970. For the next two months Bill kept up an unremitting barrage of letters in his efforts to get Doug transferred out of Vietnam. He began, on January 3, with George Romney (father of Mitt Romney) Secretary of Housing and Urban Development in the Nixon administration. The Romneys were a prominent Mormon family. In the first paragraph Bill Johnson extols the merits of a Mr. Romney who was dean of men at Utah State University when Bill was a student there. He continues:

> I enclose a copy of a letter addressed to the President of United States. Self explanatory.
>
> I am writing this letter to you, Mr. Romney, to ask: will you Mr. Romney have faith in my son as a member of the Aaronic Priesthood in good standing?
>
> I am writing this letter to request that you use whatever influence you can with the president or other authorities to speed up, dissolve or break through red tape to grant my boy another opportunity to find himself and live with himself proudly and allow a balanced future. I hold the opinion that the impossible just takes longer. He is worth all this trouble.

I know he will be given another chance; his name has been submitted to the Los Angeles Temple twice. I know help is in store.

Sincerely yours,
William J. Johnson

The Aaronic Priesthood is bestowed on Mormon boys at the age of about thirteen. As for Doug's name being submitted to the Temple, I'm not sure what this means in terms of church practices, but personally, I doubt it was true. By 1970 my father was no longer active in the LDS. However, the point was certainly worth making to a Romney: Doug was a good Mormon boy from a good Mormon home, a theme Bill would constantly invoke.

On January 9 he followed up to Mr. Romney with a rather more succinct note, leaving out religion:

> Since I have not heard from you or from the White House, I have written again. Copy enclosed. . .
>
> I am writing to you in the hope you will accentuate the speed of my request. My letters must reach the President. My boy must be saved. Thank you.

Sincerely yours,
William J. Johnson

Romney's January 9, 1970, reply crossed with this in the mail. It is crisp and formal, but he was as good as his word, ending with, "I have written to the Secretary of Defense urging him to have your son's case thoroughly investigated and indicated that I believe a different course of action is probably indicated. I hope it happens."

Secretary of Defense Melvin Laird sent Romney's letter on to Secretary of the Army Stanley R. Resor, who wrote back to Secretary Romney a full month later, February 9. This official letter—the kiss-off, clothed as smug assertion—offered absolutely nothing new, only repeated what the parents already knew: Doug's offenses and the sentence from the November 1969 court-martial, including that he had been reprieved of the five months at hard labor until his "subsequent offense" (the eight-day December AWOL) when "it was the opinion of his commander. . . that Private Johnson should be placed in confinement to serve the conditional portion of his sentence." It acknowledges that Doug was sent to Japan for treatment of hepatitis. It ends with "I have asked Private Johnson's commander to contact him and insure that he informs his father of his current status." (Which, it seems unlikely to me that the commander would contact Private Johnson with this request.)

My father's requests to political figures all got pushed through these, the bowels of officialdom, in what amounted to the five-step process:

1. Mr. Politico replied to WJJ assuring him that he had sent the inquiry on.
2. Mr. Politico did indeed send it on to ... someone, Army Individual #1.
3. Army Individual #1 may have sent it on to Army Individual #2.
4. Army Individual #2 (and possibly #1) replied to Mr. Politico.
5 Mr. Politico sent the Army reply or replies on to WJJ, enclosing a note of his own.

Invariably, the process took a full month, and (as we've seen with Romney, above) by that time whatever information or wisdom these entities dispensed, their letters to the Johnsons' house on Turrill Court provided scant or no satisfaction, much less enlightenment. More often than not, the information was utterly moot.

• • •

My father was always fond of big words and fine phrases. The letters I brought up from the safe are full of rolling prose, rhetorical gravitas, formal cadences, and sometimes strange constructions ("repulsive antipathy"). Where/how he came by these sorts of high-flown phrases, I do not know. Unlike my mother, he was not a reader, so he didn't absorb it from books. It would not have come from church. Mormons don't have learned preachers offering up weekly stentorian sermons. Instead, during Sunday services, at least when I was a kid, people, including children, would give two-and-a-half-minute talks, none of them very inspiring. (Mormon hymns, by contrast, are memorable.) In any event, my father's writing style, his rhetorical choices, imply a profound trust in the power of language to effect change. But after I brought these documents up from the basement, after I read and reread one after another, dad's letters grew monotonous, repetitively pompous, particularly as the same basic letter was retyped and went out to several individuals.

Overall, his many letters have a reliable pattern of presentation:

1. He begins with (sometimes unctuous) flattery of the individual addressed.
2. He offers the long litany of Doug's worth and why he merits this person's time, effort, and energy.
3. Then a detailed description of exactly what he wants this person to do. And why. In this latter portion his language implores, but it also commands, so much so that the letters sometime sound like outright instruction manuals: *Here's what I want you to do, sir. Make this your top priority.*

Even if these politicians resented his peremptory instructions, all they had to do was to forward Bill's letter on to Army Individual #1. When Bill's letters (with their congressional escort) reached the military, I feel certain they elicited scoffs at best. *Who the hell does Bill Johnson think he is telling me what to do? And why in hell would he think for one minute that I would give a flying fuck about his Eagle Scout, piano-playing son?* In replying to my father, these sentiments were generally cast in pale, clunky boiler-plate prose, chunks of hypocrisy bedecked in what amounts to uniform statements. My father came to recognize this, but he had few weapons against it, except to up the decibels of his next letter. This, too, was his practice.

• • •

In addition to Secretary Romney, Bill appealed to various Mormon chaplains for information about Doug. The chaplains were a washout. One of their handwritten notes, dated New Year's Day of 1970, said,

By this time I'm afraid you have heard about your son. He simply did not perform with the unit and got into more trouble . . . I feel that you have given your son every encouragement and I trust you will not blame yourself for his failure. I do hope the future will find him more responsible and mature.

Another, an LDS chaplain, wrote a much longer letter to "Brother and Sister Johnson" on January 22, which read in part:

> [I believe Doug is] going to come to grips with himself. I tried to show Doug that one can have what he is looking for and still be a member of the church in good standing. One doesn't need drugs to see more clearly or "wrap" [*sic*] more openly.
>
> If Doug is not able to deal with his problems on his own I would like to recommend that you counsel him to see a psychiatrist. . . . He's not as the vernacular goes, crazy, but a psychiatrist can help him to get things in proper prospective [*sic*].

On reading this pious palaver, I can imagine my father's reaction: *Enough with the chaplains.* He redoubled his efforts with the politicos.

Senator Alan Cranston must have sent Bill's initial letter on because there is a blatantly useless letter in the file from Lieutenant Colonel Robert Serra, Adjutant General, dated January 12, 1970. It reported that Doug's battalion had "undergone a change in commanders. The previous commander . . . is no longer available for comment regarding Mr. Johnson's inquiries." Officialese for *kiss off.*

The file includes no further letters from Senator Cranston.

On January 10 my father's campaign enlisted George Murphy, the other senator from California. Bill had a phone conversation with a Murphy aide who suggested he send a letter to President Nixon via Senator Murphy. He did. The cover letter to Murphy closes with:

> Time is valuable in this instance and I request your assistance to see that the White House takes action to bring my boy back to the West Coast for hospitalization until he is completely well and allow him to complete his military obligation in the United States.

May I have your cooperation?
Would you kindly keep me informed as to progress in this case.

Thank you.

Murphy's reply, sent more than a month later on US Senate Committee on Armed Service letterhead, was noncommittal:

February 18th 1970

Dear Mr. Johnson

Enclosed is a copy of the interim reply I received from the Commanding General, Headquarters U. S. Army, Japan in response to my inquiry concerning the physical condition and assignment of your son, Douglas.

I am sorry I am unable to send you more definite information at this time with regard to Private Johnson's assignment following his release from the hospital. You will, however, be kept informed of any subsequent reports I receive regarding his case.

Sincerely George Murphy
PS In accordance with your request I am returning Douglas' photograph. He is certainly a fine looking young man.

The commanding general's enclosed letter read:

11 February 1970

Dear Senator Murphy:

This is an interim reply to your inquiry in behalf of Private Douglas S. Johnson [ssn] presently a patient at the 106th General Hospital APO San Francisco 06503 [Japan].

Private Johnson was admitted to the 106th General Hospital on 23 January 1970 as a transfer patient from Vietnam for further treatment of hepatitis. At the time of his admittance to the 106th General Hospital Private Johnson was in no severe distress and since that time he has responded well to treatment. His present prognosis and over-all health are listed as excellent and his attending physician is of the opinion that Private Johnson will recover completely. It is anticipated that he will be released from hospitalization and returned to duty . . . within two or three weeks for further disposition.

I will advise you of Private Johnson's final disposition when it is known.

Sincerely yours
John A. Goshorn
Major General U. S. Army
Commanding

The bit here about Doug's being "in no severe distress" seems to me belied by the fact that he was airlifted to Japan. Still, the information that he would "be returned to duty" (rather than returned to prison) must have been wel-come, though my father continued to work to get Doug transferred to any duty station other than Vietnam.

There were no further letters from Murphy. However, the files include a rather bizarre exchange with an aide in Murphy's office, a Mrs. Gilberton (one of the few women in all these documents) who was an assistant in military affairs. She returned my dad's telephone call. Perhaps the fact that he actually heard her voice accounts for the less formal tone in his letter to her, which included a photograph of Doug. He closed with:

You may expect a letter from Douglas within the next few days seek-ing consideration for presidential Honor Guard duty. . .

Very truly yours,
William Jess Johnson

This last paragraph boggles the mind. Presumably Dad wrote to Doug, send-ing along Mrs. Gilberton's name and address and advising him to apply through Senator Murphy for the Presidential Honor Guard. My father must have been demented. Doug Johnson—E-1 grunt, multiple AWOLs, court-martial, military prison, a drug user riddled with malaria and hepatitis—should apply to join those clean-shaven, square-jawed young men standing at attention under White House porticos in their smart uniforms with gleaming brass buttons, their shining ornamental swords pressed to their pale foreheads, their gaze stoic, serene, unflinching, their hands gloved, their consciences clean?

It was the stuff of dreams.

• • •

In his hopes to get Doug transferred out of Vietnam, Bill Johnson persistently wrote variations on the same themes, often sending the same letter to as many as seven or eight different people. Each individually typed letter had a carbon copy. Often Bill included a photograph of Doug to show that here was a real person, not just a name and number. These photographs would need to be copied. The cost of postage (including packages to Doug), paper, carbon paper, and typewriter ribbons would have been significant expenses for the Johnsons, to say nothing of the many long-distance phone calls to Washington, DC. (At the time, as I recall, this was $2 a minute after eight a.m. and before five p.m.; their phone bills must have been staggering.)

Between 1969 and 1973 the mail going through the door slot at Turrill Court was an avalanche of white envelopes franked with the names of senators and congressmen, officials from the US Army, the White House, official chaplains, and government entities of all sorts. My parents must have come home at the end of long working days and scooped up armfuls, taken them to the kitchen table, and rifled through their contents, balancing in their hearts equal parts of fear and hope. To open these envelopes now, to read these letters on their government stationary fifty-five years later—in an era when almost nothing transpires on actual paper—is to be overwhelmed with a sense of officialdom, some of it curt and dismissive, some merely stiff and formal. But all this effort eventually brought my father into the orbit of several influential governmental allies.

Foremost was the congressman from our district, Jerry L. Pettis, a Seventh-Day Adventist Republican, a man who was active on behalf of veterans in general. In the papers spread across my dining room table there are more letters to and from Jerry Pettis than anyone else. He remained Bill's confidant, the one reliable ballast in Bill Johnson's long odyssey.

There is a big fat file of letters to and from Mike Mansfield, senator from

Montana and, at the time, Senate majority leader, known to be a skeptic on the Vietnam War. Did my parents select him for that reason? Maybe they wrote to him because Doug was born in Montana. Mansfield's file includes a tiny 1971 news clipping that describes the senator as "a rare political specimen, a quiet man," who had breakfast twice a month with President Nixon at Nixon's request.

My father also engaged with Senator J. William Fulbright of Arkansas, no doubt because Fulbright was a vocal critic of the war in Vietnam. For a time Fulbright, too, applied the power of his office on behalf of Doug Johnson.

Perhaps Bill's most unlikely ally was L. Mendel Rivers (1905–1970) a Democratic congressman from South Carolina, an intransigent segregationist for thirty years, and one of the stoutest, loudest defenders of the Vietnam War. Beginning in 1965, Rivers was the powerful Chairman of the House Armed Services Committee. My father pelted him with the same letters, arguing that Doug should be reassigned stateside to finish his enlistment. Rivers replied encouragingly, which seems odd to me given Rivers' unquestioning support of the military in Vietnam. But perhaps the timing was crucial. By 1970 Congress had begun its investigations of the 1968 My Lai massacre, American GIs accused of the wholesale slaughter of unarmed Vietnamese villagers. As committee chairman, Rivers was criticized for his role in trying to keep this atrocity under wraps and out of the public eye, in short, covering up. On December 28, 1970, Rivers died, but for a while John R. Blandford, Chief Counsel for the Committee on Armed Services, carried on as Bill Johnson's ally from that office.

• • •

When these powerful men, responding to the noisy, insistent Mr. Johnson, sent his requests on to the Army brass, the military would have been obliged to reply (however annoyed or pissed off they might be at these Congressional requests). The Army's letters, as we have seen, were uniformly stiffly worded and banally uninformative. Their contents also followed a prescribed pattern already noted: a list of Doug's transgressions, then a few words about where he was. If that happened to be prison or a hospital they closed with this same paragraph:

> I wish to advise you that your son had the services of a chaplain, a doctor, a psychiatrist, a social worker and the members of the correctional staff available to him at all times while in confinement. I trust this will be of assistance to you.

This particular assertion occurs so frequently in the Army's letters as to deserve its own title, the Bullshit Paragraph, and it will be identified as such henceforth. In actual practice the care Doug received was more along the lines we've already read from his December 30 letter: the description of his yellowing skin and constant vomiting, but the people who could help him demonstrating clearly, "I don't give a ___ about you."

In fact, for the month he spent at the hospital in Japan, Doug actually did have "access to social workers, psychiatrists, the chaplain and the chaplain's assistant." This was thanks to a Dr. Shirasu, to whom my father had written a long, pleading letter on January 29, 1970, begging him to see to it that Doug was not returned to Vietnam. There's no reply from the doctor amid these files. However, Doug's testimony at the Duddy hearing indicates that Dr. Shirasu at least provided him with professional help, though, as it turns out, to no avail. Doug testified, "On February 17 I was discharged [and sent] back to Vietnam. Even after repeated attempts with social workers, chaplains and doctors to be sent home, I was then sent to Pleiku."

All this makes me wonder, compels me to ask: Was there not some person in this whole cadre of alleged professionals, some social worker or chaplain or doctor or shrink with military or medical or merely humane insight who could look at Douglas Johnson and think: *Here is a soldier, just turned twenty, whose entire deployment in Vietnam has been a total disaster. In basic training he was fine, even "Excellent," but from the time he set foot in Vietnam his superiors have evaluated him "Unsatisfactory" in both Conduct and Efficiency. He is clearly a drug addict; his arms are like pincushions. He's been repeatedly hospitalized for malaria and hepatitis. He has had multiple AWOLs, often lasting weeks. He has already had one court martial for going AWOL and yet he did it again, landing himself in Long Binh Jail from whence he came to us. This soldier is unfit. He is a liability to the safety and well-being of our other soldiers. He is a detriment to the war effort in Vietnam. Let's send him to some post in Oklahoma where he can swab floors and clean latrines, or let him freeze his ass off pulling guard duty at the border of North Korea.*

In fact, using simple math, any of these professionals could have looked at Doug Johnson's records for the first six and half months of his deployment in Vietnam and with a glance seen the obvious: from June 10, 1969, to February 17, 1970, Doug was AWOL for 36 days, hospitalized for 116, and imprisoned for 34. If we add to this calculation the eighteen words spoken by his so-called legal rep at the November 14 court-martial, "For two weeks prior to the trial the accused was restricted to the battalion area under armed guard," that's another 14 days out of active duty. So, total circa 200 days he was not actively engaged with a unit fighting Communism.

Indeed, the Army itself took belated note of Private Johnson's spotty attendance record. General Enemark of the Inspector General's office, in his January 1971 interim denial (writing to Mr. Blandford in Mendel Rivers's office), did the math for Doug's entire time in Vietnam and drew these conclusions:

> It was determined that Private Johnson was assigned to the US Army in Vietnam for a period of 15 months. During that time he spent slightly over one-fourth of his time serving with his unit of assignment. His almost constant dependence on drugs created substantial doubts about the effectiveness of his service as an infantryman when he was with his unit. This inquiry revealed that Private Johnson was assigned to the 2nd Battalion 35th Infantry on 21 June 1969. Two days later he absented himself without proper authority and remained in an absent without leave (AWOL status until 15 July 1969.) Records of subsequent AWOL's and periods of confinement for disciplinary reasons indicated that during the period 21 June 1969 until July 1970 a period of 374 days Private Johnson could possibly have performed his duties as a rifleman only for 115 days. The remainder of the time, 259 days, he was not present in his unit.

Doug Johnson had no leave except for the fifteen days granted just after basic training when he went home to San Bernardino. Other than the month he was hospitalized in Japan, Doug stayed in-country, as the phrase has it, with no respite whatever from the war for almost fifteen months. In one of Bill Johnson's later documents seeking reversal of the Undesirable, he wrote "[Doug] applied for it [R&R] four separate times and four times it was refused. At one time he was given a choice of dates to go to Hawaii. My wife, Doug's fiancée and I were going to meet him there and it was cancelled for no reason."

Belatedly, in 1971, and in that same document to Mr. Blandford, General Enemark explained this:

> Mr. Johnson's statement that his son was not permitted and rest and recuperation (R&R) during his tour of duty was substantiated. Private Johnson would have become eligible for R&R on 10 September 1969. By that time he had been AWOL twice for a total of 32 days and was in the hospital for malaria. Subsequently he went AWOL on seven additional occasions, was under suspended court-martial sentence of confinement once, was confined for disciplinary reasons twice and hospitalized for sickness three times. Records of the dates Private Johnson requested R&R were not available, however, while he may have applied for R&R, he was seldom eligible for R&R or leave because of the infrequent times he was present for duty.

In my impassioned October 1969 letter to my father, I wrote "In a lot of ways [Doug] is still terrifically immature and juvenile. All that serves to make his current situation all the worse, psychically." True. Nonetheless, I believe if some "professional" lauded in the Bullshit Paragraph had responded to Doug Johnson's obvious mental and physical afflictions, his addiction, his whole life could have been different. Had my father succeeded in his furious campaign to get Doug posted stateside, out of Vietnam, had Doug's own pleas been heeded, it's my belief my brother would have performed creditably and could have left the Army better resembling the young man in his Basic Training photo, rather than the twenty-year-old who staggered off the plane clutching a dead man's sandal with Undesirable trailing after him like dirty toilet paper stuck forever to his shoes and his psyche.

11. "I Pray, Mr. President, That You Will Intercede"

Winter/Spring 1970

In addition to his ceaseless barrage of letters to important political figures, my father repeatedly appealed to Richard Nixon for personal mercy. Bill truly believed that the President would respond to his pleas, would come down from On High, in a manner of speaking, and make everything All Right.

My parents probably voted for Nixon in 1960, if only because he was a Californian and John F. Kennedy was from far-off Massachusetts. When Nixon ran again, in the tumultuous campaign of 1968 (roiling with assassinations, riots, armed clashes of police and protesters, tear gas, violence, arrests and a courtroom where the defendants were bound and gagged), I think my mother voted for his Democratic opponent, Hubert Humphrey. (The Kalpakians had always been New Deal Democrats.) However, I know my father voted for Nixon because at the height of his unbearable anxiety for Doug, in July 1970, Dad wrote to Senator Frank Church of Idaho, a vocal critic of the war, "I am ashamed to be a registered Republican and to have voted the same." When Nixon ran again in 1972, I believe the Johnsons voted for the ill-fated Democrat, George McGovern, even though Robert Mardian, who championed Doug's cause, was an officer of the Committee to Re-Elect the President. By then (though they would not have said so to Mr. Mardian) the Johnsons had a grudge against Nixon. The President had not lifted a hand to help Doug Johnson, though Nixon had publicly intervened in the case of William Calley, the soldier convicted of twenty-two deaths in the My Lai massacres. Within three days of Calley's guilty verdict Nixon had ordered him moved from prison to house arrest, and the whole country knew it.

But early in 1970, my father clearly believed in Nixon. In January Bill wrote to the President twice through Romney, twice through Murphy, at least once through Cranston, probably more than once through Jerry Pettis. He also wrote to the White House directly. His letters to Nixon—despair couched in flights of Emersonian rhetoric—are each slightly different, though the tone, content, and trajectory remain the same. They align with Bill's usual pattern: abject flattery followed by instructions on what the President needed to do and why he needed to do it. They appeal, as all Bill's letters do, on behalf of the fine man Doug Johnson was and would be again one day if only . . .

Of all these letters, I print just one, below, sent through Romney in early January of 1970. This particular letter alludes to my parents' shock and terror on reading Doug's December 26 soul-screed, "reaching for a hand to guide me."

President Richard M. Nixon
The White House Washington DC
Subject:
Pfc Douglas Scott Johnson
[SSN]
RA 18874941
Correctional Holding Detachment
APO SF 96491

Dear Mr. President:

    A person once said to me, "When you pray, you pray to God for help—not to one of his assistants." I now beseech you for your help, Mr. President, as Commander in Chief of the Armed Forces.

    Mr. President, you have spent the major portion of your whole adult life fighting the people of the enslaved world. Will you give me five minutes of your time to help one American boy to free his mind, to regain his confidence in himself and others, trust in his superiors and normal future after his service obligation?

My son was given a court martial last October [*sic*] for being AWOL after hospitalization. He received a 5 month suspended sentence and 2/3 forfeiture of pay. He was released from the hospital again in December and reported late. He was AWOL 8 days. My boy must make retribution to the Army and accept the responsibility for his wrong doing. I feel this is important.

My last letter from him, dated December 26th 1969 was in essence panic-stricken with fear and an impelling cry for help and compassion. He advised he was being sent to Long Binh correctional facility. Mr. President, he must not be sent to Long Binh correctional facility because he is not corrupt. A corrupt person could not write this type of letter.

The Army can and must be the guiding hand to save my boy from destruction and make him a productive citizen for a future America. My boy enlisted in the Army last January, 1969 at 19 years of age. This January at age 20 he is nearer 40. A physician here who read this letter of December 26th stated that this boy is on the verge of a complete breakdown.

Instead of Long Binh stockade, wouldn't it be better if the Army would condescend:

To place him on active duty status where he would have responsibility and extra work for 12-plus hours a day.

To place him in a job which would allow him confidence, courage and pride in himself.

To increase his Army enlistment for six month and allow him to complete his obligation with honor and integrity.

I realize, Mr. President, the demand on your time; however, in this instance there is a life at stake just as surely as a surgeon prepares his patient to correct an anatomical defect. The anesthesia has been administered.

I pray Mr. President, that you will intercede and let my boy prove his worth to himself and the Government instead of Long Binh confinement.

Sincerely yours,
William J. Johnson

To me the most poignant part of this particular letter is that Bill uses Doug's own phrase, looking for "a guiding hand." Did my father somehow believe that the Army itself could fill this need and "save my boy from destruction"? Bill Johnson worked in the medical field for thirty years, so his metaphor about the surgeon cutting out the anatomical defect rings with his professional background. Still, his allusion to the anesthesia having "been administered" is strange to me. I suspect surgeons and anesthesia were very much on his mind. Helen's health had continued to deteriorate, and in early 1970 she underwent yet another surgery. Anxiety for her very life consumed my parents in addition to their fears for Doug.

Bill Johnson's many letters to Nixon did not result in presidential intercession. Instead, his pleas were, again, run through the bowels of Army. Replies came from Army officers writing on Nixon's behalf. The Army letters quoted here (and all those amid the rest of the documents) offer little more than clumsy phrases and boiler-plate assurances, signifying nothing. Like the replies the Army sent to senators and congressmen, if they are not outright bullshit, they are the Kiss-Off cast in officialese lingo:

[Office of the Provost Marshal General]
23 January 1970

Dear Mr. Johnson

On behalf of President Nixon I am replying to your letter of 3 January 1970 regarding your son, Private Douglas Scott Johnson

The distress you are suffering as a result of your son's confinement is understood; however, it would not be proper to exempt him from disciplinary action or release him from confinement solely for this reason ...

It is further suggested that you can best help your son by writing him letters of encouragement, evidencing your faith in him, as this manifestation of confidence will assist him materially in his rehabilitation. You may be sure that the Army will do all that is possible to protect both your son's rights and well being. A copy of your correspondence has been forwarded to your son's commanding officer for his information.

Sincerely yours
Karl W. Gustafson
Major General, USA
The Provost Marshal General

Keep in mind that by January 23, the date of this letter, Doug was already in the military hospital in Japan. So the Major General had not even bothered to inquire where this grunt actually was. The two letters that followed are even more baldly uninformative:

[Department of the Army Office of the Provost Marshal General]
11 February 1970

Dear Mr. Johnson:

On behalf of President Nixon, I am replying to your further inquiries regarding your son, Private Douglas Scott Johnson.

A copy of the additional correspondence concerning your son has been transmitted to his commanding officer.

I returning the photographs inclosed [*sic*] with your 9 January letter.

The anxiety which accompanies the knowledge that your son is in confinement is understood; however, you may be sure he will be afforded every reasonable consideration consistent with the merits of his case and that his rights will be protected.

Sincerely yours
W. H. Brandenburg
Colonel MPC
Acting Provost Marshal General

The next, even more stiffly worded, has a ray of good news:

[Headquarters 16th Military Police Brigade]
AFO San Francisco 96491
16 Feb 1970

Dear Mr. Johnson,

Your letter to the president as well as a copy of the letter to you from General Gustafason has been forwarded to this headquarters.

Your son, Private Douglas S. Johnson was released from confinement on 19th January 1970 and admitted to the 24th Evacuation Hospital to Japan on 21 January 1970 for treatment. His sentence was remitted by this headquarters. This remitting has the effect of terminating the confinement portion of Private Johnson's sentence. If released from the hospital for further duty, he will be reassigned to a new unit, based upon reassignment policies existing at that time.

You may correspond with your son at the following address: Private Douglas S. Johnson [ssn] 106th General Hospital APO SF 96503

I trust this information will provide you some additional relief from the distress you have encountered incident to your son's court martial and confinement

Sincerely yours
WK Wittwer
Colonel MPC
Commanding

This letter is dated February 16. Doug got out of the hospital on February 17. So the address this Colonel offered was utterly moot, and thank you, no it did not offer "additional relief" from his parents' distress. But this line did: "This remitting has the effect of terminating confinement portion of Private Johnson's sentence."

Bill Johnson's anguished campaign of letters and telephone calls—all that ink and pleading to the President and politicos in January and February— went utterly unheeded. From Japan Doug was shipped back to Vietnam, but at least he was not returned to prison. Between mid-February 1970 and May of that year he stayed out of recorded trouble, except for two brief AWOLs in mid-April. However, he remained "Unsatisfactory" in both Conduct and Efficiency. In these, say, ten weeks, Doug did not contract either malaria or hepatitis, or any disease or condition or wounds requiring hospitalization. During this lull there's no correspondence amid the documents that came up from the basement.

Bill did not write again to Richard Nixon personally. Nixon had failed him. And later, when the absolute smash-up came in May in Cambodia, my father did not include Nixon in his barrage of correspondence that summer, though he did have some exchanges with a Mr. Finch at the White House. I feel quite certain that another reason my dad quit appealing to the President had to do with that May 25 *Time* magazine photograph, a portion of which is on the cover of this book. Doug stood, second from left, with 4th Infantry soldiers awaiting a helicopter that would take them into Cambodia, a mission that Nixon called "Operation Buy Time." The President was buying time using Doug's life as ante.

12. "If the Opium Didn't Kill Me, the VC Would"

The fullest and most detailed record of what Doug Johnson actually experienced as a soldier in Vietnam is his testimony at the Inspector General's hearing presided over by Colonel R. R. Duddy. It was the first of my father's attempts to get the Undesirable changed to Honorable. It was held at Fort MacArthur in San Pedro, California, (greater Los Angeles) on December 4, 1970, about three months after Doug returned from Nam. The hearing was instigated by Congressman Pettis on the strength of Bill Johnson's scathing October 16, 1970, letter that rang with the persistent phrase "The General was not aware." This letter laid out the reasons the Undesirable was undeserved. The hearing covered the whole of Doug's experience in Vietnam, from the beginning in June 1969 to the events in May and June of 1970 that compelled him to accept the Undesirable "for the good of the service" in August.

Fort McArthur was—still is—a sort of LA landmark, set about with graceful palm trees. Built originally in 1914, its main buildings are suggestive of Edwardian elegance. It is so picture-perfect that it has served as a set location in many TV programs, such as *NCIS*, and also films such as *A Few Good Men*. I like to think that Doug's hearing took place in one of those 1914 rooms with high ceilings, and uncurtained windows that looked out to precise plots of green grass edged by gray sidewalks. I imagine military flags in the corners, and Colonel Duddy at the head of a long wooden table, Doug and Dad on one side of the table, and the stenographer on the other.

Since I know that Colonel Duddy retired two months later, I picture him as one might a military man born between, say, 1905 and 1910. Sixtyish, spare, rimmed spectacles, wearing a starched uniform adorned with assorted medals and ribbons, clean-shaven, his graying hair close-trimmed, a thin mouth and a long nose. I know about his retirement from a letter Colonel Duddy wrote to Bill in February 1971, and from the snippy tone of that letter, I imagine the rest. My father, always cognizant of appearances, would have been impeccably dressed in a suit and tie. And Doug?

When I began work on this book I went looking for photographs from his 1970 homecoming. My dad, in particular, was a picture-taking fool, and the fam would have recorded such a joyous occasion with many snapshots. My parents' photo albums (which came to be at my house) go back decades, but there are no photographs of that homecoming. I think my mother destroyed them. Too painful. Among the documents that came up from the basement there is but one photograph of Doug in the few months after his return, a snapshot taped to a piece of paper and dated December 1970 (figure 7 in this book). It was part of the package Bill assembled for the Army Discharge Review Board in 1971. Doug is standing by the fireplace, arm resting on the mantel. No longer malnourished, he looks sturdy, fit. He is clean-shaven except for a thick mustache. Though he has fashionable sideburns, his dark hair is conventionally cut, conservative even, not at all scraggly or curling over his ears as lots of young men wore in that era. He is smiling, not grinning, but confident. He wears a sport coat and a tie. (He had just gotten a retail job in the Men's Department at Silverwoods, a local clothing store.)

Worth noting, too, is that I found amid the documents a single envelope with bits jotted down, front and back, quick, unconnected notes in my father's scrawl. "Why where did you go?" "Job in the bush?" "Point man?" "Why?" "AIT [Advanced Individual Training] is not the bush." "No problems." And, on the flip side: "Problems [illegible] in Service—specific [illegible] where, when, how, why no RR Who did you apply to Drugs info." "Not using drugs now." "Take your time." "Mens Department." "Future plans school." (This last, oddly, crossed out.) I believe that these are pointers Dad used to coach Doug before the December hearing. Dad rehearsed him, probably mercilessly. This was a high-stakes performance, and Doug would have known that. Perhaps his oddly formal diction on the transcript reflects those rehearsals. Understandably, the voice in these transcripts is not that of the kid who wrote "Groovy, huh?" in his letters. Doug uses very few casual phrases, like "I was busted." His diction throughout is studied. His answers to Duddy's ninety-six questions are short and do not wander.

The hearing began at 8:30 in the morning. Doug and Dad would have risen early. My mom would have been up too, making breakfast for them. They would have left San Bernardino before six at the latest. The distance wasn't all that far, but traffic into the city was always congested and they needed to be on time. The hearing lasted until 5:30 in the afternoon.

The transcript is twenty-one single-spaced pages, recorded by a stenographer. I have inserted paragraphs and corrected spelling. Doug offered his own opening statement, beginning, fittingly, with drugs:

I enlisted in the Army for two years. I was sent to Fort Ord for basic training . . . My real problems began when I landed in Vietnam on 10 June 1969. My first few weeks in Vietnam were marked by a substantial introduction to several things I never been faced with personally before. These things, generally known as the "world of drugs," including marijuana, opium, speed and other things such as LSD, mescaline and other hallucinatory drugs. I began smoking marijuana to release the tension of an unfamiliar and somewhat frightening situation.

I was then transferred to the 2/35 Inf 4th Inf Div, located in Pleiku in the Central Highlands of South Vietnam. I entered the bush with little or no instruction on how to conduct myself and general proceedings that take place there. I began learning rather quickly everything from how to recognize a booby trap trail to loading a ruck sack and carrying one. I began learning how to protect myself from the dangers present in the jungle . . . ambushes, malaria, booby traps.

After a short time I contracted malaria and was sent to the 71st Evacuation Hospital in Pleiku. This was approximately late July or early August 1969. From there I was sent to Cam Rahn Bay Convalescent Center at which point I was introduced to a drug known as opium in a way that I had never seen, but only heard about. This was known commonly as "main lining," which is injecting directly into the blood stream. From that point I began shooting opium first a couple of times a day and then increasing it to many times (up to 7 or 8 times a day). After a short recuperation period I was sent back to Pleiku and I again returned to the bush.

I then began catching on to the type of mind that exists in a line infantry company and realized that in order to preserve my own physical well-being I would have to be aware of the goings on around me at all times. In order to accomplish this I volunteered to walk point rather than carry a 25 pound radio and ruck sack on your back. This was the only alternative left to me in order to have complete and full knowledge of what was happening within and without my unit. I found that in walking point it became insanely difficult to cope with the situation that arose in front of me under these pressures. Not knowing if when I woke up in the morning if this was going to be the day I was going to die. I began increasing my dosage of opium to facilitate the horrible tension and fear that I was enduring. The people in my unit were aware I was using this drug. My arms had become literal pin cushions.

One time, we were going through some very dense jungle and the next thing I knew I was face to face with a VC [Viet Cong] or NVA [North Vietnamese Army] who had his AK [automatic rifle] pointed at me. I heard a click. I immediately shot him. Upon inspection of his weapon I found that his firing pin was bent, this being the reason for him not killing me.

Another time I was on a short mission with some tall grass surrounding the area and my buddies and I were within 5 or 10 feet at times from a group of NVA soldiers doing a sweep of this area. We hurriedly called gun ships [helicopters], radioed our position and the NVAs'. We were told by the gun ship that they refused to come in due to the close proximity between our position and that of the enemy. Rather than take another chance on being killed, we lied to the gun ship and told them that we had moved our position to another location and asked them once again to come in and sweep the area, thus bringing the gun ship right in on top of us, taking the chance on being shot by our own men. When the barrage was finished my friend and I both look at the ruck sack lying between us . . . this ruck sack had several holes and the canteen had two holes. . . By this time I was a scared, cautious and unsure young man. Scared to die, cautious not to die and becoming at that time, an opium addict . . .

After Doug's initial statements, Colonel Duddy questioned him extensively, ninety-six questions in all. The most substantive arose out of Doug's own testimony. With regard to the above incident, he asked:

Q: Mr. Johnson what was the density of the underbrush or growth in area where this incident took place?
DSJ: Where I was specifically there was a fairly heavy jungle ahead of us and a denser growth behind us. At the time we were on a hill leading into a valley and the only thing we had for cover was tall or semi-tall elephant grass, sometimes about 3' to 4' high. . .We could see them. At times we were in but 5' to 10' from them.

Q: Mr. Johnson did you use any devices such as smoke flares or balloons to identify your location so that the helicopter pilots could then locate you in the grass?
DSJ: None whatsoever. If we were to use any type of marking, we would have been killed. We were just too close to them. They would have seen us throw it.

Doug's replies offer further clarity about what must have been terrifying circumstances, about what he meant by being "scared shitless," though in this formal setting he does not use that phrase.

Q: Mr. Johnson, you have stated that in order to preserve your own state of physical well being that you had to be aware of the goings on around you at all times, and that the only alternative . . . was that you volunteer to be a point man, would you please clarify this statement?
DSJ: I discovered that the people in a line company often react in very unusual and many times unsafe ways and rather than going along and

not know anything, and rather than carrying a radio on my back [and] to have knowledge of what's going on, the only other way is to walk point. In this way I was notified of any and all changes, situations, and other things going on within the company and everything that we knew that was going on around us. In other words, I didn't want to walk blindly into something and be killed because I was too stupid to know what was going on around me.

Q: Mr. Johnson, in your position of a point man in the bush, how many people were you able to maintain contact with and see?

DSJ: The only person I maintained contact on a constant or semi-constant level was the radio man and the compass man. The only people I could see in very heavy jungle were my slack man and occasionally one or two other people. On a flat, thinly vegetated area, I could usually maintain contact visually with more of them, sometimes all of them.

Q: Mr. Johnson, would you please explain the term slack man?

DSJ: Slack man is the first person behind point man. In other words, he takes up the slack of the man walking point, who is usually a pretty good distance ahead of the group.

Q: Please estimate what this distance you are referring to is in yards.

DSJ: Depending upon the terrain, it could be anywhere from twenty to thirty yards to two or three feet. Sometimes, late at night you have to hang on to the guy in front of you because you can't see. If you let go, you have to stop because of the intensity of the dark.

Q: Mr. Johnson, you have referred to the use of opium during the period you were a point man. Can you tell me whether it made you more alert in accomplishing your mission? You have referred to it as a method to facilitate the handling of the horrible tension and fear you were enduring.

DSJ: I used opium for several reasons. One, being it relaxed extreme nervousness and tensions that build while walking forward leading some people through an area where you don't know if you are going to live or die before sunset. Secondly, I used opium because I didn't care at that point whether or not the opium killed me. My reasoning at that time was if the opium didn't kill me, the VC would.

Q: Mr. Johnson, in your father's letter to Congressman Pettis dated 16 October 1970 he states that you were a point man for a seven-month period. Were you in fact a point man for a seven-month period and if so, did you ever ask for relief from that assignment because of the tensions you were under?

DSJ: I was in fact a point man for a total of seven months. Now, this wasn't one straight seven month period without stop. When I was in the bush I was a point man. I considered many times requesting relief from this position, but I was thwarted by the thought that if I were relieved I would be in the same place that I was when I first got out there, following blindly.

Regarding the events that led to Doug's going AWOL in December, 1969, he testified thus about his experience in late November of that year:

I contracted then what they thought was malaria, and was sent to a hospital where I was later found to have hepatitis. I was again sent to Cam Rahn Bay Convalescent Center and given five days hospitalization before being sent back. I went back to the bush. At this time our company was operating approximately due west of Pleiku City, about a click [kilometer] and a half from the Cambodian border. Within a short time I had been in Cambodia about three or four times and on one of those times we were sent in by chopper on a huge assault. The enemy fire was so great that many of the choppers turned away, with the exception of a few. One of these few was my chopper. Shortly after the landing, the body count of American dead soldiers came roughly to 17. We were then transferred to an area in close proximity to Ban Me Thuot, which was several miles south of where we were near the Cambodian border. We were in this area when I contracted hepatitis and was sent to Nha Trang Hospital. In Nha Trang I was introduced to two more drugs to which I had not been exposed before. These were LSD and speed. I began using speed to alleviate the necessity for opium and found myself using the two together in order to provide a different result than that to which I was accustomed.

(This hospitalization preceded the eight day AWOL chronicled in his December 26, 1969, soul-shrieking letter.)

In addition to Doug offering many candid descriptions of his drug abuse, Colonel Duddy questioned Doug about drugs:

Q 41: Were you ever treated by US medical authorities for the use of drugs?
DSJ: They put me in the hospital once for one and one half days.

Q 42: Do you remember specifically where or when?
DSJ: I was in the hospital once for a day and a half at An Khe. I was still using drugs while in the hospital. In other words, they gave me a bed for a night and kicked me out the next day.

Q 43: You refer to the use of speed and opium in your statement. Can you be more specific as to the dates?
DSJ: I was using from the time I got into Vietnam. From the time I was introduced to opium I was mainlining. That means for about five and half months and then I began mainlining speed for the duration of my time overseas.

When I read this, I cannot help but hear a note of irritation in Doug's voice, even on the page, as if he were trying not to throttle Colonel Duddy with the obvious: *Don't you get it? Don't you hear me? I've been telling you that I'd been doing drugs nonstop from the time I set foot there, that I tried all sorts of drugs in different combinations, that I never ceased doing drugs. How can I possibly make this more plain?*

Q 44: Mr. Johnson, how was it possible that you obtained the amount and varying types of drugs while under combat conditions?

DSJ: Either through the Vietnamese or other GIs. When they would go into the rear they would bring back everything they could get their hands on.

Q 45: Did you have to pay for the quantity of narcotics you stated you used?
DSJ: No.

In answer to Duddy's Question 79, Doug said that in April 1970 he was told by a nameless officer that his rank would be upgraded, that he would be returned to an E-3. (He had been demoted to an E-1 at the November court-martial.) This did not happen. Perhaps the failure to reinstate had something to do with two brief AWOLs, mid-month in April. In any event Doug remained at the lowest grade, the gruntiest of the grunts, an E-1 for as long as he was in the Army.

Some of Colonel Duddy's ninety-six questions seem to me especially odd, as if the whole purpose here was merely to test and elicit trivia. Question 83: "Do you recall the name of the doctor who performed your final physical at Fort Lewis, Washington?" Doug: "No." Indeed, the questions often switch from topic to topic without transition or building toward any greater understanding of events. For instance, Question 51 asked when Doug was incarcerated in Long Binh Jail. He answered succinctly. "The 28th of December 1969 to the 9th of January, 1970. The second time was June and July 1970." Immediately following, in Question 52, apropos of nothing, Colonel Duddy asked, "Do you recall any of the names of the individuals you contacted while you were in Japan attempting to have them assist you in not returning to the Republic of Vietnam?" Doug replied, "The only one I can remember is my doctor, Dr. Shirasu, who gave me access to social workers, psychiatrists, the chaplain and the chaplain's assistant." (No doubt Dr. Shirasu was memorable because he actually *did* grant Doug access to professional help.)

On this, the small stuff, Doug was uniformly vague. His replies to Duddy's inquiries of "Can you recall [places, dates, names]" were almost all simple and negative, "No." Even when he offered something beyond "No," his replies were iffy, inexact. When asked, "Can you recall the approximate date of your second confinement at the Cam Rahn Bay Convalescent Center?"

Doug replied, "It was getting close to Christmas, '69 because one of the guys was carrying a plastic Christmas tree with trimmings on it." These failures to remember details would later be to Doug's detriment. In making their reports, the Inspector General's office would use these failures to undermine his credibility.

The rest of the testimony at the December 4 Duddy hearing concentrated on the events of May and June of 1970, which is to say, his experience in Cambodia. We will come to that in a later chapter. Before April 30 —when Nixon admitted publicly to the invasion—Doug Johnson had already been part of "three or four" incursions into Cambodia. To the psychiatrist who treated him after his return home, he said it was five. This psychiatrist believed that these forays cumulatively drove my brother to madness in May 1970. He wrote:

> [Doug] reports that on five occasions he was in Cambodia on special assignments. He finally refused a 6th mission. He was sent anyway and at the Cambodian border left his group and went AWOL. I want to emphasize that his refusal to go at this time had not to do with unwillingness to do his duty, but was a sign of his flagrant psychological breakdown at which point his judgment had deteriorated beyond his control. Such behavior was the final desperate effort to remain integrated at all costs and to prevent further deterioration into insanity.

. . .

For reasons that remain unclear to me, Doug and Dad, at their own request, returned to Fort MacArthur the following week, December 10, to alter one brief passage of Doug's testimony. Colonel Duddy and a stenographer were again present. At 8 a.m. Duddy reminded Doug he was still under oath. He had but one pointed question, clearly at the request of the Johnsons:

Duddy: Mr. Johnson, do you have any further testimony that you would like to offer?

DSJ: Yes sir. On page 8, Question No. 12, the question is asked, if I recall the names and ranks of my platoon leaders or Commanding Officer. During my assignment to CO. Company D, 2/35 Inf, my Platoon Leader was an E.5 and my Commanding officer was a Captain, however, I do not recall their names. It is not Captain Hughes.

(Witness was excused)

By 8:25 a.m. it was concluded and they left.

I am particularly perplexed by this minute exchange because the testimony hardly differs from what Doug originally offered with regard to Question 12, which was: "I only recall one person's name, but he wasn't there when I transferred. He came later. His name is Cpt. Hughes."

Why would they go back to Fort MacArthur to make such a small but clearly—to them—significant change? Their copy of the transcript wasn't even mailed to Turrill Court until December 11. This suggests to me that on their drive home on December 4 Doug and Dad mulled over his reference to Captain Hughes and something about it, something about Captain Hughes, rankled them to the point where they would set up a new appointment and drive back into Los Angeles on December 10 to correct it. (Doug can cite the actual page 8 and Question 12 probably because the stenographer found it for them and read it back.) The whole exercise had a singular, specific purpose: to remove Captain Hughes from Doug's testimony. But why was this fleeting reference so important? I wonder if perhaps "Captain Hughes" was a name that Doug and Bill Johnson definitely did not want entered into the record, someone they wanted, in effect, *erased entirely from the record* so that the Inspector General would not seek him out, so that "Captain Hughes" would not be asked to corroborate or comment on Douglas Johnson at all. If so, might he have been the person referred to in Doug's October 29 letter, "I have this stupid Captain who is trying to get me in jail and a Bad Conduct Discharge." As this person, too, is nameless, these questions have no answers.

• • •

On April 30, 1970, Richard Nixon went on television to announce the incursion of American and South Vietnamese troops into Cambodia. Put bluntly, Nixon finally copped to, announced publicly the invasion of Cambodia. But it had begun the year before, in March 1969, in a secret operation called Operation Menu, known only to Nixon and a few select others, certainly not known to Congress or even to certain members of Nixon's cabinet. A reporter, William Beecher, broke this story in May 1969 on the front page of the *New York Times*, writing that "small teams" of US reconnaissance forces were infiltrating Cambodia "to assure that accurate information can be obtained to provide 'lucrative' targets for the bombers." Two weeks later the Nixon White House asked the FBI to tap Beecher's phone and the phones of other journalists, according to Beecher's obituary in that same paper in February 2024.

Nixon's announcement churned a society already seething with civil unrest. This was a volatile political moment, and even if Nixon didn't know it, members of his cabinet did. It's said that Secretary of Defense Melvin Laird was against the invasion of Cambodia because it would further inflame antiwar sentiment. Laird was proven correct. Protests—and governmental response to those protests—escalated in intensity, with sometimes violent clashes. On May 4, 1970, armed National Guardsmen at Kent State University in Ohio fired into a crowd of protesters, killing four students. On May 15, state and local police opened fire on a dormitory at Jackson State College in Mississippi, killing two men and injuring twelve. Outrage and disbelief at these murderous incidents raged all over America. The May 25, 1970, issue of *Time* magazine covered the Jackson State shootings, calling it "Kent State II." *Time* also published a multipage spread with text, photographs, and maps detailing the Cambodia invasion.

Peggy Johnson opened that magazine and saw the color photo of eleven nameless, disheveled soldiers. The caption read, "At an airstrip in South Viet Nam Central Highlands, US 4th Infantry troopers await helilift to join Operation Pacify One aimed at rooting North Vietnamese troops out of a rugged base area in NE Cambodia."

My sister remembers Mom uttering strangled shrieks as she rummaged through a drawer looking for a magnifying glass to scour the photograph of the GIs. Yes—there, there, unmistakably, was Doug wearing a head covering, a grin on his face, his hand raised in the peace sign. Mom began to scream, mad with grief and anxiety. She telephoned me in Delaware, sobbing, "Open the *Time* magazine! There, the color picture! It's Doug! It's him! Look at it! It's Doug and they've sent him into Cambodia! Oh, God! They've sent him into Cambodia."

PART III

<table>
<tr><td>A</td><td>Playlist</td><td align="right">B</td></tr>
</table>

Teach Your Children	CROSBY, STILLS, NASH & YOUNG
Carry On	CROSBY, STILLS, NASH & YOUNG
(Four Dead in) Ohio	CROSBY, STILLS, NASH & YOUNG
Eight Miles High	THE BYRDS
All Along the Watchtower	JIMI HENDRIX,
	BATTLESTAR GALACTICA VERSION
War! (What is it Good For?)	THE TEMPTATIONS, EDWIN STARR
Darkness, Darkness	THE YOUNGBLOODS

13. "Please in the Name of God, Do Something Today"

From the time they saw the photo in the May 25 *Time* magazine until mid-June, Doug's parents knew absolutely nothing of, from, or about their son. They certainly did not know that he had already been sent into Cambodia several times before "Operation Pacify One." And they did not know that this time, in May, yes, he got into the helicopter with the other soldiers in that photograph, but once in Cambodia, Doug did not join the fight against the Viet Cong. This time he went AWOL.

Doug had been in Vietnam since June 10, 1969, and standard practice dictated that he ought to have rotated out on June 9, 1970, to be given leave and fulfill his enlistment elsewhere. Why did this not happen? Papers unearthed from the basement offer no clear answer. Perhaps, (as in the Army's reasoning for denying him R&R) they counted AWOLs, jail time, and hospitalizations against him. Perhaps it had something to do with being "busted just before my DEROS [Date of Estimated Return from Overseas]," as he testified at the Duddy hearing (one of his few specific timing references). He went AWOL on May 22, showing back up on June 8 when he was arrested and taken to "Long Binh jail [for] the pretrial confinement. Upon arrival there without any preliminary measures or questions, I was placed in maximum security where I remained for 12 or 13 days." So much for going home. Imagine his mental anguish, the crash-and-burn of any equilibrium, knowing on June 9 that he ought to have been with the family and the fiancée. Imagine his parents' anguish as that Tuesday, June 9, came and went with no word. Bill and Peggy Johnson woke each morning sick with unspeakable foreboding and went to bed each night sick with unspoken grief.

His parents first approached the Red Cross, seeking information. Among the documents there are faded copies of two telegrams. (Spellings are left as I found them.) The first is dated June 18:

> RE PFC DSJ [ssn] SVCM [serviceman] FATHER WILLIAM REO AND DATE OF SVCMN RETURN SVCMN WAS DUE HOME 9 JUNE FONED SVC MOTHER BY MARS 26 APRIL STATED WOULD BE DELAYED GAVE NO REASON FYIO SVCPARENTS CONCEREND DUE TO PREVIOUS PROBLMES SVCMAN HAD WITH MARIJUNA

The second was sent the following day, June 19:

> San Bernardino California re: pvt DSJ [ssn] Presently USARM Correctional holding DET . . . Milauth [Military authorities] adv svcmn in pre-Trail confinement above address. Charged AWOL During Cambodian campaign Use narcotics dangerous drugs states SVCMN has seen psychiatrist and hospitalized for drying out use own descression release info to father however seems he fully aware svcmns problems recommend father write direct svcmn or milauth.

My father did so immediately, that very day, writing to the company commander:

> Dear Sir: It is with deep regret and humbleness that I write this letter to request your consideration in giving particulars concerning my son, Douglas S Johnson, PFC [ssn] formerly under your command.
>
> I was advised today via Red Cross Health and Welfare Report that Douglas is in a correctional holding detachment in pre-trial confine-

ment. Red Cross suggested I write to you for further information and disposition of this case.

Will you be kind enough to advise me at your earliest convenience regarding charges and disposition I am indeed grateful for your cooperation in this matter.

Very Truly Yours,
William J. Johnson

There was no reply.

The pitch and intensity of my father's letters that summer of 1970 escalate to near-insane. Reading them, I was reminded of the Tim O'Brien story "The Things They Carried," which I assigned to students when I taught Creative Writing. The narrative gathers momentum as the reader moves into it; the reader feels the weight, the burden, the velocity, stress and terror that the characters endured. The same is true of my father's letters; they gather momentum, fear and rage. One could truly say, all hell broke loose. As June moved into July, Bill slathered letters on one and all, far and wide, military, politicos, chaplains. These had his usual pleas and instructions, but not the rhetorical flourishes. Bill laid out his questions with bullet points, demanding answers. The tone and content changed again in mid-July, the letters awash in rage and unleavened desperation. "Please in the name of God, do something today," he wrote to Congressman Mendel Rivers. At the peak of his anguish, Bill became increasingly unhinged; his letters are enraged and incautious. He recognized—and had lost all patience with—the persistent Mr. Politico/Army runaround, their hypocrisy, their bullshit. On July 13, 1970, he thanked Senator Fulbright for sending his [Bill's] letter on to the Army, but added, "However, Mr. Fulbright, this is where the red tape starts and in time you will receive a very polite and formal letter signed by an officer that wants to impress you and advising that in essence this matter is referred." Bill accused the Army of the "premeditated murder of my son," of negligence and the "most perpetuated injustice of all time in the history of the US Army." He was rabidly angry and insistent and reckless, so much so that in replying to him Senator Fulbright included a stiff reprimand:

The Dept of the Army has assured me that the matter will be

thoroughly and fairly evaluated. I am sure you must realize that a US
Senator or anyone else other than the President cannot give the Army
a direct order with regard to a particular matter.

My father's incessant incendiary comments to Army brass and lawmakers
might have had consequences he did not anticipate. History has documented
that the Nixon administration was actively and widely using phone surveil-
lance on many of its perceived adversaries. The Johnsons felt certain that
summer that their phone was being tapped; Helen and Mom watched fear-
fully from the kitchen window as a panel truck parked down the street and
men worked on the phone lines for days.

In the letters of this summer, 1970, we see the first repeated use of Bill's
signature phrase, "I stand before you without shame or trepidation." However, this phrase suggests to me its opposite. In fact, he was facing them,
writing with shame *and* trepidation. Shame that a good Mormon boy, Eagle
Scout, piano prodigy, son of a good home should have been reduced to court-
martial and drug addiction and was jailed for the second time in a notorious
prison. And trepidation, fear, that the Army could do what it liked with
Doug Johnson—let him rot in prison, uncared for, even die there alone and
unmourned—and that his father would be powerless to save him.

• • •

In a single envelope in the basement I found a thick sheaf of papers stapled
together, with "In The Order They Were Received" written in my mother's
neat hand across the top. Below I list them in chronological order by date. I
ask the reader to keep in mind that dates on the replies here reflect when the
letters were *written*, not when they were received by the Johnsons. Some of my
father's letters, notably the long ones of July 6 and July 16, went out to perhaps
ten or twelve different people. Though I have edited these two letters, they are
mostly intact. For the rest, I quote only brief excerpts to give the tenor of Bill
Johnson's increasing desperation. They start on June 20, the day after my parents read the notice from the Red Cross advising, "Charged AWOL During
Cambodian campaign Use narcotics dangerous drugs states SVCMN has seen
psychiatrist and hospitalized for drying out use own descression."

IN THE ORDER THEY WERE RECEIVED

June 20: WJJ to company commander he had written to on June 19:
refers to a newspaper article about a California Polytechnic
valedictorian who had had a drug problem as a young person but
was granted clemency by a judge. "Asking that same clemency for
my son."

June 23: WJJ to former high-school teacher asking for a character
reference for Doug.

June 23: WJJ to District President of the SE Asia Latter-Day Saint
Mission. This long letter addresses the recipient as "Brother
Smith" and asks for the church chaplain to find Doug and send
information. He closes, "I am praying you will help in this fight to
save a young man from the depths of depression of hell. I'm afraid
the military [will] report <u>after</u> it is over."

June 23: WJJ to Company Commander again asking for "medical
rehabilitation for [Doug's] drug problems."

June 30: Reply from the Latter-Day Saints, SE Mission who will send a
letter seeking information on Doug.

July 2: WJJ to Frank Church, senator from Idaho, asks for nothing.
No mention of Doug. Final paragraph: "Keep up the fight. Keep
up the good work. Keep it up for the sake of our country. I am
ashamed to be a registered Republican and to have voted the same.
Don't let up and keep fighting." Senator Church (1924–1984) was a
vocal critic of the war.

July 6: WJJ to staff chaplain, quoting the Red Cross telegram cited
above. "I plead no contest for my son. No one in his right mind
would go AWOL in Cambodia two weeks before his rotation date.
I am trying to ascertain:

Is my boy in pretrial confinement? Is there to be a trial? I want the
name of his defense counsel.

If a trial has been held, what was the outcome?

July 6: WJJ to the Confinement Officer: "I am advised that my son, Pfc.
Douglas S. Johnson is being held in pre-trial confinement. . . . I am
requesting the following information:

Has this trial been held? If so what was the outcome. If not, what is the date of the trial?

Name and address of his defense counsel.

When may I expect the Army to return my son to the US?

Is my son hospitalized?

July 6: WJJ to Senator Fulbright. This long letter reads in part, "I feel that you and Senator Mansfield are my only hope. I have been the route of correct channels through my Congressman, Representative Jerry Pettis beginning May 26 and after at least 20 telephone calls to Washington DC, to this date I have had no reply, no information whatever . . . I feel that with each day that passes my son dies a little more . . . Mr. Senator, this boy must be exonerated of all charges and returned to the United States for psychiatric and medical treatment if he is to be saved from the pangs of hell . . . I strongly feel the Army has been extremely negligent in their handling of this situation. At this stage, sir every second of every minute is important to my boy's salvation." Ends with "I am eternally grateful to you."

July 6: Same letter as above but addressed to Senator Mansfield, including the information that Doug was born in Great Falls, Montana.

July 6: Same letter as above, with a few tweaks, addressed to Robert Finch, Bill's contact (such as it was) at the White House. "I am writing to you to plead for help in saving my son from the gallows of hell . . . You will fight for justice and will understand my fighting for my son when negligence and injustice have occurred on the part of the Army in this instance. . . . I feel that with each day that passes, he dies a little more." It concludes, "I put it to you that every second of every minute is important to my boy's salvation."

July 6: WJJ to Mr. Hulbert [music teacher] seeking letter for a character reference.

July 8: WJJ to Representative Mendel Rivers, chair of the Armed Services Committee. Same long letter that went to Fulbright, Mansfield, and Finch. Includes the same four questions. Ends with the imperative of Doug's salvation and eternal gratitude.

July 9: Reply from Senator Fulbright: "One of my great concerns about

our country's involvement in the conflict in SE Asia is the effect it
has caused in the lives of so many of our young people."

July 11: Reply from Irwin C. Loud Jr., Chaplain (Maj) USA, USARV
Installation Stockade Chaplain that Doug is not in confinement.
Offers an address in B Company 2 of the 12th Infantry.

July 12: Paul Kleinwachter's first letter to WJJ. Bill probably received it on
July 18 or 19. (Their exchanges are developed in the next chapter.)

July 13: WJJ to Senator Fulbright thanking him for his reply and sending
his letter to the Army's attention. He continues with the quote
already noted about red tape and "polite and formal" hypocrisy.
"My son is in the throes of a situation worse than death and he nor
I [can] wait for the red tape or polite answers. . . . Since May [2]6th
I have been unable to ascertain

His unit of assignment

What are the charges

Name and address of his military counsel

If the trial has been held, where and what is the verdict and
sentence meted out? . . .

I am confident my boy could be exonerated and hospitalized
in San Francisco next week by a direct order from somebody to
the Army. Will you please help me find that person and fight to
accomplish what must be done as well as rushing to me the answers
to the above questions."

July 13: WJJ to Mike Mansfield. Same long letter and same four
questions.

July 13: Telegram from Mansfield [responding to the letter of July 8]
"Contacting officials and will advise as soon as I have anything to
report. Regards."

July 16: WJJ to Pettis offering the address he had received from the
chaplain. Closing line: "I stand before you without shame or
trepidation where my son's fate and future is in your hands."
This same letter went out on this date to Mendel Rivers and
Mansfield and Fulbright and Mr. Finch at the White House, all
with the same closing line: "I stand before you without shame or
trepidation."

This flurry of letters written on July 16 was meant to give each of these politicos the new address for Doug that Bill had received from the LDS chaplain. He no doubt thought it would help to find the correct person to write to: that is, the (mythical) person who could, with a stroke of a pen, get Doug sent to the States for treatment. With each letter, Bill also enclosed a copy of the following letter he had written to the Battalion Commander, the Commanding General, and the Company Commander of Doug's unit at that APO. This letter is long, garrulous, pleading. I have edited it slightly:

July 16

Dear Sir

I have been informed through American Red Cross channels that my son Douglas was released back to your unit, pending court martial proceedings.

I am only partially cognizant of the heavy burden that you bear as [assignment] and the grave decisions that are yours alone in fighting to protect the lives of American soldiers, as well as trying to save the Republic of Viet Nam.

I am writing to you sir, as Battalion Commander in humbleness, gratitude, honesty and earnestness.

Sir, this is the second court martial my son will have received in the matter of 14 months in Vietnam. You and the court may ask yourselves why should the court be lenient to the point of exoneration in this situation when the first time apparently failed? Perhaps Mr. Commander I can answer your intelligent and natural question in this letter.

When Douglas was in infantry training he wrote us that one particular day during dress parade when the colors passed, it brought tears to his eyes and a lump in his throat and he said to us in this letter, "I don't think that two years is a long time to give to your country." With this type of patriotism there must be room in the court's heart for leniency.

The American government has spent hundreds of billions of dollars and thousands of American lives so far in its bid for saving South VN from communism. My plea is to save one American at no cost to the government. If my son is not allowed to finish his enlistment with honor and integrity six months before the end of his enlistment period . . . [A long description follows of Doug's losses and impaired abilities that will be the result.]

May I state several reasons why he should be exonerated from the charges because if they are true, he obviously did not know what he was doing.

Douglas has never been in trouble in his life except in VN

No one in his right mind would go AWOL in Cambodia two weeks before rotation home date (9 June 1970) least of all in Cong country. (I understand from ARC [American Red Cross] that this is the charge.)

[Long paragraph about how drugs destroy judgment.]

[No drug problems before being sent to Vietnam.]

[Many character references are on their way.]

Cost of his exoneration to the Army is zero. This in itself would save the future of one American boy. Isn't this why America is in Viet Nam?

[Doug enlisted at age 19 and is an "honorable young man with firm desire to serve his country willingly."]

[Doug was an Eagle Scout.]

May I beg your indulgence and that of the Court, sir. . . . You and the court, sir are in command of his next 45 years of life or more. Could you find it within your heart and mind to save my boy from the pangs of repulsive antipathy and allow him his earned leave with further assignment in the United States.

I pray in the name of Jesus Christ that you will be guided and directed in this trial to save Douglas from the throes of hell. Amen. I thank you.

Very truly yours,
William J. Johnson

PS I must fight—and I will fight for the right—I will give my all to save my son.

With this PS I think my father intended to forewarn the Army that if they failed to reply or respond, this campaign would not cease: Bill Johnson would find justice for Doug. This same letter (minus the postscript) went on

July 16 to the Inspector General's APO and also to the Chaplain of the 4th Infantry. Both of these letters use the "stand before you without shame or trepidation" phrase and both end with this paragraph:

> Sir, I will fight with every means possible and enlist the aid of every private and governmental source available to gain rehabilitation, honor and an honorable discharge after his tour of duty. Douglas is worthy of your help.

These letters also advise recipients that on July 7, Bill had hired an attorney. I have no idea how my father knew or came to know of this attorney; he was retired military. I will not identify him or his firm because my parents' association with them was money and time squandered.

The firm's four letters are all tone-deaf verging on witless. On July 9 they wrote a stiffly worded letter on lawyerly letterhead to PFC Douglas S. Johnson at the address provided by the chaplain, inquiring after his whereabouts and the upcoming trial. In closing, they add, with an implied *tut tut*, "I will appreciate a prompt reply from you." Really? *Doug, are you perchance rotting in a military prison, or maybe you're AWOL again, off in some jungle or another, but please do reply forthwith.* On July 15 the firm wrote again to Doug "to provide help and assistance to you, should you require it." *Should you require it? What the hell kind of question is that? Why do you think you were hired?* Again, they close: "I will appreciate a prompt reply from you," as if they are setting up an invitation to tea and need to know how many cupcakes to order. Also on July 9 they wrote to the office of the Adjunct General at the Pentagon asking for information on Doug's whereabouts on behalf of his parents. Oddly, the last line here is: "Our Cost Check No. 7387 in the amount of $1.50 is enclosed for the customary charge for this material." This statement leaves me baffled and no reply is included in the file. Enough said of lawyers.

The list continues:

July 14: to WJJ from Mack M. Dugger, Administrative Officer, replying on behalf of the "Commanding Officer," who states, "Your son was confined at the United States Army Vietnam Installation Stockade on 15 June 1970 in a pre-trial status. He was charged with violation of [AWOL] and Article 113—sleeping on guard. On 1 July 1970 your son was returned to his parent unit, Co B 3/12th In 4th Inf Div AP SF 96262 after his Commanding Officer had deemed pre-trial confinement no longer necessary." The letter finishes with: "I wish to advise you that your son had the services of a chaplain, a doctor, a psychiatrist, a social worker and the members of the correctional staff available to him at all times while in confinement. I trust this will be of assistance to you."

This is the very same Bullshit Paragraph the Army had sent repeatedly. Indeed, nearly all of the letters the Army wrote in the summer of 1970, whether to Bill or a senator or a congressman, closed with this Bullshit Paragraph, implying that in Long Binh Jail, long famous for its horrors, a whole phalanx of uniformed angels, helpful nurses, competent doctors, and bespectacled shrinks hovered near Private Johnson, eager to listen to any problems he encountered, that social workers freshened up the flowers in his prison cell, and that correctional staff saw to it that his personal library was well-stocked with cheerful self-help volumes.

> July 15: A long, informative letter from David Folkman, Jr., Major, USAF and President, Southern Vietnam District (of Latter-day Saints). He begins "Dear Brother Johnson" and goes on to say that he has not spoken with Doug directly, but has clearly had long exchanges with Paul Kleinwachter about Doug's health and well-being, particularly with regard to drugs. Paul has said Doug will have a good chance to get hold of himself when he gets out of Vietnam. Folkman says that the court-martial will be held in the next few days. (This did not happen.)
>
> July 16: To WJJ from Kenneth Hodson, Major General USA, The Judge Advocate General, replying "On behalf of Mr. Finch." This was the response to my father's long, impassioned letter of July 6 to his contact in the White House. Hodson continues, "I have no recent information about the status of his case other than your letter. I

have asked his command for information necessary [and] shall write again."

We heard nothing further from this dude, ever, or from Finch.

> July 16: From Mendel Rivers acknowledging receipt of WJJ's letter of July 8. He has taken it up with the Army and will reply when he hears.

> July 17: From Senator Fulbright acknowledging WJJ's letter of July 13. In the second paragraph is Fulbright's previously quoted sharp rebuke to Bill's recognition of the Army's usual blather and hypocrisy.

> July 19: Bill replies to Paul Kleinwachter's introductory letter, including a copy of his Battalion Commander letter.

> July 19: WJJ to George Romney, Secretary of Housing and Urban Development. He begins his letter with a quote from the Book of Mormon: Moroni, Book 10 Verse 20, about faith, hope, and charity. He thanks Romney for his intervention because "within a very short time last January after you took action, Douglas was on his way to Japan for treatment of the severe hepatitis he had at that time. I begged the Army not to return this boy to Viet Nam for fear of what has since happened." He goes on "If they confine this boy he will either kill himself or be a vegetable and I call that premeditated murder of my son . . . I am desperate. The trial may be over. My son enlisted and has served his year in VN. He deserves an Honorable Discharge but at this point I cannot and do not really care as long as he comes <u>now</u>. I will pay his medical psychiatric costs. I want my boy home and exonerated. Please please help."

There is no reply from Romney in these files.

> July 19: WJJ to Mendel Rivers's office, Attn: Mr. Hogan. The letter reads, in part,
> If Doug is given confinement in LJB I feel he will either kill himself or be a vegetable. I call that premeditated murder of my son at the hands of military justice. This trial, sir, if allowed

to render a decision other than complete exoneration is most perpetuated injustice of all time in the history of the US Army. . . . I am desperate. My wife is on the verge of a complete nervous breakdown. My boy at this time may be damaged beyond the limits both psychosocially and physically and physiologically. My son served his year in VN. He deserves an honorable discharge. I gave to the Army of the United States of America a man for a two year enlistment. Due to the conditions that have prevailed, the least I can expect from the Army of the United States of America is the return of the same son I willingly sent and who willingly went. Please in the name of God, do something today.

July 21: Reply from Mansfield regarding a phone a call from WJJ.

July 23: Reply from Mendel Rivers: "I have received your most recent correspondence and again contacted the Army with regard to the case of your son . . . As word is received I will let you know."

July 25: WJJ to David Folkman, LDS chaplain, with heartfelt thanks for his help and meeting with Paul Kleinwachter. Bill, too, has been in touch with Paul. Bill has sent copies of *all* the character references (probably about eight) to the whole galaxy: Pettis, Rivers, Fulbright, Mansfield, Finch, Romney, and others. "The San Bernardino County Medical Association is sending a letter asking for a just trial and no confinement, but rather 30 or 45 days' leave, which [Doug] has coming, and reassignment to duty in the States . . . as John Paul Jones said, "I have not yet begun to fight." . . . I further pray that someday our Douglas will make you a very proud man to be able to say that you helped him in his hour of need."

July 27 1970: Western Union Telegram to WJJ from Commanding General

THIS MESSAGE IS SENT IN RESPONSE TO A REQUEST FROM HONORABLE MENDEL RIVERS THAT YOU BE ADVISED REGARDING THE HEALTH, WELFARE AND PRESENT STATUS OF YOUR SON, PRIVATE DOUGLAS JOHNSON [SSN], COMPANY B 3RD BATALLION 12TH INFANTRY, THIS COMMAND. DOUGLAS IS PRESENTLY WITH HIS UNIT AT CAMP RADCLIFF

AN KHE REPUBLIC OF VIET NAM. HE IS AWAITING
TRIAL BY SPECIAL COURT MARTIAL AS YOU WERE
ADVISED BY HIS APPOINTED COUNSEL, CPT PAUL
KLEINWACHTER BY LETTER AND IN TELEPHONE
CONVERSATION WITH HIM ON 22 JULY 1970. YOUR SON
IS IN GOOD HEALTH. PRIOR INQUIRIES RECEIVED
FROM THE HONORABLE L PETTIS CONCERNING
DOUGLAS WERE ANSWERED BY ELECTRICAL
MESSAGE FROM THIS COMMAND ON 29 JUNE 1970.
REPRESENTATIVE PETTIS WAS ADVISED IN OUR
MESSAGE OF 23 JULY 1970 THAT THE TENTATIVE
DATE FOR DOUGLAS TRIAL WAS 26 JULY 1970.
HOWEVER, THE TRIAL HAS BEEN DELAYED PENDING
RECEIPT OF LETTERS ATTESTING TO DOUGLAS
GOOD CHARACTER WHICH WILL BE USED IN
MITIGATION BY HIS DEFENSE COUNSEL. I HOPE THIS
INFORMATION IS OF ASSISTANCE TO YOU
COMMANDING GENERAL 4TH INFANTRY DIVISION

Marshall McLuhan famously proclaimed: "The medium is the message," so perhaps here it is the medium—that is, a telegram—that accounts for the peremptory tone. The inference, however, telegram or not, is unmistakable: that the Commanding General and the Army itself are annoyed-unto-truly-pissed-off with Bill Johnson and his barrage of letters, his sending nosy Congressional lackeys to make inquiries to probe the health and where-abouts of one hapless grunt awaiting court-martial. These military men have dealt with these incessant requests and inquiries, and they're sick of it. This distraught father should shut the hell up and let them get on with their jobs. They have a war to run.

Indeed, Bill's Congressional allies also seemed fatigued unto annoyed. One can hear the note of exasperation in the replies even from those people who had been supportive.

July 28, 1970: Reply from Mendel Rivers to WJJ. It reads, in part:
We have had detailed discussions with the Army on this matter

and understand they have an extensive file of correspondence from
you and are completely aware of your concern over the situation. . . .
I am in no position to inject myself or this Committee into the
judicial process or influence those responsible for the review of the
case.

These politicos who implied that Mr. Johnson should shut up and let military
justice take its course clearly underestimated my father's commitment to his
son. Only the ever-active, sympathetic Congressman Jerry Pettis understood
the stakes for the Johnsons. His last sentence states the truth my father had
stressed all along.

July 28: Reply from Jerry Pettis to WJJ enclosing a copy of a letter
Pettis wrote to Major General William A. Becker, Chief of
Legislative Liaison, Department of the Army: "For some time
now I have been working with your office via telephone on behalf
of my constituent, Mr. William J. Johnson. . . . I would sincerely
appreciate any advice you might be able to offer providing Private
Douglas S. Johnson the opportunity to complete his enlisted
service in an honorable fashion. I cannot stress too strongly
that this young man's entire future will be determined by the
Department of the Army in the action which will be decreed by
the court which is scheduled to convene on August 3rd."

No reply from Major General Becker exists amid these documents.

• • •

At the very back of the "In The Order They Were Received" list is a hand-
scrawled log of long-distance phone calls Bill made on Doug's behalf. The
phone log, which I suspect is incomplete, records calls made, Pacific time.
The long-distance fees would have been staggering. Across the top of this
list Bill wrote: "July 25th, I have written a total of 61 letters to 21 different
individuals, retained an attorney and worked 3 weeks full time (vacation)."
If my father was as intemperate in these phone calls as he was on paper

(which I suspect he was), the Johnsons' phone might well have been tapped that summer.

7-7-70 At 8 Am Called Fulbright's office DC also Mrs. Del-Balzo, Mike Mansfield's office also Miss Jones Bob Finch's office at the White House. Asked specifically to intercept letter mailed 7-6-70 and be given to addressee in each case stated that if that is accomplished then cost of telephone calls would be well worth the money.

July 14 Called DC Mendel Rivers office at 9 AM. Got in touch with a Mr. Hogan who is handling case. Called back at 2 . . . Will do all he can and stated feel free to call any time.

July 14 Called White House Talked to Miss Jones sec'y to Bob Finch. advised call SF

July 14 Called chaplain returned call and suggested I give chaplain time and write Inspector general same APO and request info and help

July 15th 10 AM Sgt Harris called with new address for Pvt DSJ

Called San Pedro talk to Lt. Col chaplain

Hired [name withheld] attorney Riverside July 7

July 14 Called Sgt Harris at Norton AFB [in San Bernardino] who will try to find out something or get Doug on the radio

July 14 Talked to Mr. Garner at RC [Red Cross] and no info on subject

July 16 rec'd call from Mr. Hulburt who anxious to write letter of character reference for Doug

July 16 called chaplain at 4th Div general and address. He advises he will return call if he can find it. 4 PM 5 PM no call returned do not expect any

July 17—6:30 AM called Mr. Hogan at Armed services. [Mendel Rivers's office] Was transferred. Mr. Hogan advises nothing new at this point will do all in his power to help. Advised him of copy of letter we wrote to CO was forthcoming

July 17 6:30 AM called Mike Mansfield Mrs. [illegible] will re instigate [illegible] of Doug's change of address. She could not recall the original letter. I asked specifically if she would show letter to Senator Mansfield and take action to bring this kid home and I don't think there's much time left. We must have something done now.

July 17 Western Union sending wire to SF and mailed $1.54/15 words fast
cable .34 for each word overnight cable service 3.74 for 22 words
will not send cable too expense and no guarantee of delivery only
to Saigon.

. . .

This was also the summer that Ed's mother in Wisconsin wrote my parents
five anguished letters in succession (July 11, July 13, July 14, July 17, August
24). Her letters make plain that she and Peggy Johnson also spoke on the
phone. Her son Ed and Doug were prisoners in Long Binh at the same time.
I assume that Doug gave Ed our phone number and address and that Ed sent
them to his mom, who started their connection. Her letters are by turns
bewildered and angry and forlorn. She counsels my mom to be brave, to be
strong, but to be careful. She herself was dealing with the Red Cross, not
contacting her Congressman because she was afraid of stirring up trouble.
She clung to caution: "You don't know how dirty they [the Army] can be. No
one to help the poor boys."

The most heart-rending of all her letters is the last one, sent Special
Delivery, postmarked August 24. Ed also received an Undesirable discharge
and was afflicted by drugs. Her letter is addressed to Peggy alone, and her
warnings are clearly born of her own immediate experience:

> Ed got home—what a shock—spent 8½ weeks in jail . . . You raise a
> good Christian child and this is what the service does . . . I intend to
> see he gets an Honorable Discharge. He earned it . . . It's such a shame
> and a dirty disgrace to think the boys are treated so rotten . . . Peggy, I
> hope you can have the courage to stick with Doug. There will be many
> trying days. Just be patient. I shall keep you informed about the prog-
> ress I _hope_ to make.

Ed's mother never wrote to Peggy again. But my mother took her advice
to heart: She did have the courage to stick with Doug for thirty years, and
indeed there would be many trying days ahead.

14. "An Outstanding and Very Beautiful Individual"

July 1970

The fact that Paul Kleinwachter was assigned as Doug's attorney testifies to some cosmic bright light in what was otherwise pervasive darkness. Paul gave Doug Johnson the only ray of hope he had had in months, maybe since he had set foot in Vietnam. And Paul gave Doug's parents a cogent, clear, true conduit of information undiluted by stale-phrase bullshit or buck-passing. Moreover, Paul actually dealt with Doug, saw him frequently. The same could not be said of anyone else with whom my father corresponded. Paul Kleinwachter opened communications with Bill Johnson on July 12. From that point on, Bill's letters to senators, congressmen, and Army brass remained intense, determined, even panicked and anguished, but his exchanges with Paul, though urgent, were cooperative rather than combative.

Paul Kleinwachter was twenty-five years old when he went to Vietnam. He had grown up in Inglewood, California, a Los Angeles suburb, and attended Northwestern University, graduating with a degree in history with the class of 1966. In the meantime his father, who worked for North American Aviation, was transferred to their division in Tulsa, Oklahoma. After college, Paul enrolled at the Tulsa School of Law and graduated in December 1968. He passed the Oklahoma Bar Exam and joined the Army in 1969.

Paul Kleinwachter, 1970, Washington State. Photo credit: Pam Kleinwachter.

Stationed at Fort Lewis, he worked in the Judge Advocate General (JAG) office from July of 1969 until he left to join the 4th Infantry Division in Vietnam in May of 1970, the very month that Doug Johnson got into trouble (again).

Around July 1 Doug was released from Long Binh and sent back to his unit at the 4th Infantry's sprawling Camp Radcliff, near the town of An Khe. Paul was assigned as his attorney some time in early July. Paul Kleinwachter was not simply a dutiful attorney; he responded to Doug on a human level, recognized his suffering, as well as the effects and the toll of his drug abuse. At the Duddy hearing in December 1970, Doug described him thus: "My lawyer, Paul Kleinwachter, [is] an outstanding and very beautiful individual. I requested to see a psychiatrist. I was granted this and found out the psychiatrist totally ignored me. I then began going to see Paul Kleinwachter on a regular basis, not only for legal assistance but for personal relief from the tension that I was under. . . . I would visit him [Paul] and spoke to him not only of legal matters, but of personal frustrations and worries and other things that were on my mind and bothering me. He did this for me on his own time." Paul was one of only three people Doug actually named in the whole of his Duddy testimony. Paul Kleinwachter was the closest thing to an actual friend that Doug had in Vietnam.

Camp Radcliff itself had only just been carved from the jungle a few years before. Interested readers can go to the internet and look for "Staff Film Report 66" and at 26:17 watch extensive 1965 footage of the military quickly establishing this base, originally for an Air Cavalry Division. When the 4th Infantry took over in late 1969, Camp Radcliff remained basically unchanged from its beginnings: rugged, ramshackle, slapped-together wooden structures, sleeping quarters called hooches. Paul kindly shared with me his recollections and slides, pictures he took in 1970. He remembered a sort of trench, an open ditch that ran alongside the path to the mess hall where waste liquids collected, coagulated, soured, and smelled. Earthen dugouts were scattered throughout Camp Radcliff for personnel to retreat to in case of attacks. One such dugout was very near a battered building, bleached to a khaki color, marked "Court." What might have once been a window was boarded up by 1970. Nearby was a low, rambling wooden structure where Paul and his colleagues worked seven days a week. Ten lawyers shared this space, along with support staff and a lieutenant colonel and a major who oversaw operations; these two had small offices cordoned off from the others. There were windows, placed high, with slats rather than glass. Paul's small, plain metal desk was tucked into a corner and dominated by a large portable fan to ease the heat and humidity. Paul and his colleagues sat on metal folding chairs.

In addition to his caseload, Captain Kleinwachter took the time and care to write to Doug's father. His first letter is formal, but not curt or dismissive or blatheringly uninformative as were most of the letters from Army men:

July 12 1970

Dear Sir:

By way of introduction my name is Paul Kleinwachter and I am a lawyer and as a member of the Judge Advocate General Corps of the Army I have been assigned to defend your son Doug at his forthcoming trial. He is charged with being absent without leave from 10

May to 15 May and from 11 [i.e., 22] May to 8 June. In addition he is further charged with sleeping while on guard duty on 16 May and possessing one tablet of a drug called binoctol. These charges have been referred to a special court martial where the maximum possible punishment which could be adjudged is confinement at hard labor for 6 months, forfeiture of ⅔ pay per month for 6 months and reduction to Pvt. E-1. It should be added that a punitive discharge cannot be adjudged.

I have talked with Doug on numerous occasions and we have established a good working relationship and a basis of understanding. Although I am not at liberty to divulge information of a confidential nature without your son's consent, I can tell you that we intend to plead guilty to the AWOL charges and not guilty to the others if and when the case comes to trial.

Right now Doug feels that he wants to be released from the Army as soon as possible. We have discussed thoroughly many ramifications and implications of his receiving an administrative discharge from the Army prior to his normal termination of service and he appears very set in this decision. Doug has the right if he wishes to request that he be discharged from the service in lieu of being tried by court martial. At this time I am in the process of determining whether such a request would be granted if it were submitted. Until this matter is satisfactorily resolved the trial will be delayed. Of course if this resignation is submitted and accepted there would be no trial and in all likelihood Doug would receive an undesirable discharge from the Army.

At Doug's insistence I have not mentioned his use or misuse of drugs. Suffice it to say that I feel he has a problem in this area and I am determining the extent of the medical and/or psychiatric help which is available to him.

I hope I have answered some of the questions you have re: Doug and I will try to keep you informed as the case progresses. In addition please feel free to contact me directly at any time.

In reply my father wrote on July 19:

Dear Captain Kleinwachter:

I am enclosing copy of a letter I have sent to Battalion Commander, Company Commander, Commanding General Fourth Infantry Davison and others, including congressmen and senators.

Captain, I am writing this not only as a concerned father on the outcome of this trial, but am far more concerned about the mental and physical health of my boy, not only today, for his mental and physical outlook in the years to come.

Since Doug has been in the service, he has not had what I would call an even break. If Doug had been sent to any other part of the world, or assigned any job, even in Viet Nam, other than with a gun, he would never have caused trouble for himself or others. In this respect I would give odds of 10,000 to one in any amount.

The whole of my son is in your hands. I have retained an attorney whom you have heard from already, for your use as you see fit. I will back you through private and governmental agencies and individuals.

Captain Kleinwachter, if you will save my son from the fires of hell I will be eternally grateful. Perhaps some day the time will come somewhere, sometime, somehow, either thru me or mine, I will be able to repay you in some way.

If you want something from me fast, call via MARS or commercial telephone [family phone number]. I will accept the charges.

Very Truly Yours,
William J. Johnson

Other references I found among the letters indicate that Bill and Paul spoke on the phone often in this fraught period of time. In the midst of Bill's later struggle to get the Undesirable changed to a Medical discharge, my dad quotes from these phone calls: "Defense Counsel Paul Kleinwachter advised me on the telephone last summer that my son was very ill, both in mind and body and that there was <u>absolutely no help for him there in Viet Nam and that he had been in that country too long</u>." Clearly, Paul was trying to help Doug on a human level, not simply as his defense counsel.

Having established a supportive relationship with Paul, Bill set out to aid in Doug's defense for the court-martial that still loomed. He wrote the following [edited] letter to the entire galaxy of important political men he had thus far assembled: Pettis, Mansfield, Fulbright, Rivers, Finch, Romney, and the LDS chaplain. Basically he is asking for *them* to write instructions to the military court,

July 24th

Dear Sir:

In less than eight days the Military Court of Justice will convene, the Army of the United States of America vs. Pfc. Douglas S. Johnson [ssn] Co B, 3/12 Infantry, 4th Infantry Division.

Time is running out. Would you please read this letter [name] and act on it today. Tomorrow may be too late for Captain Kleinwachter to use it in his defense of Douglas ...

I am enclosing copies of character references, originals of which I have sent to Captain Kleinwachter ... [Everyone got copies of all the character references, probably eight of them.]

At this point [name] I have been able to ascertain the answers to the questions referred to in my recent letter. I submit the following information:

1: Defense Counsel: Captain Paul Kleinwachter

2. Charges: a. Possession of one tablet of binoctal,

b. AWOL 10 May–15 May

22 May–8 June

c. Sleeping on guard duty—16 May

3. Trial to be held about August 3.

4. Defense will plead guilty to the AWOL charges and not guilty to the other charges.

In my recent letters and phone calls to you I feel I have stated with clarity our concern for our son and why he must not and I repeat <u>must not</u> be subjected to imprisonment in any stockade, and further I have stated the detailed reasons why Doug should be allowed his earned leave and reassignment ...

The Court is entitled to impose upon him a sentence. If confinement is part of this picture the confinement must be suspended. I repeat, the confinement must be suspended. If the Court could find justice served and allow Doug then to return home on his earned leave and reassignment in the United States,

Doug would pay his debt to the Army.

Doug could hold his head high and finish his tour of duty with honor and integrity

It would save the life of a young man mentally, physically and morally and allow him to be a productive citizen.

Doug's defense counsel, Captain Paul Kleinwachter is capable, interested in this case and is earnestly trying to save Doug from the pangs of hell.

I beg and plead for your cooperation, [name]. Will you, [name] write a letter to the Court asking for the Court to consider

Suspending stockade confinement in the event it is ordered.

Allowing Douglas his earned leave and reassignment in the States for the remainder of his service enlistment (6 months)

Please address [your letter] to the Court c/o Captain Kleinwachter. This letter must reach Captain Kleinwachter immediately or the trial will be over.

I hope this is my last appeal ...

Sincerely yours,
William J. Johnson
Enclosures
PS Perhaps you noted the recent court-martial in
Viet Nam of Lt. Duffy of Claremont, California.
He was found guilty of premeditated murder and
given a <u>suspended</u> sentence and a fine.

I would guess that Jerry Pettis and probably Mike Mansfield and the LDS chaplain did as my father requested. But Mendel Rivers, Senator Fulbright, and George Romney were distinctly unsympathetic after Bill's rants about the "premeditated murder of my son."

Even this impassioned imploring on Doug's behalf could not assuage my father's fears. The following day, July 25, Bill personally wrote a long, eloquent, elaborate defense of Doug, which he sent to the court through Paul. Like most of my father's letters, this invokes the usual litany of Doug's worth and waxes rhapsodic about the productive life that yet lies before him if only the court will heed his father. It reads as if Bill Johnson saw himself as Atticus Finch, actually looking these men in the eye, standing before them, regaling, beseeching.

25 July 1970
To the Court—United States Army
Headquarters 4th Infantry Division
Office of the Staff Judge Advocate
c/o Captain Paul Kleinwachter
Defense Attorney for Douglas Scott Johnson APO San Francisco 96262

Gentlemen of the Court:

By way of introduction, let me introduce myself. My name is William J. Johnson; I am the father of the above-named defendant.

I should like to state at this time I appreciate your position on this Court as the body of men who must make a fair judgment of another man on trial. I am writing this letter in lieu of attending trial, for myself, my wife and three other children, for those concerned individuals who wrote character references and for all the other individuals who steadfastly wish to actively participate. I offer you, gentlemen of the Court, the following facts and data.

The defendant, gentlemen of the Court, is 20 years old and enlisted in the Army at age 19. He enlisted without hesitation to serve his country willingly. In a letter Doug once wrote, "I don't think that two years is long enough to give to your country." When Doug enlisted he was healthy, physically and mentally and morally sound. He displayed confidence, eagerness and a lust to excel in any situation that confronted him in his training. In six months Doug received orders for Viet Nam. He honored his orders and left for Viet Nam with fear in his heart, bewilderment and a <u>definite forced</u> display of positive emotions, -- a feeling of patriotic devotion to duty. The defendant's behavior pattern in Viet

Nam is entirely out of character with the Douglas we have loved, raised and guided for 19 years.

Prior to Viet Nam the defendant was never in a position or experienced problems that he was unable to cope with. Situations and conditions in Viet Nam were his first experience in which he was forced, physically, and from a patriotic standpoint, to comply with, but psychologically was blocked. Gentlemen, I make this statement to you in all sincerity and earnestness. I do not hold the Army responsible for Doug's present situation and neither do I hold Doug responsible for his present situation. It is obvious that the pressures, conditions and strain of Viet Nam were too great for Douglas to bear. My extremely deep concern is three-fold

His physical and mental health.

His feelings for himself in honor, integrity and self-confidence

His future as a successful and good citizen.

Doug has had at no time in his life any difficulty with the law of our land. His worst offense with the law was a ticket he received for parking too far away from the curb. He has had no violations of any kind.

Douglas belongs to the Church of Jesus Christ of Latter-Day Saints (Mormon) and is a member in good standing.

Douglas is an Eagle Scout, and remained active in scouting his late teens in Explorers, as assistant scout master and assistant aquatics director at Boy Scout Camp.

Douglas was returned to a fire base after hospitalization in Japan. Apparently this fire base duty was tolerable and here he was able to cope with existing conditions. He wrote quite regularly, wanted film and food and awaited anxiously his rotation home date, 9 June 1970 with plans and parties arranged on this end. Then came Cambodia.

Gentlemen of the Court, I ask that you weigh in your minds and base your decision of the trial on the fact that you and you alone are in strict command of the next 45 years of this defendant's life. The decision you render here today will affect this young man forever. You can make a just decision and still save my son from the pangs of hell, and allow him to finish his Army commitment with honor and integrity. I am aware the Court is entitled to impose a sentence. If confinement is part of this picture, I earnestly plead that the confinement will be suspended. If the Court could find justice served and allow Doug to return home on his earned leave and reassignment to the United States,

Doug would pay his debt to the Army

Doug could hold his head high and finish his tour with honor and integrity.

It would save my son mentally, physically morally and allow him to be a productive citizen.

The very most important fact that I am concerned with is the mental and physical health of my son. After careful and somber reflections of all the facts of this case, I sincerely and earnestly hope you will find it in your hearts to find the defendant not guilty.

Gentlemen of the Court, my son's life and future are in your hands. He is 20 years old with a full lifetime ahead of him. He has never had any kind of trouble with law, military or civil before going to Viet Nam. He is essentially a fine young man with great potential to the military, to his country and to himself.

Gentleman, I trust my son's future to your fair and just deliberation, with wisdom and love in your hearts,

Sincerely yours
William J. Johnson

To me this letter rings with something of the pathos, the poignancy of Portia's famous speech in *The Merchant of Venice*, "the quality of mercy is not strain'd, It droppeth as the gentle rain from heaven." His repeated hopes that the court will act from the heart are pathetic. "I sincerely and earnestly hope you will find it in your hearts to find the defendant not guilty." His last sentence, that the court should act with "wisdom and love in your hearts" is a cry from a man deluded. Perhaps Bill Johnson saw himself not so much as Atticus Finch as a gladiator. "I must fight—and I will fight for the right—I will give my all to save my son." This oration was never read to the court because there was no second court-martial. Instead, Doug took the Undesirable "for the good of the service."

• • •

My father's pleading Statement to the Court probably arrived on Paul's desk before August 1. At that same time, Paul Kleinwachter was inundated with character references from Doug's teachers, friends, and neighbors, including my long letter of July 25 (reprinted in chapter 4). I try to imagine all this paper overflowing Paul's narrow desk as he read through them. The careful wording in his August 2 letter to Bill suggests that he had read my father's impassioned statement to the court. Paul clearly wants Bill to understand what the few options were and how those options might work and the limitations within which he is working on Doug's behalf. The letter is formal, but not stiff or cold:

Dear Sir,

I am in receipt of various of your letters and appreciate the interest and zeal you have expressed in your son's case. Be assured that I also am doing my utmost to insure that his present dilemma is resolved in a manner satisfactory to both Doug and you.

Upon returning from Pleiku last weekend, I called Doug to my office to further discuss the pending court martial and to show him the letters that I had received from you and [the character references]. He was very appreciative of the efforts you are making in his behalf, although I think there may be some differences between you and Doug's idea concerning what constitutes an appropriate disposition of his case. Doug is primarily preoccupied with staying out of the stockade and being discharged from the Army in that order. To accomplish both of these objectives will necessitate the acceptance of Doug's resignation for the good of the service and it is toward this end that I am working. Approximately two days after I last corresponded with you, I was informed by the battalion adjutant that in all likelihood, LTC McKee, the commanding officer of the 3rd Bn. 12th Inf would recommend that Doug's request for discharge be disapproved. Now, were this action to be taken it not necessarily be fatal since the commanding General, 4th Infantry Division, is the ultimate authority; however this possibility that a discharge would be approved would drop appreciably. Since then, your letters, as well as those from various Congressmen have been received which have brought to light many aspects of your son's background and history not formerly available to the command. In addition, since LTC McKee has been in the field, I have personally spoken to the battalion adjutant and executive officer concerning Doug and the nature and processing of a discharge under AR 635-200, chapter 10. With the unit now fully informed, I am very hopeful that upon reconsideration, a favorable recommendation will result. In any event, I'll have an answer in several days.

Initially, the idea to resign from the service originated with Doug. He recognizes that if his resignation is accepted he will probably receive an undesirable discharge certificate from the Army. Because of the type of discharge which usually results, I make it a practice not to mention a Chapter 10 to the accused unless he raises the possibility himself. Doug and I have thoroughly discussed the serious implications which could result if he is discharged under conditions less than honorable. I have explained to him on an item by item basis in any instances the nature of the Army and Veteran benefits he can expect to lose, in addition to the problem he might encounter in applying for a job. He seems to have his heart set on teaching English or a related subject at a college or university some day. He realizes that with an undesirable discharge the number of doors open to him in this field will be limited.

Insofar as the trial is concerned, it is being held in abeyance pending the decision of Doug's battalion commander. In the event that a court martial becomes a necessity, I am in receipt of approximately ten letters of character reference you have sent, as well as the family pictures, all of which will be used accordingly. Doug will be found guilty of the AWOL charges and as such the letters of reference would be pertinent for sentencing purposes. Now, under our present military justice system neither the court of officers nor the military judge, depending on who hears the case, has the power to order a sentence to confinement suspended. This right exists only in the convening authority who in this instance would be the commanding officer of 3d Bn, 12th In, although the court or judge is at liberty to recommend suspension if it is felt appropriate. The letters of reference would not only be used in court but brought to the convening authority's attention prior to his taking his action in the case, however, I could not be optimistic that confinement would be suspended. In the event that confinement is not suspended Doug would probably be administratively separated while at the stockade.

I have seen Doug twice this week and his physical appearance and mental attitude were both good. I understand that today he went to Qui Nhon to take a physical examination which is part of the processing of his request for discharge. If the request for discharge is accepted, Doug could be out of the Army in approximately two weeks from now.

I hope this letter has answered some questions you have had regarding the status of Doug's case. As developments occur, I will make every effort to keep you informed.

Sincerely,
Paul J. Kleinwachter
Cpt, JAGC
Defense Counsel

Reasoned, measured as this letter is, my parents could not have taken much comfort from it. The bit about what the court could decide regarding confinement surely blighted their hopes. For Bill and Peggy Johnson one line shone out of this letter, a little beacon in an otherwise murky and threatening darkness. "If the request for discharge is accepted, Doug could be out of the Army in approximately two weeks from now."

15. "The Problem of Course Is What Should Be Done with Private Johnson"

August 1970

Doug asked for the Undesirable discharge, despite Paul's having explained to him how it could severely limit his future. But before moving to that precipice, on August 16 Paul wrote a remarkable letter to Doug's commander, asking that he be granted an "AR 635-212 [that] authorizes a general discharge for alcoholics." He wrote this having spent time with Doug, having seen firsthand the toll that drug addiction had taken on this soldier's very fiber. Paul later shared this letter with my father, who would use it extensively in his long fight for Doug's exoneration.

To me, this letter is remarkable for its balance. I'm also impressed that Paul clearly did his research in seeking out some solution for Doug that did not involve an Undesirable or a second court-martial. Paul's argument here, or perhaps better said, his plea, was that the General should recognize that the root of Doug's problems, the root of the crimes charged against him, was drug addiction. In a lawyerly fashion Paul acknowledged the Army's rights and the limits of their obligations to men like Private Johnson, drug addicts, but there ripples underneath the standard prose Paul's recognition of my brother's suffering, that in fact his essential humanity was being eroded away. Of all these papers and documents, it is

163

the only firsthand contemporaneous account of what Doug was like under the influence of drugs.

> SUBJECT: Request for Discharge for the Good of the Service
> RE: Pvt Douglas Johnson
> Commanding General
> 4th Infantry Division AP SF 96262

I feel you have before you a question for discharge for the good of the service which should be approved.

The applicant, Douglas Johnson, has developed a serious drug problem since coming to Vietnam. Although this individual is charged with but one specification of drug possession and none of drug use, his entire existence centers around the use of amphetamines and other habit forming barbiturates. He has developed a strong psychological as well as lesser physiological dependence on the drug commonly known as speed. I have seen Douglas Johnson on several occasions while he was "speeding" and frankly it was frightening and pathetic to see such a sight. For a period of time he was in Japan convalescing from hepatitis which is an illness oftentimes contracted from inserting an unclean hypodermic needle into oneself, and occasionally has been sent to the 17th Field Hospital to dry out his system.

From speaking with various Army doctors and psychiatrists, it is my understanding that the Army by and large does not engage itself actively in drug rehabilitation. As we know the Army does not nor should it carry the responsibility for rehabilitating drug addicts. That is not one of our missions, although we do what we can to be socially responsible in as many area of human relations as possible.

The problem of course is what should be done with Private Johnson. Due to his sickness he is no longer a vital functioning member of his unit. The Army recognizes the need to discharge this type of individual administratively in AS 635-212 which provides in part that drug addicts may be separated as being unfit for military service. . . .

I have attached for your consideration a few of the many letters I have received in the past few weeks concerning the defendant's background. [Character references.] From all indications Private Johnson was a conscientious, hard working young man with high aspirations prior to coming to Vietnam. Whatever his reasons were, he is now a drug addict. We can't blame the Army for this unfortunate occurrence, but I feel it does give rise to a social obligation on the Army's part to separate this man from the service so that he can receive the necessary treatment which might someday allow him to be a responsible citizen again.

I hope that consideration will be given with a view toward discharging Douglas with a general rather than undesirable certificate. To date he has been in-country almost 14 months. When he has not been turned on with drugs, his service has often been creditable. The offenses with which he is charged are all directly or indirectly related to his drug problem. His periods of AWOL were precipitated by his desire to obtain and use speed. In fact, while he was gone he mainlined to the extent that he hardly slept, and upon returning he fell asleep on guard. His total involvement with drugs does not excuse his offenses, but perhaps a sick, sick individual who is badly in need of treatment. AR 635-212 authorizes a general discharge for alcoholics, and I feel that in the near future drug addiction will be classified with alcoholism in this manner.

Your consideration of the above matter will be greatly appreciated.

• • •

The CO rejected Paul's reasoned plea:

On 20 August 1970, the applicant's [Doug Johnson's] Commanding Officer recommended approval of the applicant's request for discharge for the good of the service; that he observed the applicant on several occasions and had yet to see him clean or in proper uniform; that he refused to comply with the most basic of requirements and personal hygiene and recommended an Undesirable Discharge.

Why not just end this pronouncement "for the good of the service"? Or cite Doug Johnson's sorry military record? Or his repeated

AWOLs? Why add this observation about cleanliness? That Private Johnson was *dirty* seems here to have been crucial for not heeding Paul's carefully argued position that Doug needed treatment for his sickness/drug addiction, conditions that should be dealt with medically. To me, the general's observation about personal hygiene is an infamous addition to the Undesirable that implies further troubling questions. The wording suggests that the Commanding Officer of the 4th Infantry *asked* Doug to comply with these "most basic of requirements" and that Doug refused outright. What are the "most basic of requirements?" A shave? A haircut? A pressed uniform? On what "several occasions" did the Commanding Officer have the opportunity to observe or reprimand the slovenly Private Johnson? Was the general present when Italian photographer Ennio Iacobucci took the picture that appeared in *Time* magazine? The eleven nameless grunts in that photo don't look especially well groomed. Was he present when Doug fetched up on December 26, 1969, after eight days doing God-knows-what God-knows-where and railing about his "new philosophy"? Maybe the CO had the opportunity to criticize Doug's lack of hygiene as he popped some speed and LSD and hoisted himself into the helicopter, preparing to be point man. Or perhaps the general saw him, slouched, skinny, strung-out, shambling between two MPs after an arrest? Perhaps the CO saw Doug in Long Binh Jail, there among the foot-long rats, and found him understandably filthy. None of these seems likely to me, and yet, his wording stands: he "observed the applicant on several occasions . . ."

In the margin of this page, my dad scrawled: "On August 30th the appl[icant] [Doug] was sick, drugged, a broken individual and it was this same CO who put him in LBJ." General Burke is the CO under discussion here. That he had some particular animus against E-1 Doug Johnson is, in my opinion, apparent from the infamous addition itself. My father was clearly aware of this.

I also cannot help but wonder if the general opted for the truly harsh penalty, the Undesirable, because he was pissed off with dirty Private Johnson, but even more pissed off with all the goddamned Congressional inquiries, the bothersome intrusions from nosey congressmen and senators butting into Army business (when the Army had a war to fight), asking a lot of dunning, dipshit questions about this grunt and requiring a bunch of time-consuming rote replies accounting for this E-1's whereabouts and well-being ("your son had the services of a chaplain, a doctor, a psychiatrist, a social worker and the members of the correctional staff available to him at all times while in confinement"). Was the general even further pissed off with Private Johnson's noisy, blathering, interfering father, the instigator of all this Congressional inquiry? How dare Bill Johnson assault everyone with his letters and phone calls and telegrams? How dare Bill Johnson deign to instruct the Army on what we can and cannot do? "Confinement must be suspended. I repeat, confinement must be suspended." Who the hell does this asshole think he is? We are the fucking Army! The Brass! The war professionals!

What if my father had been more circumspect? What if he had been more like the Wisconsin mother who stepped back from making trouble? What if he had not pestered and relentlessly provoked? What if he had not called out the Army for the injustice he saw perpetrated against his son? Would the general have been more likely to heed Paul's solution to the problem of Private Johnson? To give Doug, as a drug addict, the discharge routinely handed out to alcoholics? To assign this traumatized soldier a General or Medical discharge? Might the general's wrath at my father's incessant dunning of the military (and obliging senators to do the same) have lain at the root of his decision to scorn Paul's reasoned approach and go for the Undesirable? Clearly, these questions have no answers. Nonetheless, they are worth asking. This infamous addendum seems to me knowingly brutal, crass, poorly ballasted, and without any truly defensible military rationale.

In the Army's many later skirmishes with my father, they inevitably point out that according to official documents that he signed, Doug *requested* the Undesirable discharge. He *knew* what it meant. Paul Kleinwachter had *told* him what it meant. Moreover, Paul had *told* Bill Johnson what it meant and Mr. Johnson was in favor of it. All true. But in August 1970 Doug Johnson didn't know anything except that he wanted the hell out of Vietnam, "that wretched country." Bill Johnson only knew that Doug's "life was at stake and I would rather have him alive than dead regardless of the discharge." In July

Bill declared to George Romney, "I want my boy home and exonerated." By August he would settle for having his son home.

• • •

Once the discharge had been agreed upon, there followed, of necessity, the red tape to remove Doug from the Army, including a physical examination and signing many documents. In the midst of these preparations, the Red Cross informed the Johnsons that Doug had gone AWOL again and could not be found to attend to these particulars. The parents went bonkers. *We are so close to getting him home! It's finally all arranged! All is in order, approved except for paperwork, and it cannot be completed because Doug is AWOL again? Off to God-knows-where doing God-knows-what? OD-ing himself into some kind of drugged-up, vegetative coma from which he may never emerge? How can that be?*

On August 14 Bill wrote to Paul (as a follow-up to a telephone conversation they had just had), throwing caution and manners and everything else to the wind, in essence begging Paul to babysit Doug, to park him in a corner of the office and (the mind boggles) give him "some responsibility."

Captain Paul Kleinwachter
Headquarters 4th Infantry Division Office Staff Judge Advocate
APO San Francisco 9626234
August 14 1970

Dear Paul,

Thank you for your consideration and help this evening. I sincerely appreciate your understanding, patience and thoughtfulness.

Since our discussion this evening I have given a great deal of thought to the fact that Doug is free lancing so to speak [i.e., AWOL]. Would it be possible to have Doug report to your office daily and place him in a position of some responsibility until he is released? This in itself would be a great beginning in mental therapy. I am making this request as a friend and I hope you will be able to honor it in the same light.

May I at this time also request another moment of your time to put forth extra effort to expedite this discharge through the channels in order that Doug can come home at once. As per our telephone conversation I feel every minute that Doug is in Viet Nam is one minute gone, and in that minute he could be under medical and psychiatric care. This one minute could be very important.

I predict Paul that the day will come when you will be proud of Doug and will be gratified that your work and time spent in helping him were not in vain. If you have a few minutes free, I would appreciate your keeping me informed [about] events there.

Please ask Doug to write to his family. We love him.

Sincerely yours,
William J. Johnson

This last line is especially pathetic: There were just days before Doug would leave Vietnam and still the Johnsons had not heard Word One from him.

On the strength of their phone conversation that took place on August 14 and clearly before he received the above letter, Paul wrote to my father on August 15:

I believe there is a lot of good in Douglas that can be saved with proper treatment. Concerning the Red Cross reports of his being AWOL, don't put much stock in them. What they mean by AWOL is that the unit can't locate him at that time. Now technically he is AWOL but I feel sure Doug is around the area somewhere, probably visiting with people.

As I explained on the phone the paperwork on Doug's discharge has been completed but he has to be found now to sign [off on] the physical examination he took several days ago. Once this is done, Doug can be home within a week assuming the General approves the discharge.

The unit has informed me that they will assign an escort to him until he physically leaves the division and hopefully Vietnam. We want to insure that he leaves and it is done safely.

I'm sorry for the brevity of this letter but I'll try to keep you informed

> in this manner until this case is resolved. If I can corner Doug I'll have him write a letter home.

I think Paul wrote this to be kind. The whole note has a soothing, reassuring tone and quality, and my parents might have even wept to read "I believe there is a lot of good in Douglas that can be saved with proper treatment." Paul's gentle observation that Doug is "visiting some people" sounds as though he is sharing teatime anecdotes with friends. But "If I can corner Doug" suggests to me that Paul guessed what my brother was up to.

When Doug was still unaccounted for four days later, my father was yet more frantic. Bill wrote again to Paul, this time marshaling the vain, strange, crazed hope that Vice President Spiro Agnew would somehow step in and take charge:

Dear Paul,

> I have just talked to Vice President Agnew's Office in Washington D. C. He will be in Viet Nam this weekend and will inquire of the 4th Infantry Command about the status of Doug. I am advised that the Vice-President will talk to someone to expedite the proceedings to return Doug home. Also I sent a personal wire to the Commanding General requesting "Doug be placed under guard to expedite release."
>
> . . .
>
> I am making arrangements to have Doug admitted to the University Medical Center at Loma Linda for medical and psychiatric treatment.
>
> I understand from ARC [American Red Cross] that the paper work of five congressional inquiries is being held up because they cannot locate Douglas. Wouldn't it be possible, Captain K, to hold Doug in some kind of custody until this paperwork is completed and he can be placed on a plane for return to California?

I can't even fathom the depths of my father's despair that he should *ask* for Doug to be "held in some kind of custody until this paperwork is completed." This is the man who insisted "Confinement must be suspended." The letter continues:

Please have patience with me in this case, Captain, because as I have advised before, I will not quit until I have my boy in my hands. The Army's responsibility ends when he is turned over to me at Travis AFB or Oakland.

I am indeed grateful for your help and will be forever indebted to you for your consideration and your untiring efforts on my son's behalf.

Sincerely Yours
William J. Johnson
PS Please advise me of his arrival time and place,
so I may be there to meet him. Thank you.

There was a flurry of official exchanges in the next few days while Doug was chased down and the papers were signed. Finally, on August 23, 1970, my brother flew to the States, not to a base in California, but to McChord Air Force Base, Washington, where his father met him on the tarmac and embraced his son and the dead man's sandal that Doug clutched.

• • •

Had the Army agreed with Paul's reasoned appeal, Doug could have had the General discharge that was routinely handed out to alcoholics. The VA could have helped provide medical treatment for his addictions, help that would have eased the stresses of his reintegration into family and civilian life. Whatever his physical and mental problems, Doug could have moved through the following years without the indelible stain, the shame of Undesirable. The Army rejected this. They offered the Undesirable in exchange for avoiding the second court-martial. Had that trial gone forward, Paul's careful letter to my father makes clear that "an order of a sentence to 'confinement suspended' belongs only to the Commanding Officer of the 3rd Bn 12th In," and though the many letters of character reference would have been available to the court," Paul "could not be optimistic that 'confinement would be suspended.'" If (as seems clear) there was animus toward Doug, he would doubtless have been sentenced to confinement. Furthermore, at least to me, Paul's letter to my parents implied that if confined, Doug would be separated from the service with an Undesirable or Dishonorable discharge in any event. Moreover, if the court-martial had confined him to prison, Doug might well have gone irretrievably insane or perished, or both. The doctor who treated him at Loma Linda Hospital in September 1970 wrote that Doug's physical condition was so dire that he could not have lived six more months as he was. The Loma Linda psychiatrist described a mind crumbling into insanity. Confinement in a military prison might have been a de facto death sentence, not for murderous mayhem, rape, robbery, rampage, grievous assault on another human being, or war crimes. Doug went AWOL. He slept on guard duty. He was filthy.

Agreeing to the Undesirable saved Doug's life. Even at this great distance in time, more than half a century, even taking into account all the time, tears and energy, all the ink and paper, the money my parents would lavish, seeking to get the Undesirable discharge changed to Honorable and all the heartbreak, the time and tears and energy that they would expend in seeking treatment for Doug's ailments and addictions, and even acknowledging the sad paths that the life of Doug Johnson took, the anguish he caused his family and the people who cared about him, I think they made the right choice. Given the Army's clearly punitive attitude toward Private Johnson and the power they had over him, yes, the Undesirable discharge was the best option. Get him out of Nam. Bring him home.

16. The Undesirable Is Undeserved

Summer 1970

What really happened to Doug Johnson in May and June 1970?

The papers unearthed from the basement safe have several versions of the events that led to Doug's Undesirable discharge, testimony given both orally and in written form. Some are more specific than others, but the basic facts remain consistent. Private Johnson did not go AWOL *in* Cambodia, but rather, once the unit landed there (and presumably set out to find and destroy the Viet Cong), he "caught a chopper" back to An Khe in Viet Nam, where he lived for days with some unnamed ARVN soldiers (Army of the Republic of [South] Vietnam), translators he knew.

The testimony below is from his hearing before Colonel Duddy at Fort McArthur on December 4, 1970:

Although I had no written order to report to the 3/12 Inf 4th Div I reported and at that time the 3/12 was pulling bunker guard on Camp Enari at Pleiku which was to be turned over to the ARVNs very soon. As a result of the letter I wrote home and action upon my father's part, I received a Congressional Inquiry as to my general state of health and whereabouts. Shortly after that the whole division moved from Pleiku to An Khe, about 60 miles east of Pleiku.

173

Shortly after the move we were informed, while still in the bush that our division would be moving into Cambodia soon. At the time of this announcement I had 20 days left until my normal rotation date back to the United States. I went to the Battalion doctor, who in turn sent me to the Division Surgeon. The Division Surgeon did absolutely nothing. In desperation I returned to the Battalion Doctor and turned myself in for being strung out on speed and asked for a written profile to keep me from going past a firebase and into the bush. Dr. Cantrell, who was the Battalion Doctor, granted this request and wrote on a prescription form in handwriting, a profile that I, Douglas Johnson, was to go no further into the bush than a firebase. The reasons he stated on the profile were because of my past history of malaria twice and hepatitis three times. I then went to a firebase named Firebase Marty . . .

This firebase was mortared very heavily by 4.2 mortar rounds, 81 mm and 60 mm mortars. From this firebase there was to be sent out a company of men to try and locate the position of the enemy mortar tubes. At this time I was chosen to go out and I argued the point and displayed my profile to a Sgt. Major. I was instructed by the Sgt. Major to give my profile to a Sgt. E7 who would hold it for me until further notice. This I complied with. The E7 may have turned the profile over to the Sgt. Major who seemed to me very much against me due to my rank as an E1 and the fact that I had long hair. Later on that afternoon the Sgt Major and several other officers, including a Captain, a Major and I believe, a Colonel, were shot down over the area in which the mortar tubes were located. Everybody in the chopper except one door gunner was killed.

We then changed locations to another firebase where I worked on the chopper pad, sending out re-supply to various companies that requested them. The whole battalion then went back to base camp [Camp Radcliff] in An Khe for the big push into Cambodia. At this time I was informed that I was to be going to Cambodia also.

I told my LT and CO that I had a profile exempting me from going any further than a firebase. This was ignored. I was told to either produce the profile or be sent. I, in turn, began searching the battalion for the E7 to whom I had given my profile. I was sent everywhere on base by different people, but still could not locate the Sgt to whom I had given my profile. All during this time I was mainlining speed and as a result I had become a mental and physical wreck.

Colonel Duddy asked clarifying questions of Doug:

Q62: Did you make any attempts to contact Captain Cantrell once you were directed to produce the profile which you state he gave you?
DSJ : Yes, I did try to contact him. I was informed that he had been transferred to Cam Rahn Bay Convalescent Center.

Q: Did you attempt to contact him at Cam Rahn Bay Convalescent Center?
DSJ: There was no way I could.

Q: By that, what do you mean?
DSJ: The only way to contact him would be by telephone and that requires permission.

Q: Did you ask for permission to contact him, and if so from whom?
DSJ: Yes. I did ask for permission. It was denied. I don't know [by] whom specifically. It was an officer in the S1 office.

While Doug's description here is coherent, not much imagination is required to picture a skinny speed freak racketing all over Camp Radcliff, wildly banging on flimsy doors, cage-rattling unsympathetic officers, pleading to use a telephone, searching for a lost scrap of paper with a handwritten note that he had handed over (as ordered). No great reserves of empathy are needed to picture a strung-out soldier desperate to find Dr. Cantrell's note, a man becoming progressively more unhinged until finally, if he failed in this quest, he would surely be put on a chopper and sent, up, up, and away over the jungle, weapon in hand, scared shitless.

Doug's testimony continues:

In desperation I went AWOL and began living with some ARVN soldiers who were good friends of mine. After a week I returned to the unit, was placed under guard and notified that I was

No 1 going to be court martialed for AWOL and

No 2 I was going to on guard duty regardless of the fact I was pending court martial.

Anyone pending court martial, as I was told, was not to be given a weapon or to be placed in a position of normal duty. I was informed then that I was going to be placed on guard on the chopper pad. At this I informed my CO that I had not slept in six days and that I was pending court martial and that there was no possible way I could stay awake all night. He completely ignored me and placed me on guard duty anyhow and then came out and caught me asleep on guard. He notified me that this charge would be added on to my previous cm charges and at this I panicked and again went AWOL.

I returned to the ARVNs' house where I was living before and stayed there with them. I became increasingly dependent on the use of drugs to maintain my sanity. I was losing weight at a rapid rate and the use of these drugs became my only concern. I began staying awake 24 hours a day and seven days a week and continued this until I was caught. When the MPs caught us I weighed 128 pounds.

Instead of being placed in a hospital I was placed in a detention cell and then transferred once again to Long Binh jail [for] the pretrial confinement. Upon arrival there without any preliminary measures or questions, I was placed in maximum security where I remained for 12 or 13 days.

I was taken out of solitary and placed in a pretrial area of the stockade where I encountered tensions, especially racial that I had not believed possible. I was beat up once by Puerto Ricans and once by a group of Negroes. I was then sent back to An Khe where I was placed under 24 hour guard and left there with permission only to see my lawyer and go to the rest room.

Later, Colonel Duddy specifically asked about the beating incidents:

Q 73: During your second confinement at the Army facility in Long Binh you refer to racial tensions, do you recall the dates of the assaults made upon you and whether or not any action was taken?
DSJ: I don't recall any dates and there was no action taken whatsoever.

Q74: How do you know action was not taken?
DSJ: Because it was never reported and if the guards did see it, which they must have since they had visual access to the whole stockade, then they never reported it either.

Q: Did anyone come to your assistance during these assaults and if so do you recall their names?
DSJ: Yes, people did come to my assistance. They were friends of mine whom I had met at the stockade. The only names I remember are nicknames.

Doug's testimony continues regarding his time after returning to Camp Radcliff:

My lawyer, Captain Paul Kleinwachter [is] an outstanding and very beautiful individual. I requested to see a psychiatrist. I was granted this and found out the psychiatrist totally ignored me. I then began going to see Paul Kleinwachter on a regular basis, not only for legal assistance but for personal relief from the tension that I was under.

I found out through my lawyer that my father had begun making inquiries as to my whereabouts, my state of mind and my state of health, due to the fact that I was long past my rotation date and yet not returned. I was relying upon drugs heavily during this time. I had not written home in approximately three to four months and I had gotten to the point where I was not even reading the mail I was receiving from home. Any thoughts that occurred to me concerning my mother or father, my sisters and brother, and especially my fiancée were excruciating. So much so that the very inkling that I was going to be thinking about home threw me into an uncontrollable and very horrible depression. Thus the reason for my using amphetamines to erase my mind from the agony I was experiencing.

Through my lawyer I requested a 212 [General] discharge and my unit turned it down in favor of court martialing me. I was then informed, again from my lawyer, that I could request an undesirable discharge in lieu of court martial. At this point the only thing I cared about was leaving that wretched country, getting home and trying to regain my sanity.

Once again Congressional Investigations were sent out on me and my unit granted me the discharge. I was given what was supposed to be a physical and sent under armed guard to Cam Rahn Bay for my rotation home. Somewhere between Cam Rahn, South Vietnam and Fort Lewis Air Force Base, Seattle Washington my records were lost by the E5 assigned to carry them. This included my 201 [health] file and finance records. . . .

The core, the most significant piece of information in this testimony is this: Doug had a handwritten note from Dr. Cantrell that he was too ill to be moved into combat. This medical exemption took precedence over any orders. A sergeant major ordered Doug to hand over Dr. Cantrell's note to a sergeant E-7. He did so, and it was never seen again. In my father's fight to get the Undesirable changed to Honorable, he would insistently contend that had Dr. Cantrell's note not been destroyed, had that note been heeded, Doug would *not* have been sent into a combat situation in Cambodia and he would *not* have gone AWOL and there would *not* have been a second court-martial and thus, *no need to accept the Undesirable discharge to avoid the court-martial.* The Undesirable was undeserved. Unjust. This would be the foundational rock of my father's campaign in the coming years, though he would need to prove it time and again and the Army would fight and deny him at every turn. The Undesirable discharge might well have been "for the good of the service," but it was a wrong perpetrated against Doug Johnson by the Army itself.

PART IV

A

Playlist

B

The Weight — THE BAND
Imagine — JOHN LENNON
Born Under a Bad Sign — JIMI HENDRIX, CREAM, ALBERT KING
What's Going On? — MARVIN GAYE
Our House — CROSBY STILLS, NASH & YOUNG
Another Brick in the Wall, Part 1 — PINK FLOYD
Theme from The Mission — ENNIO MORRICONE
Wander My Friends — BEAR MCCREARY
FROM BATTLESTAR GALACTICA

17. "The General Was Not Aware"

Like a piece of physical, spiritual, mental and emotional flotsam following the shipwreck of the self, Doug Johnson washed up in San Bernardino. He was quickly admitted to Loma Linda Medical Center, and his father drove out to see him daily for the ten days he was a patient there. "At Loma Linda Doug and I sat on this hospital lawn and talked," Bill later wrote to Jerry Pettis. "When he told me of the killing and the bloodshed, he buried his face in his hands and sobbed and sobbed and sobbed. I put my arm around him and gave him comfort."

In these talks with Doug my father learned of "acts incompatible with his conscience." He also learned of many incidents that heretofore Dad could not have known, incidents that would fuel his long struggle for justice for Doug. Among them were the plane crashes in December 1969 that kept Doug from returning to his unit for eight days after being hospitalized at Nha Trang, being wounded in the hip by shrapnel, being wounded again when falling debris left a large cut beside his eye, and climbing down a ninety-foot helicopter ladder to rescue a wounded buddy. But the single most important piece of information Doug shared was the story of Dr. Cantrell's handwritten note that had vanished. The events obliging Doug to accept the Undesirable ought never to have happened, or, in the phrase my dad would persistently use, "could have been completely averted." My father was seething with righteous rage: Dr. Cantrell's note had been lost or willfully destroyed, and thus, the Army could fling this devastated kid back into society with no recognition of his military service. This was an absolute injustice.

Within a mere six weeks following Doug's return (and despite the many other strains the family lived with) Bill Johnson picked up his weapon of choice: that is, the pen. He wanted the Undesirable discharge reversed to an Honorable or at least a Medical. On October 16, 1970, he sent a letter that would form the basis of his struggle for the next few years. Copies went to Jerry Pettis, Mike Mansfield, and Mendel Rivers. (Fulbright and Romney seem to have dropped out after my father's rants about "premeditated murder.") Knowing that General Burke had sent a wire to each of these politicos informing them that Douglas Johnson had been deemed Undesirable, Bill was about to set everyone straight. Throughout this letter his use of the phrase, "The General was not aware" reads like a tuning fork. Ping! Every time he hits it: *Listen up!*

October 16th 1970

Dear Senator Mansfield:

It is with unbounded joy and physical and mental relief that I write this letter. I find this letter difficult to write since phrases are inadequate to express to you our family's intense gratitude and appreciation for your patience, understanding, active participation, attitude, and relentless cooperation in maintaining the key position to actually saving the life of my son. I wish you to know that we as a family are and will be eternally grateful.

I met the plane when Douglas returned to the States at McChord AFB near Seattle. He was a pathetic sight, Senator Mansfield. He weighed 130 pounds instead of his 175. He was dirty, hungry, mentally and physically very ill and could absolutely not believe he was back in the world. The E-5 enlistee the Army assigned the responsibility to carry Doug's 201 file was remiss and his whole file was lost somewhere between Viet Nam and Fort Lewis. His health records, finance records etc. were gone. (He was not given any funds at discharge from the finance section and has not been paid at this date. He has sent two letters for request for payment without reply as of this date.) On the second day, after a physical examination and after a temporary file had been made up, Douglas was discharged under Article 635-200 as undesirable. His discharge reads, "Undesirable Discharge from the United States Army."

August 30 I admitted him to the Loma Linda University Medical Center under the care of [doctor's name] M. D. and a host of others in all departments. He was a patient for ten days. His file at the Hospital looks like a book. He had jungle rot under the calluses of his feet; he has an extremely enlarged spleen, enlarged liver and was found to be anemic as well as in a general state of malnutrition. When Doug was released from the Department of Internal Medicine he was assigned to Dr. [name] Chief of Psychiatry. (Enclosed is a copy of the hospital bill which does not include doctors' fees.)

From the wire you received from General Burke of the Fourth Infantry Division, one would quite readily suspect that Doug was an incompetent soldier. What the General was not aware of, was the following:

The General was not aware that a doctor, Captain Cantrell, had written a letter in April 1970, stating that Doug was not to go farther out into the bush than the fire base where he was then assigned because (1) Doug had only 20 days left before rotation date home and (2) he had had malaria twice and hepatitis three times. A sergeant E-7 took Doug's letter and <u>never turned it in</u>. It was never found again, even after Doug inquired for it. And Doug was sent to Cambodia. Dr. Cantrell was transferred to Cam Rahn Bay and was not available to substantiate the order.

The General was not aware that Doug was point man for a seven month period, most of them rated as an E-1 instead of E-3. In 15 months in Viet Nam he was never allowed an R and R or a leave ...

<u>In order to retain his sanity and do what he was required to do,</u> <u>acts which were incompatible with his conscience, he used drugs</u>. The Army was aware of it and no one did or said anything about it. It was

and should have been the responsibility of the Army to return him to the States when this problem became apparent. He never used drugs before he enlisted and he is not using drugs now. Doug lived hand in hand with death, Senator Mansfield. In our talks he breaks down and cries over things he had to do and what was done to him. For instance [incidents described earlier: Doug's killing a VC whose gun had a bent firing pin, lying about his group's location to a helicopter backup team, and finding their rucksack and canteen full of holes from American guns]. Doug climbed down a 90 foot ladder from a chopper to rescue another soldier, picked up the man and climbed back while machine gun fire was going on. At one time his friend standing by his side was hit in the head and killed. While under fire Doug picked up his body and carried him back to the chopper on his shoulder. Doug states he does not know why he was not killed.

The General was not aware that Doug had gone into Cambodia three or four times before the big publicized push. On one of those missions, the enemy fire was so heavy that many choppers turned back (but not Doug's) and 17 men died before they hit the ground.

The General was not aware that Doug was never given R and R. He applied for it four separate times and four times it was refused. At one time he was given a choice of dates to go to Hawaii. My wife, Doug's fiance and I were going to meet him there and it was cancelled for no reason.

The General was not aware that Doug received shrapnel wounds in his hip—had they been one inch over, he would have been paralyzed from the waist down. He also has a scar on his face below and above his eye, Senator Mansfield. After the hit in his hip they bandaged him up and sent him back. Doug is still uncomfortable sitting down and can sit in one position for a very short period of time only.

Regarding the AWOL's referred to in the wire, the General was probably not aware of the circumstances. On August 14th I talked to Captain Paul Kleinwachter in An Khe for half an hour. He advised me that the times when Doug was considered AWOL he was not AWOL at all. He was not in his unit and the clerk could not find him, so they marked him AWOL.

Last December when Doug was put in the stockade for being late reporting from Nha Trang Hospital back to Pleiku, the circumstances were completely beyond his control. That day (and this story was in our newspapers and *Time* Magazine) an F-4 Phantom jet crashed and a Vietnamese airplane crashed into a school, killing many of the children. There were fires and telephone lines were down. Doug tried to make contact with his CO in Pleiku and absolutely could not. When he arrived late the CO stated, "Do you have anything to say?" Doug answered, "Yes." And the CO stated, 'I don't want to hear it. Get out.' He confined Doug to prison. Ten days in solitary confinement for something over which he had no control.

While court martial charges were pending last summer, he was assigned guard duty. I understand that an individual pending court martial charges is not to carry weapons or be placed on active duty. He advised his superior of this and was still ordered to guard duty. He had been on drugs and it was physically impossible to stay awake. He was then jailed at Long Binh and put in solitary confinement with maximum security. Thirty days later he was ordered back to An Khe. He was hospitalized for only 1½ days and spent the other 28½ days in confinement. (I was informed by the Red Cross at the time that he was hospitalized for the thirty day period.)

At Loma Linda Doug and I sat on this hospital lawn and talked . . . [Doug sobbing as he recounted what he'd done and seen.] . . .

The Following are key points why Douglas does not deserve and should not be faced with a tag of undesirable discharge for the next 45 years of his life.

> Doug served his country in Viet Nam for more than the full
> required period.
> He spent 14½ months in VN without an earned R and R or a
> leave.
> He spent the required number of months there to qualify for an
> early out honorable discharge of 150 days.

In his professional opinion Dr. Cantrell wrote a letter which in effect was an order that the Army was not to send Doug back to Cambodia at the time of the big push because (a) he had only 20 days left before his rotation date back to the states. (b) He had had malaria twice and hepatitis three times.

When Doug was released, he was mentally and physically extremely ill. He still makes regular visits to the hospital. Dr. [psychiatrist] advised me today that Doug should have professional help for at least six months. I am enclosing letters from physicians expressing professional opinions as to the extreme need for a reversal of his Army discharge in order to assist them in their treatment of Doug's mental health problems.

I am writing this letter for three reasons, Senator Mansfield:

I thank you with all the graciousness and humbleness I can express.

My son does not deserve this undesirable discharge. He went to war as his country commanded. He did what was asked of him to do and he did it well. Doug made the statement, "I was the best point man in Viet Nam for nine months . . . the very best . . . none better." Doug did his job. He did not shirk his duty. I do not think Doug will be completely well until he has received an honorable or a medical discharge. This entire episode could have and would have been averted except for the unfortunate circumstances which followed his being forced to go into Cambodia again in spite of Captain Cantrell's written order that he should not be sent.

I make a formal request to Congressman Pettis to please take the necessary steps to reverse this discharge of Pvt. E-1 Douglas Scott Johnson under the reasons outlined in this letter from a 635-200 discharge to an honorable or a medical. Any assistance you could give in this endeavor would be sincerely appreciated. When this reversal is a reality you may in all sincerity and honesty say, "I helped," because as the saying goes, no man ever stands so straight as the man who stoops to help a boy.

Sincerely yours,
William J. Johnson
Enclosures

In November Jerry Pettis alerted the Johnsons that a hearing had been arranged at Fort McArthur for December 4, 1970. In the transcript of that hearing the officiating Colonel Duddy, forming his questions to Doug, refers often to "your father's letter of October 16th."

Even before the Duddy hearing my father was not idle; he knew he must prove that the medical profile existed. He must find the doctor who wrote it. Bill turned to the one individual in the Army who had responded to Doug with understanding and compassion. To Paul Kleinwachter he wrote on October 26, in part:

> As you can well imagine, Paul, I am in the process of reversing the undesirable discharge either to honorable or medical. I am hoping you will be willing to help in this endeavor. Last April a Doctor Cantrell (Captain) who was stationed at An Khe, wrote in longhand a profile for Doug which in essence restricted him to the fire base where he was then assigned (L Z Marty) due to (1) short period of time left before Doug's regular rotation home date, and (2) history of hepatitis twice, and (3) malaria twice. Dr. Cantrell's order was directed to the company CO and Doug submitted it to an E-7 sergeant who either lost it or destroyed it. Doug could never find the profile and the CO apparently did not receive it. Dr. Cantrell was transferred to Cam Rahn Bay and Doug was unable to verify the profile.
>
> My question is, would it be possible to locate Dr. Cantrell and get a statement from him to the effect that he did in fact write the profile for Doug about the latter part of April 1970. This statement is an extremely important document in our pursuit of the medical discharge. Doug must not be forced to face the future with an undesirable discharge.
>
> If you could be of any assistance in this endeavor, we would be grateful.

As weeks rolled by with no reply, I'm sure Bill's heart fell with disappointment. Then Paul's handwritten reply arrived:

Dear Mr. Johnson:

> I have been back in the states for 2 weeks while my wife had an operation and just returned to the Division yesterday. Your letter dated

26 October was here and I have discovered certain information today which may help Doug per your request.

Captain Cantrell was to DEROS [Date of Estimated Return from Overseas] from Vietnam 7 Oct 1970. After he left the 4th Div last May his orders indicated he was assigned to the 86th Medical Group at APO96491 which is Long Binh. I can't find an 86th group in listing of units in Vietnam so will probably have little or no luck running down further info on Cantrell in Vietnam. However, his orders did list a [name] as his next of kin. I understand that she is his sister and she resides at [city in northern] Calif. I assume from the name that she is married. Perhaps you can trace him through his sister.

For your information his full name is Frank L. Cantrell [ssn]. I hope the above allows you to find him and that he will remember Doug.

If I can be of further assistance don't hesitate to write.

Sincerely,
Paul

PS Since the division is pulling out soon I am being reassigned. After 25 Nov. I will be working at Nha Trang with IFFV in case you need further help. I don't know my address there but the APO is 96350

My parents must have wept with relief. Thanks to Paul, the possibility of exoneration gleamed!

November 29 1970
Captain Frank L. Cantrell, MD.
c/o [sister]
[Northern] California

Dear Dr. Cantrell:

Let me begin by introducing myself. My name is William Jess Johnson. I am the father of Douglas Scott Johnson, formerly of the 4th Infantry Division, Vietnam. I was able to locate you through Captain Paul Kleinwachter, Doug's defense counsel of the Judge Advocate's Office, 4th Infantry Division at An Khe. We have a problem with which we hope you will be able to help. In order that you may recall Doug and his situation at the time, I will condense a few of the facts relevant to this problem in order to help you recall your part in this episode. . . .

Doug refused to go again [into Cambodia] on the basis of your hand-written profile. Doug advised a sergeant major and an E-7 as well as a captain that you had written a profile on or about April 15, 1970, at Camp Radcliffe to the effect that Doug should not be assigned farther into the bush than the fire base at which he was then assigned. He advises that the profile stated that because of Doug's past history of hepatitis and malaria (and the fact that he was due for rotation date home on June 9), he was not to be sent farther into the bush. Doug advises that a sergeant E-7 in his company took the profile from him, and from then on, no one could find it or had any knowledge of its whereabouts. He advises further that you had been transferred and he could not contact you.

On August 25th 1970, Doug was discharged from the Army as undesirable in lieu of standing court martial. We are in the process of reversing this discharge either to medical or honorable on the recommendations of our Congressman, Representative Jerry L. Pettis, plus assistance from Senate Majority Leader, Mike Mansfield, Representative L. Mendel Rivers, [psychiatrist] M.D. and [doctor] M. D. Chief, Department of Internal Medicine Loma Linda University Medical Center.

If you remember Doug and the fact that you did write the profile would you be kind enough to advise this information in a letter addressed "To Whom it May Concern"? . . .

Dr. Cantrell I sincerely hope you will be able to remember writing the aforementioned profile since I cannot emphasize strongly enough the extreme need for this letter since it may mean the difference between 45 years of success or 45 years of depression for this young man.

May I hear from you at your very earliest convenience? I sincerely thank you for your time and consideration.

Very Truly Yours
William J. Johnson

Bill wrote separately to Cantrell's sister on that same day that "since I am unable to locate him directly . . . If you would be kind enough to forward my letter to Dr. Cantrell, I shall be very grateful." Dr. Cantrell's sister sent his letter on. Within days my father received a reply:

8 December 1970

Dear Mr. Johnson:

Enclosed you will find a statement that may be of value to Douglas.

I remember Douglas well and want to wish him a speedy recovery to good emotional and physical health.

Sincerely,
Frank L. Cantrell
Captain, MC
U. S. Army

And in the envelope with that:

8 December 1970

TO WHOM IT MAY CONCERN:

On or about 17 April 1970, acting as Battalion Surgeon for the 3rd Battalion 12th Infantry of the Fourth Infantry Division, I most certainly did write a profile for PFC Douglas S. Johnson.

The profile was handwritten because proper medical forms were not readily available inasmuch as we had very recently moved from Camp Enari, Pleiku to Camp Radcliff, An Khe, and Republic of South Vietnam.

The profile stated that because Douglas Johnson was still in the process of recovering from repeated relapses of hepatitis and malaria, that he was to be stationed at the fire base and not be subjected to the rigors of rifle company duty.

It is unfortunate that some individuals in position of leadership, i.e., in Douglas' case, choose to manipulate or conveniently "lose" medical recommendations.

I was transferred to Cam Rahn Bay on 4 May 1970. The medical administration of the 3rd Battalion, 12th Infantry, Fourth Infantry Division became the responsibility of my replacement on 1 May 1970. Perhaps further information could be gained by contacting him.

If there are further questions regarding this matter, please inform me.

Sincerely,
Frank L. Cantrell
Captain, MC
U. S. Army

Vindication! Proof! Signed statement from the doctor! Doug had a medical release that would have spared him being sent into Cambodia, would have spared him going AWOL! This indisputable truth would surely reverse the Undesirable and secure him an Honorable discharge.

Dear Captain Cantrell:

> I can never tell you how happy we were to receive your letter and statement. Please accept the sincere thanks of our entire family—we shall always be grateful to you. Your letter will undoubtedly hold the key to a reversal of Doug's discharge.
>
> On December 4th Doug and I spent a grueling 10-hour day at the Inspector General's Office at Fort MacArthur at which time Doug made a 21 page sworn statement concerning his activities in Viet Nam.

However, the Fort MacArthur hearing had already taken place. Dr. Cantrell's letter substantiating Doug's assertion was not part of the record. My dad wrote a swift emphatic note:

December 14th 1970
Office of Inspector General
United States Army
Presidio
San Francisco California,
Attention: Colonel Moon

Dear Colonel Moon:

Enclosed is a copy of a letter from Captain Frank L. Cantrell, M. D. United States Army, M. C. Dr. Cantrell's letter verifies Doug's previous statement that Dr. Cantrell did in fact write a hand-written profile which stated that Doug was not to go farther out into the bush than the fire base where he was then assigned, due to his medical history of malaria and hepatitis.

[A short paragraph to accompany a copy of the May 25 *Time* magazine article about invading Cambodia.]

I submit the enclosed for your consideration in reversing the discharge of Douglas Scott Johnson from undesirable to honorable or medical.

Very truly yours,
William J. Johnson

Colonel Moon never replied, not even to acknowledge. However, Dr. Cantrell's letter did go into Doug's file. When, in early 1971, the Inspector General's office wrote their Interim and Final reports, they acknowledged that Captain Cantrell had indeed written such a letter. They did not dispute that. But beyond that? *Nada.* Their evasive judgment reads thus:

Mr. Johnson's statement that Captain Cantrell issued a profile slip for Private Johnson was corroborated by Dr. Cantrell and Private Johnson. It could not be determined who lost the profile slip, but Dr. Cantrell testified under oath that he issued the slip to Private Johnson. Private Johnson, in his sworn testimony, could not remember the name of the individual to whom he allegedly gave the profile. Such a profile would have been valid for a maximum of two weeks. In this regard, it must be pointed out that Mr. Johnson's comment that "this entire episode could have and would have been averted except for the unfortunate circumstances which followed his being forced to go to Cambodia again in spite of Captain Cantrell's written order that he should not be sent" was not substantiated.

Their dismissal of Captain Cantrell's letter—discrediting even the evidence they allowed!—would have made Bill Johnson apoplectic. Not only would they paste "allegedly" over Doug's actions, but General Enemark went on to contest the whole notion of Doug's unit being in Cambodia at all:

Private Johnson's company was attached to another battalion with a similar mission during this time frame. According to the official 4th Infantry Division records and the sworn testimony of the battalion commander concerned, no elements of the battalion went into Cambodia. Private Johnson was not ordered to go to Cambodia; consequently, Mr. Johnson's comment that the reason for Private Johnson's second court-martial was based on his refusal to go to Cambodia was not correct.

Put that in your pipe and smoke it, Mr. Johnson.

The Inspector General's findings were first issued in an Interim January 1971 report written by Colonel Hughett and then, finally, the matter was definitively settled in March, with General Enemark's Final. The two documents were unanimous in their findings. Colonel Hughett's report more closely addressed the particulars. General Enemark's sometimes repeated it verbatim. The judgment of both was emphatic: "Mr. Johnson's allegations are baseless and without merit."

The inquiry revealed no evidence to indicate that there was any impropriety involved in Private Johnson's discharge. Obviously, Private Johnson's father, Mr. William Johnson, does not accept this decision.

I can all but hear my father reply, on reading this, "You're goddamn right I don't."

18. "Shame and Trepidation"

<u>Early 1971</u>

The Inspector General's reports, Interim and Final, were brutal defeats, striking down my father's arguments point by point. Doug and the parents must have suffered a chaotic range of devastating emotions. Bill Johnson would have taken these defeats personally, and in this he was justified. The wording of these two reports refers often to *refuting* Mr. Johnson's claims, *denying* Mr. Johnson's allegations, just as at the Duddy hearing, the Colonel had constantly invoked "your father's letter of October 16th 1970." It's as if Duddy, Hughett, and Enemark acknowledged that Doug Johnson might be the subject of these undertakings, but Bill Johnson was the adversary.

Once past his immediate anger, Bill would have had to reassess his approach. Writing letters to congressmen and senators—basically crying out, "For the love of God, do something!"—that was a very different undertaking than this new battle. Politicians would, indeed must respond to the thrashing of a noisy constituent, a vociferous citizen. The Army? They had no such obligation to civilians. They were their own entity with their own agenda, their own evidence to present in rebuttal.

My father would also have winced to see that he had been overhasty in his presentation. For instance, with regard to the AWOL in December 1969, when he maintained that Doug could not get back to his unit because of an airplane crash in the vicinity, Colonel Hughett wrote a long, detailed denial, including:

It was determined further that Mr. Johnson's allegation that an aircraft crash in Nha Trang in December 1969 prevented his son from returning to his unit was not true. Mr. Johnson referred to an article in <u>Time</u> magazine which allegedly described the incident. A review of <u>Time</u> issue files for December 1969 and January 1970 was conducted. No such story appeared in those issues. A cross check was made of <u>Newsweek</u> issues for the same period with negative results . . . His allegation about being unable to get transportation to his unit and being unable to contact his unit by phone for seven days, although abounding in plausible details, was a complete fabrication.

The fact is, and my father would admit this to Jerry Pettis, the incident was not noted in *Time*. Bill had a clipping of an Associated Press article about these two plane crashes in December 1969, and he mistakenly attributed the information to the magazine. The oversight had cost him.

Copies of the Inspector General's reports, Interim and Final, also went to Jerry Pettis, to Mike Mansfield, and to Mr. Blandford in Mendel Rivers's office. (Rivers had died in December 1970.) On receiving Colonel Hughett's interim report in January my father wrote a crisp note to these three men. "Please be advised that in the next few days I shall submit to you a rebuttal . . . including a photostat of a newspaper article confirming the airplane crash in Nha Trang in December of 1969 which he [Hughett] states did not occur."

But some of the Inspector General's conclusions could not merely be laid at the door of an incorrect reference to a news article. The contention that "Doug climbed down a 90 foot ladder from a chopper to rescue another soldier, picked up the man and climbed back while machine gun fire was going on" was met in these reports with dry derision:

The feat, as described, would have required an extraordinary physical effort for a man in the best physical condition. Climbing unburdened up a rope ladder into a helicopter is difficult due to the downward wind forces of the rotor wash. Experienced aviation personnel queried on this subject stated that they had never heard of a soldier carrying a wounded man up the rope ladder into a hovering helicopter. During the inquiry,

Private Johnson was interviewed. He alleged that this incident happened just prior to his return to the United States. At that particular time, Private Johnson was malnourished and dependent upon drugs. The feat described under the circumstances was physically impossible and did not, in fact, occur.

In my mother's hand on this document is a note that this incident did not happen just before Doug's return in August, but earlier, in May or June 1970, when he would ordinarily be rotating out and going home, when, presumably, he would have been more fit. Personally, I doubt that his physical condition in June was significantly better than in August, and the feat does have the ring of action-movie heroism. Whatever the truth of it, Bill would drop this incident from later iterations of his campaign. What he would take from both the Interim and the Final reports was their own wording as to *why* this incident did not happen: Doug was "malnourished and dependent on drugs." Bill has underlined this phrase and scrawled in the margins, "Why didn't Army discharge him when in fact, they knew he was sick?" This question would come to be central to his later appeals.

The two wounds my brother sustained, once by shrapnel in the hip and once by flying debris near his eye, were met with skepticism. Hughett asserts, "it would appear that the alleged trauma would have required a short period of hospitalization." Ordinarily, true, one would think such wounds would have required hospital time, though the intense pressures of combat might have altered these circumstances. Doug testified at the Duddy hearing that he received no more than a shot of morphine and then went back into the field. Duddy had pressed Doug on the dates of these injuries and Doug was characteristically vague. Hughett correlated these dates with the Army's record of Doug's various AWOLs, confinements, and hospitalizations and found that "Since Private Johnson's statement was unsupported by any corroborative evidence, there was no reason to doubt the validity of the 4th Infantry Division Congressional correspondence. The allegation was without merit."

Nonetheless, Doug Johnson, on his return from Nam, had a scar beside his eye that he carried all his life. Late in life, he had difficulty walking. But mention of these wounds would not make it into my father's later appeals for reversal.

As for the Army not tending to Doug's drug problem, the Inspector General addressed that thus:

> The allegation that the Army was aware of Private Johnson's drug problem and did nothing about it was not substantiated. The 4th Infantry Division had an active drug amnesty program in effect during the period Private Johnson was assigned to the division. The nature of the program precluded the keeping of formal records on individual cases; therefore, it could not be conclusively ascertained that Private Johnson ever turned himself in for assistance under the program. . . . [A list follows of Doug's various drug infractions, including heroin found in his footlocker.] The inquiry revealed further that Private Johnson was interviewed and counseled concerning his use of drugs on both occasions when he was confined in the United States Army, Vietnam, Installation Stockade.

We will revisit General Enemark's assertions about drug programs in a later chapter. Here, however, let us ask: Was this counseling in confinement part of the Army's standard Bullshit Paragraph so often tacked on to their official communications? "You may be assured that while confined Private Johnson had the services of a chaplain, doctor, psychiatrist, social worker and the members of the correctional staff available to him to help solve any problems he encountered."

As for Doug's physical fitness for duty,

> The inquiry revealed further that in a 9 April 1970 letter the Division Surgeon reported that Private Johnson received a careful examination including several blood tests pertinent to the evaluation of his liver. The tests and physical examination revealed that the liver had returned to normal function and was healthy.

Doug left the hospital in Japan in mid-February; after that, in March and April 1970 he had only two recorded infractions, AWOLs from April 16 to 18 and 18 to 21. Moreover, these were the months in which he seems not to have been in combat situations. In May, with the new "big push" into

Cambodia, his situation changed significantly. After a year in Vietnam Doug ought to have rotated out on June 9. But with a mere twenty days to go, he was ordered (again) onto a chopper to Cambodia. His testimony at the Duddy hearing is explicit on this. By July and August, as we have seen from Paul's correspondence with Bill, Doug's physical health had deteriorated and his mental health had crashed into drugged despair. Here, again, is Paul's assessment from August of that year, that Doug's

> entire existence centers around the use of amphetamines and other habit forming barbiturates. He has developed a strong psychological as well lesser physiological dependence on the drug commonly known as speed. I have seen Douglas Johnson on several occasions while he was 'speeding" and frankly it was frightening and pathetic to see such a sight.

With regard to Doug's mental health, General Enemark declared: "Further, in a report dated 9 July 1970 the Division Psychiatrist reported that during an interview, Private Johnson spoke clearly and coherently with no evidence of a thinking disorder or other signs of psychosis." Reader, please note that General Enemark does not quote this Division Psychiatrist. He only surmises, paraphrases. Because of the mere paraphrasing, I would add that Doug allegedly "spoke clearly and coherently with no evidence of a thinking disorder or other signs of psychosis." In support of my "allegedly," I here quote the private psychiatrist who treated Doug once he was home:

> [H]is refusal to go [into a mission in Cambodia] at this time had not to do with unwillingness to do his duty, but was a sign of his flagrant psychological breakdown at which point his judgment had deteriorated beyond his control.

General Enemark does not quote this Division Psychiatrist's report, but he does assign a date to it "9 July 1970." This date might very well align with the occasion Doug referred to at the Duddy hearing when he testified, "I requested to see a psychiatrist. I was granted this and found out the psychiatrist totally ignored me." (After which he turned to Paul Kleinwachter.)

General Enemark concluded his paragraph about Doug's mental health by further paraphrasing the anonymous Army psychiatrist: "Private Johnson was diagnosed as having an immature personality influenced by drug abuse."

Wow! What penetrating insight! At twenty years old Doug Johnson was an immature personality! General, you must be a freaking seer! And "influenced by drug abuse." Did this thoughtful assessment arise from Doug's frank testimony before Colonel Duddy of a seven-week free-fall into addiction (from his June 10, 1969, arrival in Nam to August 1969 when "my arms had become literal pincushions"), his telling of persistently mainlining heroin and speed, ingesting LSD, and smoking marijuana for fourteen months? Or is "influenced by drug abuse" a tepid, timid, even cowardly euphemism? General Enemark's careful tiptoeing will come under further scrutiny in a later chapter of this book.

These two IG reports left Bill Johnson badly shaken. Point by point, he was utterly defeated. He spent that spring writing two blistering rebuttals, which he mailed not only to the Inspector General's office, but to Mansfield and Pettis, as well as Mr. Blandford in Rivers's office. His rebuttal draft of February 19, 1971, is four single-spaced pages of outrage, opening with "I was appalled at some of the flagrant statements made and signed by very responsible persons from the IG's office." Bill cites Doug's testimony, chapter and verse, at the Duddy hearing. He cites newspaper and magazine articles. He underscores more than once that Doug was never supposed to be in Cambodia because he had Dr. Cantrell's letter in hand (until he gave it over on being asked to an E-7, no "allegedly" about it). "Basis for the undesirable discharge was in lieu of court martial; reason for the court-martial was his refusal to go [to] Cambodia. <u>His basis for refusal to go was valid, medical and has since been substantiated and corroborated by Dr. Cantrell</u>" and the private psychiatrist, quoted above, whose professional evaluation he included.

Bill's rebuttal of General Enemark's Final, dated April 19, 1971, is even more impassioned and outspoken: six pages, single-spaced, culminating in a long line of paragraphs charging "impropriety" of every imaginable sort, the first of which reads:

> I charge the US Army and those officers responsible for the welfare of my son as committing an atrocious impropriety when they allowed,

yes, forced an undesirable discharge on Private Johnson instead of a medical. I include Lt. Col McKee and General Burke in my accusation. Both share the guilt and neither has any apparent regard for human life, specifically the life of my son. Captain Paul Kleinwachter requested a 212 discharge from General Burke and it was refused. General Burke preferred a 635 200 [Undesirable] discharge instead.

While Bill's stinging rebuttals no doubt gave him some satisfaction to be kicking the IG's ass, they were not useful in reversing the Undesirable. The IG's office was finished with the Johnsons. Their last word: Doug could appeal to the Army Discharge Review Board. For all the energy and the work that went into Bill's rebuttals, they effectively functioned as rehearsals. He would include both of them, intemperate as they were, in the package he put together in the spring of 1971 for the Army Discharge Review Board.

• • •

The defeats administered by the IG's office also exacted an emotional toll on my father that was not altogether apparent in his long, passionate rebuttals. Bill Johnson's sense of shame on behalf of his son deepened and his trepidation heightened. He was terrified that his allies might have lost faith in the cause: saving Private Johnson. And it's true that in 1971 and 1972 we heard no more from (and I can find no letters to) Senator Fulbright, Mr. Finch at the White House, or Mr. Romney.

The core of Bill Johnson's argument from the beginning—not just of this fight, but from the moment he first picked up the pen in 1969—rested on the absolute, unassailable fact that Doug was a young man worth saving: sterling character, an unblemished past, a bright future, moral, upstanding. The portrait the Inspector General painted of Doug was damning. By their account Doug was a wastrel, a lying, whining, cowardly, self-aggrandizing, disobedient little shit, "an immature personality influenced by drug abuse." Who was to be believed?

Bill Johnson's greatest fear was losing the support of Jerry Pettis, who had been part of this struggle, a ballast, an ally from the very beginning. In the archive I found a photostatic copy of an easily readable handwritten note to

Jerry Pettis. At first I wondered who wrote it. Not my mother; she had elegant penmanship. Surely it could not have been my dad. His handwriting was so bad, so unreadable, often illegible, that when I was in the seventh grade a teacher had refused to accept a note from him. I cannot remember what the note was about, but she accused me of having faked it. I pleaded innocent, but she said no adult had handwriting that bad. When I went home and told my dad, he got into a froth. Mom could not type the note because she had just given birth to Brian and was still in the hospital. Dad wrote this teacher a brand new, carefully penned letter, setting the teacher straight, where he actually used the word "perspicacious." I had no idea what the word meant, and when he told me, I remember being pleased because he had said it about me. On those (very rare) occasions when I hear or read "perspicacious," I still smile to think of this incident.

So when I unearthed this handwritten document and noted the recipient, I realized that it was intended to be read as is, a brief, heartfelt longhand note enclosed with a formal letter. Thus, it had to be legible:

My dear Mr. Pettis,

> I am writing to you a personal and confidential note that does not belong in reply to the IG's office.
>
> I daresay you were aghast and bewildered upon reading the IG's Interim report. You are probably wondering what a waste of time and effort in trying to [save] a person of that caliber.
>
> Mr. Pettis, let me assure you at this time your effort and interest have not been in vain. Douglas is a fine young man, responsible and gainfully employed and intends to attend university in September. He has high hopes, ideals and worthwhile goals that someday will be achieved.
>
> From the tone and substance of the IG's report they want to put Doug against the wall and forget. If the IG's information and report were based on facts, I could understand it, but this is not the case. I have substantiated my rebuttal with undeniable positive proof and therefore absolutely <u>refute</u> the allegations made by the IG's office. They (the IG) made statements <u>without proof</u> and I make rebuttal with facts and enclosures.

I literally beg you, Mr. Pettis, to stay with me on this case and apply personal pressure and your influence with the authorities to speed up, dissolve or break through the red tape to reverse this discharge.

I predict the day will come when you can point with pride that your interest and help was a major factor in the greatness of Douglas Johnson.

Mr. Pettis, in his next letter, graciously assured Bill of his ongoing support for Doug. He would continually prove that support in the struggles that still lay ahead.

. . .

Following Mendel Rivers's death in December 1970, the Johnsons would have had scant use for whoever became the next congressman from South Carolina because this person would not be the powerful chair of the Armed Services Committee. However, Bill had some exchanges with Mr. Blandford in Rivers' office. Blandford (probably unknowingly) did Bill a favor when he sent the original of a four-page, single-spaced letter from General Enemark dated January 29, 1971, "an interim reply to the inquiry of the late Honorable L. Mendel Rivers." Much of it was verbatim what would be on the Interim and Final reports that were sent to my father. However, there are some significant points present that are not found elsewhere. They are worth noting.

Colonel Enemark states: "The undesirable discharge certificate issued to Private Johnson in lieu of trial by court martial was appropriate under the circumstances and Mr. Johnson was so advised. Private Johnson's poor Vietnam record was the basis for his undesirable discharge." I am struck here by a significant omission: that there is *no mention whatever* of Doug being dirty or disheveled, not in uniform, unhygienic, etc. This observation, this infamous addition, was the creation of General Burke.

There is also no mention of drug abuse as a basis for the Undesirable. But it states that "Private Johnson was also under investigation of possession of marijuana and heroin which was found in his footlocker. That investigation was discontinued upon his return to the United States for separation." Other than the tablet of Binoctal, drug possession is not listed among the charges that would have been addressed at the second court-martial, had it convened.

If there were other drugs, other drug charges, why were they not part of the original complaint? This question would arise again.

In his final paragraph to Mr. Blandford, General Enemark writes, "Due to the transfer of many of the individuals involved and the need to locate Private Johnson's permanent records, a firm completion date [for the inquiry] cannot be established." The records that Doug's guard had lost between Vietnam and Fort Lewis in August had not been found by January 1971. My father wrote to Mr. Pettis on February 19, 1971, with astringent understatement, "Also, I would agree to the need to locate Private Johnson's permanent records."

General Enemark, however, did not wait to find Doug's lost records before issuing a final report in March which found that Bill Johnson in the wrong in every possible instance and that the Army had acted with complete propriety: Doug Johnson was deservedly slimed with the Undesirable.

• • •

The timing of the Inspector General's final report in March 1971 coincided with the verdict finally rendered in the court-martial of Lt. William Calley and thirteen other American soldiers accused of murdering, raping, and rampaging through the village of My Lai in March of 1968. They killed little children, killed wailing babies, killed women and girls, killed defenseless old men, burned homes. For months the My Lai court-martial consumed news outlets. Of the fourteen men tried, Calley was the only person convicted. He was sentenced to life imprisonment—of which he served three days because President Richard Nixon intervened. Nixon ordered Calley released from custody and put under house arrest, where he remained for three years before being paroled in 1974. I can only imagine my parents' wrath and sorrow when they heard that Nixon had bestowed presidential mercy on a slayer of children when their entreaties on behalf of Doug had come to naught.

William Calley died in 2024 as I was writing this book. As I read his obituaries revisiting the atrocities of My Lai and the names of the other soldiers, brass and enlisted, who were never punished, men who presumably collected their Honorable discharge papers, perhaps even their pensions, upon leaving the Army, did I wonder anew at the crimes for which Doug Johnson was deemed forever Undesirable? I did.

. . .

After the Inspector General's scathing dismissals in January and March of 1971, my father would spend that year collecting and presenting reams of material to myriad persons to substantiate two separate appeals, one for an Honorable discharge, and one for a medical discharge. Even though the materials he gathered are voluminous, Bill would pare down his presentation. There would be no more references to Doug's heroic act picking up a fellow soldier from a hovering helicopter or to Doug's wounds suffered in combat. However accusatory his rhetoric, the core of his arguments would rest upon four major points:

1. Doug ought never to gone into Cambodia in May. With Dr. Cantrell's letter he had a valid reason not to go into the fighting.
2. Doug's physical and mental health had been ravaged by disease and drug addiction.
3. Doug's crimes, such as they were, ought not to blight the next fifty years of his life.
4. Doug had fulfilled the terms stemming from his November 14, 1969, court martial and it should not have any bearing on the Army's decision regarding an Honorable or Medical discharge.

Bill would repeatedly insist that in November 1969 Doug accepted responsibility, paid his fines, took his demotion, even served a portion of his prison sentence (until he was airlifted to Japan). The Army accepted all this. Thus, any reference to this court martial as an evidentiary reason *not* to reverse the Undesirable was the equivalent of "trying a man twice for the same crime."

My parents put all this together. They sent it out. They waited.

These years, 1971, 1972, must have seemed to Doug and his parents as though they were passed in a perpetual waiting room, the sort with stale air, fluorescent lighting, and long-outdated magazines, where flies hover, where tinny Muzak tunes play in loops and everyone sits on unforgiving plastic chairs and no one's name is ever called.

19. The Wait

<u>1971 to Spring 1972</u>

The letters and other materials my father assembled in 1971 and 1972 seeking a reversal of the Undesirable are often distraught and angry, but they are not nearly as desperate as those he wrote in summer 1970. He also sent fewer letters in 1971 and 1972. With Doug now at home Bill could more easily use the phone to reach the people he wanted to pester and cage-rattle. Clearly, he was every bit as relentless on the telephone, judging from a snippy note from Colonel Duddy, which makes clear that the Colonel has had just about enough from Mr. Johnson.

March 22 1971

Dear Mr. Johnson:

> As I informed you during our telephone conversation last week I have been retired from the US Army since 28 February 1971, so that the information which follows does not reflect an official US Army position.
>
> First I suggest you write an office letter to the US Army requesting their position in this matter.
>
> To date, my research has not disclosed any regulation or provision in the MCM which prevents an individual pending CM charges from not being utilized in his normal role as a soldier or officer.

From my own experience I can assure you that many times, based upon the circumstances, individuals have not been restricted while pending CM charges. This type of decision must be made by the commander at the time and under the circumstances facing him. Actually this is in keeping with our Civil proceedings, as you know.

Sincerely
Duddy
Robert R. Duddy
Col. USA, Ret

(In his new materials Bill would excoriate the officer who put the self-confessed-drugged-up Private Johnson on guard duty, but he would not insist that it was against regulations for a soldier facing a court martial to be armed or given normal duties.)

My father's efforts to secure a Medical discharge were primarily conducted on the phone, once again with Jerry Pettis guiding the effort. Material that was mailed included written testimony from the Loma Linda doctor and the psychiatrist the parents hired after Doug came home. The medical doctor wrote:

> On examination we found him to be extremely malnourished, to have an enlarged liver and spleen and a severe mental depression. It was obvious that he was at the breaking point psychologically and psychiatric care was immediately requested for his assistance. Laboratory studies indicated him to be anemic. His sedimentation rate was markedly elevated. There was evidence of liver damage upon laboratory investigation. It is doubtful that this man could have survived for 3 to 6 months under the previous circumstances. It is my opinion that Douglas was in extreme need of medical care and should have received a medical discharge from the service rather than an undesirable one. It would be my recommendation that he be given a medical discharge and I certainly believe that his medical condition at the time we saw him would justify this.

And from the psychiatrist (some of which I have already quoted elsewhere):

I want to say that this man is psychiatrically extremely disturbed. His diagnosis at the present time must be considered psychotic depressive reaction chronic, very severe. His behavior as it is recalled in a careful chronological recollection in Vietnam resembled more a schizophrenic reaction which is of a much more profound disintegrative quality. This may have been contributed to by his drug usage in the service, but it is more likely to have resulted from the profound variety of living in combat experiences during his 16 months in Viet Nam. Most of which was spent on patrol with his platoon in situations of very great hazard and terror. Nine months of this time he was "point" man, a position of remarkable responsibility and nearly unbearable hazard. He reports that on five occasions he was in Cambodia on special assignments. He finally refused a 6th mission. He was sent anyway and at the Cambodian border left his group and went AWOL.

I want to emphasize that his refusal to go at this time had not to do with unwillingness to do his duty, but was a sign of his flagrant psychological breakdown at which point his judgment had deteriorated beyond his control. Such behavior was the final desperate effort to remain integrated at all costs and to prevent further deterioration into insanity.

For a Medical discharge the Army insisted Doug must have a physical, which was conducted on November 19, 1971, at the Letterman General Hospital in San Francisco. Bill went with him. When Bill and Doug left the Letterman Hospital they were under the impression that the Medical discharge would go through. Although there is no document to this effect in any of these files, Doug and Dad believed this, or at the very least, they had been led to believe it. But in early 1972 Jerry Pettis wrote to Bill:

I have been in telephone contact with the Surgeon's General's office of the Department of the Army here. I am informed that the medical board at Letterman found your son questionably unfit and that on February 14 the Central Physical Evaluation Board, which is a part of Walter Reed Army Hospital, found Douglas physically fit.

The appeal for a Medical discharge was denied. Was it denied because they deemed Doug physically fit in November 1970, or were they casting this judgment back to August? There's no way of knowing. The records that would have detailed his ravaged health remained lost. Without these records, how could the Army substantiate his physical condition in the summer of 1970? And certainly the portrait that emerges from the Loma Linda doctor and the psychiatrist who attended him in September 1970 emphatically describes a young man beset with physical and mental trauma.

• • •

The second avenue my father pursued was approaching the Army Discharge Review Board for a change to Honorable. In April 1971 he put together an elaborate package that included all the work he had done in rebutting both the interim and final IG decisions and additional information.

ENCLOSURES

1. Picture of applicant [Snapshot from December 1969 at home.]
2. Statement of applicant
3. Letter to Board of Review from father of applicant
4. Statement from Frank L. Cantrell, Capt. MC, US Army
5. Statement from [doctor] MD, Dept Internal Medicine, Loma Linda University
6. Statement from [doctor] MD, Psychiatrist,
7. Copy of WJJ letter to Jerry L Pettis US Congressman 10-16-70 ["The General was not aware"]
8. Letter from Inspector General dated 1-29-71 interim report
9. WJJ Reply to Interim report addressed to Congressman Pettis 2/19/71
10. Photostat of newspaper article Nha Trang plane crash, December 1969
11. WJJ annotations on IG Letter for IG dated 2-18-71
12. Chronology from Inspector General's office
13. WJJ reply to second IG report dated April 19 1971
14. Affidavit from Applicant

15. Time Magazine issue May 25 1970 showing picture of Applicant
16. Copy of [WJJ] letter addressed to Dr. Shiroshu [*sic*] 106th General
    Hospital [Japan] 1-29-70
17. Letter to Military court from Applicant's sister 7-25-70
18. Character letters originals of which sent to Viet Nam summer 1970
    [six of them]
19. Sworn testimony of applicant

Number 14, "Affidavit from Applicant," is a terse five-line statement sworn and signed in front of a notary that Doug's unit was, in fact, sent into Cambodia, no matter what Colonel Hughett and General Enemark might aver to the contrary.

Number 19, however, "Sworn testimony of applicant," is a massive document, basically everything Doug had said at the Duddy hearing. But here it is written, not spoken. And here it is incontestably *not* written by Doug, but by his father. The events the writer selects for emphasis, the rhetorical flourishes, invoking "Gentlemen of the Board," "without shame or trepidation," "high moral standards," all that and more is pure Bill Johnson. To me, this raises a question: Why didn't Doug write his own sworn testimony? He was clear enough, cogent when he spoke at the Duddy hearing. Perhaps Doug did write a statement and my father found it insufficiently eloquent. My sister, Helen, however, is of the opinion that Dad simply did it without asking for Doug's input.

Writing as Doug, Bill's empathy for what his son suffered has alarming conviction and immediacy. He reiterates time and again the misery, even the madness of being "placed in a detention cell. I was drugged, sick, and had a feeling of absolute hopelessness." He writes of being "required to do, acts which were incompatible with my conscience, I used drugs. (I would like to interject that I did not use drugs before entering the Army, and I am not now using drugs, nor will I ever again use drugs.)" Being in the

Stockade in solitary that threw me into the very depths of despair, helplessness and hopelessness. Drugs became a satisfaction and a way of life. I had given up all hope. I felt that, since I had been vindicated of previous charges, it was unjust, unfair, and against military justice to force me into solitary pre-trial detention. All this for a five-day AWOL charge. I was mentally and physically ill and in a state of horrible depression and shock.

In his concluding paragraphs Bill Johnson, although writing as Doug, once again echoes Portia from *The Merchant of Venice*, pleading:

> Gentlemen of the Board, I testify to you every statement I made was the absolute truth and nothing but the truth so help me God. I am now a new man physically and mentally, and I am completely recovered. I do not have any desire whatsoever to use any type or kind of drugs. I have regained my ideals, desires, and my goals. Before Viet Nam, I played concert piano. I certainly do not play that well now, but do enjoy playing the piano for myself, family, and friends.

> I conduct myself on the highest plane and in keeping with my family's principles and in line with my Church's standards (Church of Jesus Christ of Latter-day Saints, Mormon), and I believe in the scouting principles. I am an Eagle Scout. I have never had any problems with the law before Viet Nam nor since discharge. I am gainfully employed and also a student at California State College at San Bernardino.

> Gentlemen of the Board, with earnestness and sincerity, I beg of you to study my case with all thoroughness and pray that in your evaluation you find it acceptable to reverse the 635-200 Undesirable Discharge to an Honorable one. I am now 22 years old and beginning a life. Gentlemen, without shame or trepidation, without qualification or reservation I openly plead for an even chance at life without a cloud of Undesirable Discharge for the next 45 years of life.

> Everyone at some time or another in his life can think of at least one situation in which he was given a chance by someone known or unknown to him, which became the turning point that placed him on the road to a productive and meaningful life. You, Gentlemen of the Board, are in that position now, in evaluating this discharge. Please give me this opportunity in order that this cross I bear can be lifted and discarded.

> It is my prayer that the day will come when I can be instrumental in some way, either being wholly responsible or a part of an accomplishment for

which you, on this Board, can take credit for giving me the opportunity when I was 22.

Gentlemen, I have faith and trust that you will make your decision to reverse the Undesirable to Honorable.

My father asked Jerry Pettis to submit this enormous appeal package on his behalf. And then, once again, they waited.

• • •

Did it really take a year for the Army Discharge Review Board to assess these materials? Their curt denial offers no clues. A letter dated April 19, 1972, arrived addressed to Doug:

> This is in reference to your application for a review of discharge in which Congressional interest has been expressed. The Army Discharge Review Board, after careful consideration of your military records and all other available evidence has determined that you were properly discharged.
>
> Accordingly the Secretary of the Army has directed that you be advised that your request for a change in the type and nature of your discharge has been denied.
>
> Interested parties and your counsel have been informed of the board's decision.
>
> Sincerely
> Verne L Bowers
> Major General

Bill instructed Jerry Pettis to ask the Army Discharge Review Board for the minutes of the meeting that denied Doug's request and the names of the officers on that board. They would reply that there were no minutes. None were kept. *Nada.* Really? It took a fucking year to come to this decision and there were *no supporting documents at all*? Did my father's massive package supporting Doug's right to an Honorable discharge get lost somewhere in the entrails of the Pentagon? Did it end up being a doorstop? Did someone put a fan atop it and then forget it was there? Did someone spill an urn of coffee on it, obliterating all the pages? Upon being asked for the reasoning behind their denial, the Army simply retreated into the power they had to say, *No. There are no notes of this year-long undertaking and there are no names,* as though the whole had dissolved into thin air, leaving not a trace behind.

• • •

Dad wrote, Mom typed and filed. Thanks to her skills, these files exist. And yet, from these files Doug himself is oddly absent. I'm sure he and his parents had long confabs—questions asked, questions answered—but, judging from the actual documents at hand, Doug does not seem to have actively contributed to the struggle to get the Undesirable changed to an Honorable. A few official papers, brief, typed inquiries that bear his signature, that's all I have. Perhaps Doug left the fight to his father and mother because he could not bear to revisit all that anguish and he needed his energies to navigate a new life. And perhaps for that very reason, the parents didn't ask him to contribute more than he did. After enrolling in San Bernardino State University Doug was taken up with new challenges, new classes, and new friends, none of whom knew anything of the Undesirable. The woman who later became his second wife, who was friends with him in these college years, never heard the word Undesirable with regard to his discharge, not even when she was married to him.

In one of Doug's letters to Dad written from the pits of Long Binh Jail, he describes himself as a "natural optimist." Even so, these repeated defeats at the hands of the Inspector General's office and the Army Discharge Review Board and the denial of the Medical discharge must surely have left my brother depressed, even crushed, his equilibrium undermined. I have no doubt that the parents tried to shore up his confidence, assuring him of eventual success. Their own sadness, fatigue, depression must surely have been profound. As I read and reread all the materials documenting these successive defeats—absorbing the work, the time, effort, energy, the proverbial blood, sweat, and tears my parents poured into seeking an Honorable discharge—the song that keeps playing in my mind is The Band's doleful ballad "The Weight." The lyrics are oblique but unmistakable. The grizzled

Johnson family, Christmas 1971.

singer is weary, beaten, seeking rest, resolution, some sort of safe harbor, but the answer is always defeat, denial, and failure, an echoing *No No No*. However, these emotions are not readily evident in the papers I brought up from the basement. These are letters to outside entities and official persons, not journals or diaries recording inner doubts or emotional turmoil. And yet, I think that turmoil and its toll are visible in a studio family portrait my mother insisted on at Christmas 1971 when I was briefly home for the holidays. Compared to the 1967 family group, where an element of spontaneity is clearly visible on everyone's faces, here no one evinces any such thing. The Johnsons are assembled, well-dressed, smiling, but an air of fatigue suffuses the whole. Dad looks especially tired; his closed-lipped smile is tense. Doug, unsmiling, has a haunted look about the eyes. Mom's smile, seemingly pinned in place, looks unconvincing and her lacquered, rigid hairstyle adds to the implied tension. Even Helen and fourteen-year-old Brian look drained. They all look on edge, except possibly for me, but then I was home only briefly for the holidays in 1971. I didn't live there.

20. The Epidemic

Spring 1972

By April 1972 the Army had had four opportunities to consider Doug Johnson's fate. Sequentially, the first was the judicious, reasonable case made by Paul Kleinwachter in Vietnam, "What should be done with Private Johnson?":

> The applicant, Douglas Johnson, has developed a serious drug problem
> since coming to Vietnam. Although this individual is charged with
> but one specification of drug possession and none of drug use, his
> entire existence centers around the use of amphetamines and other
> habit forming barbiturates. He has developed a strong psychological as
> well lesser physiological dependence on the drug commonly known as
> speed . . .
>
> Due to his sickness he is no longer a vital functioning member of his
> unit. The Army recognizes the need to discharge this type of individual
> administratively in AS 635-212 which provides in part that drug addicts
> may be separate as being unfit for military service.

The general refused. On August 20, General Burke slapped the Undesirable on Doug, adding that he (the general) "observed the applicant on several occasions and had yet to see him clean or in proper uniform; that he refused to comply with the most basic of requirements and personal hygiene."

I have come to wonder why my father—with his painstakingly detailed appeals—did not use that dirty and disheveled bit to call the general's judgment into question. Bill Johnson certainly called other aspects of his judgment into question. "The General was unaware . . ." he wrote again and again, his "tuning fork" phrase of the October 16, 1970, letter. It's possible, though not likely, in my opinion, that in concentrating so heavily on what the general was *unaware* of, my father missed, failed to note what the general was all too well aware of—what the general had apparently seen for himself. I also think it's unlikely, because in Bill's own hand, scrawled in the margin of the general's document, my dad has written: "it was this same CO who put [Doug] in LBJ." Clearly, Dad believed the general held some sort of animus against Doug, information my father probably learned in his talks with Doug at Loma Linda. Why didn't he use that perceived animus as one of his weapons in favor of an Honorable? For this I have only conjecture. Perhaps it entailed some incident that reflected badly on Doug. Perhaps it would have been too hard to prove. Perhaps Bill was confident that the actual documented facts, especially Dr. Cantrell's letter, were sufficient.

The Army's second consideration of Doug's fate was the Inspector General's investigation. Their reports, Interim and Final, in early 1971 absolved the Army in every way and in every instance of any possible infractions, conceding nothing. Mr. Johnson's allegations were unsubstantiated and Doug's accounts, "while abounding in plausible particulars," were simply untrue. The Army would acknowledge not one shred of Mr. Johnson's evidence to be valid. (But let me remind the reader that neither their Interim nor the Final makes any reference whatever to the general having "observed the applicant on several occasions and had yet to see him clean or in proper uniform," etc.)

Third, the request for a Medical discharge, informally OK'd at the Letterman Hospital in San Francisco in November 1971, was denied by Walter Reed Hospital bureaucracy in Washington, DC, early the next year. In a letter to Mr. Pettis, Bill asked, "If one medical board approved the discharge, why then was a second board included in the case? The Medical Board at Letterman examined and interviewed Doug. The second board reviewed the case on paper." There was never an answer to this question.

Fourth, the Army Discharge Review Board declined the application in

April 1972. My father noted their timing (without remarking that it took a year):

> Congressman Pettis, I feel the Army Board has truly and drastically erred . . . They were surely aware that Secretary Laird's change of policy [regarding GIs with drug problems] would be released on May 12 1972, yet it appears they hurriedly sent the letter of denial prior to that date.

Among the documents unearthed from the basement is a May 12, 1972, clipping of the AP wire service story of this policy change:

> The armed forces have since stopped issuing dishonorable discharges solely for drug use or possession. Servicemen holding bad conduct or dishonorable discharges for using or possessing drugs may now appeal for an honorable discharge under a new policy announced yesterday by the Pentagon.
>
> The Pentagon said Secretary of Defense Melvin R. Laird has ordered that these ex-GIs may now request a review of their cases. The order does not apply to those men punished for selling drugs.
>
> Laird's order was similar to the one issued last August covering administrative discharges granted under less than honorable conditions because of possessing or using drugs . . .
>
> Officials said the new ruling affects only about 200 men who received bad conduct or dishonorable discharges for drug use before July 7, 1971.

Given that Doug separated from the Army before July 7, 1971, he ought to have come under this umbrella of forgiveness. But he didn't. On May 30, 1972, Lieutenant Colonel Vilas wrote to Jerry Pettis, "The character of his separation was based on his overall military record which included several instances of misconduct. The use of drugs was not the primary consideration in his request for separation or in the type of discharge he received." Officially, then, Doug was given the Undesirable for his lousy military record and "instances of misconduct."

But the role of drug addiction in Doug's military life cannot be overestimated. General Enemark's observation that Doug had an "immature personality influenced by drug abuse" is utterly insufficient to the circumstances. At the Duddy hearing Doug gave copious, frank references to his persistent drug use: "I was using ever since I got into Vietnam. From the time I got introduced to opium, I was mainlining. That means for about five and a half months. Then I began mainlining speed for the duration of my time overseas."

Yet each of the Inspector General's detailed denials (Interim and Final) would claim:

> The allegation that the Army was aware of Private Johnson's drug problem and did nothing about it was not substantiated. The 4th Infantry Division had an active drug amnesty program in effect during the period Private Johnson was assigned to the division. The nature of the program precluded the keeping of formal records on individual cases; therefore, it could not be conclusively ascertained that Private Johnson ever turned himself in for assistance under the program.

Really? An "active drug amnesty program during this period that precluded the keeping of formal records on individual cases?" What the hell kind of active program is that? If they didn't keep records, how could they possibly know whether or not Private Johnson applied? Interim and Final denials further add, "[Doug's] almost constant dependence on drugs created substantial doubts about the effectiveness of his service as an infantryman when he was with his unit." So which is it to be, dude? Was there a program for drug amnesty? Might it have included soldiers who had "constant dependence on drugs?" Men who are drug addicts are ineffective infantrymen, yes or no? It is difficult to parse out what is actually being said here.

In fact, slowly—and for reasons we shall shortly better understand—there were, as early as 1970, changes to the Army's treatment of drug addiction. In February 1971, in Bill's lengthy rebuttal to the Inspector General's Interim report, he reported: "On Thursday, August 20, 1970, an Associated Press release appeared in the San Bernardino <u>Telegram</u> by Correspondent Carl C. Croft from Washington, which states, "A Pentagon task force recommended

<u>today</u> establishment of a trial program to grant amnesty to U. S. servicemen who stop using illegal drugs and seek help in kicking the habit."

In a twist of ironic chronology, August 20 1970 coincided exactly with Doug's acceptance of the Undesirable "for the good of the service." Bill's rebuttal continued, citing a second news item that, in another ironic overlap, corresponded with the date of the Duddy hearing: "Also, on Friday, December 4, 1970, the San Bernardino Evening *Telegram* reprinted a New York Times News Service piece saying that the US Army had reversed its 'drug punishment policy for rehabilitation.' And the Army, in a reversal of its traditional policy of strict punishment for drug use, was trying to help them through a new experiment called 'Operation Awareness.'" Remember, too, that when Paul wrote his August 16 letter to the General seeking a AR 635-212 for Doug that "authorizes a general discharge for alcoholics," he added, "and I feel that in the near future drug addiction will be classified with alcoholism in this manner." Indeed, he was proved correct, particularly if "Operation Awareness" was already or about to be underway in a matter of days.

• • •

For some better understanding of Doug's actual on-the-ground-experience with drugs, we can turn to the pages of *U.S. Army Psychiatry in the Vietnam War: New Challenges in Extended Counterinsurgency Warfare* by Norman Camp, MD (Borden Institute, 2014.) Despite the book's dry, daunting title, the contents are eye-popping. It is available for anyone to download and read on the internet. Look it up.

Chapter 9, "Substance Abuse in the Theater: The Big Story," observes that "In early 1970, a new and far more pernicious problem arose following the emergence of a very efficient Vietnamese heroin marketing system and the enthusiastic embrace of heroin by the lower-ranking troops in Vietnam. Within a short span of time, concerns [were voiced] about rapidly accelerating heroin-related arrests, medical problems, and overdose deaths" and goes on to say that, by the time the problem was recognized, "heroin use, as widespread misconduct, was also heroin use as medical epidemic" (321, 341).

Doug Johnson was caught up in this epidemic. Yes, he was "an immature personality influenced by drug abuse," but he was a victim nonetheless.

I stumbled upon *U.S. Army Psychiatry in the Vietnam War* doing what I thought was a cursory internet search for Binoctal (possession of which was one of the charges against Doug). I ended up spending uncounted hours thrashing particularly through the pages of Chapter 9, "Substance Abuse in the Theater." This long, shocking, informative chapter (pages 321 to 373) documents the Army's lackluster, confused, inadequate response. Complete with footnotes and appendices and statistics and charts, with input and photos from doctors and patients, it chronicles the widespread use of heroin by enlisted soldiers in Vietnam particularly in the years 1969 and 1970. The Army might have cheerfully dubbed their efforts "Operation Awareness," but the evidence in Camp's book indicates that this was a total misnomer. Doug and others were caught in a web of what might have been willful ignorance or, at the very least, belated recognition that by 1970 heroin addiction, especially among enlisted men, was a problem of gargantuan proportions, a veritable epidemic, so much so that:

> By 1972 the Army in Vietnam shifted to an unprecedented hybrid medical/law enforcement model: soldiers with positive urines were "quarantined" for observation, detoxified as needed, and returned to the United States as patients. This peaked in July with an annualized rate of one out of every eight soldiers medically evacuated back to the United States for this reason (322).

Wrap your mind around that. One in every eight soldiers medically evacuated for addiction by 1972. Who was left to carry on the fight against Communism in Southeast Asia? The closing line of chapter 9 resonates with sad, even tragic implications: "[I]n the end this insoluble medical/morale problem [heroin use] within the ranks became the Army's Achilles' heel and emblematic of America's failure in Vietnam" (366–67).

Furthermore, the book links the use of heroin among the troops to growing home front anger and disillusion with the war that had spread to the men who were fighting it, that the "accelerating rates coincided with the widespread antagonism of lower ranks toward military authority and the US mission in Vietnam" (366).

Chapter 9 considers the course of this epidemic in chronological phases, including the "Transition Phase (1968–1969): A Growing Polydrug Problem

(Pre-Heroin)" and the "Drawdown Phase (1970–1972): The Shift to Heroin." My brother's months in Vietnam (early June 1969 to late August 1970) overlapped with both of these. In essence, Doug succumbed to this epidemic before the Army itself was fully aware of the extent of the problem. *U.S. Army Psychiatry in the Vietnam War* shows that basically, and certainly by 1970, the Army had no clear path, much less protocol—possibly not even true understanding—of the extent of heroin use among its troops. Doug Johnson, who was just fine before he went to Nam, was, within seven weeks of arrival, shooting up "seven or eight times a day" for months on end. He was not alone.

When at last the Army became aware, the response was all too little, too late. In describing the military's unsuccessful efforts to establish "a system for case identification and monitored detoxification in a medically supportive environment" these soldiers faced real difficulties, among them, that:

Confirmation of the presence and extent of [narcotic] withdrawal requires monitoring of objective signs or laboratory measures.

Medical facilities in Vietnam had no reliable laboratory means for ensuring drug abstinence in soldiers undergoing withdrawal until roughly 1 year after the epidemic began.

Inpatient facilities could not be kept free of illegal drugs.

Soldiers in Vietnam defended their drug use as being justified by the circumstances (service in Vietnam), or as generally not problematic; thus, their motivation for abstinence was very low.

Medical observers noted that the withdrawal syndromes for many soldiers could be mild and managed through dispensary-level care.

Despite these features, soldiers claimed that the likelihood of unbearable withdrawal symptoms necessitated their continued use. And, if pressed, especially when they were threatened with prosecution for drug possession, they demanded hospitalization (for both detoxification and isolation from drug suppliers).

By this time soldiers were so antagonistic to military authority and opposed to serving in Vietnam that identified heroin users welcomed removal from military duties as a medical diversion; thus heroin use alone served as an "evacuation syndrome"

The incidence of heroin use became so high that if inpatient hospital-level service was provided for all users, that is, without identifying those in need of 24-hour monitoring and care, the hospitals could be overtaxed, which meant that the care of other patients could be compromised (341–42).

Each of these echoes experiences that Doug made plain at the Duddy hearing. Drugs could be found anywhere. He was introduced to the cocktail of speed and LSD at the Nha Trang hospital. That "Soldiers in Vietnam defended their drug use as being justified by the circumstances" might be rendered more colloquially as "scared shitless." As for "motivation for abstinence was very low," in Doug's words:

> I used opium for several reasons. One, being it relaxed extreme nervousness and tensions that build while walking forward leading some people through an area where you don't know if you are going to live or die before sunset. Secondly, I used opium because I didn't care at that point whether or not the opium killed me. My reasoning at that time was if the opium didn't kill me the VC would.

As for Doug's being treated in a hospital, repetitive bouts of hepatitis ought to have signaled to any of the professionals lauded in the Army's Bullshit Paragraph that drugs lay at the root of his woes.

Q41: Were you ever treated by US medical authorities for the use of drugs?
DSJ: They put me in the hospital once for one and one half days.

Q42: Do you remember specifically where or when?
DSJ: I was in the hospital once for a day and a half at An Khe. I was still using drugs while in the hospital. In other words, they gave me a bed for a night and kicked me out the next day.

Q43: You refer to the use of speed and opium in your statement. Can you be more specific as to the dates?

DSJ: I was using from the time I got into Vietnam. From the time I was introduced to opium I was mainlining. That means for about five and half months and then I began mainlining speed for the duration of my time overseas.

Q44: Mr. Johnson, how was it possible that you obtained the amount and varying types of drugs while under combat conditions?
DSJ: Either thru the Vietnamese or other GIs. When they would go into the rear they would bring back everything they could get their hands on.

Q45: Did you have to pay for the quantity of narcotics you stated you used?
DSJ: No.

Drug addiction played a crucial role in my brother's sorry record in Vietnam, a role the Army never did acknowledge. They conceded in the Inspector General's report that Doug's "almost constant dependence on drugs created substantial doubts about the effectiveness of his service" (itself something of a bullshit euphemism). So why was he not treated? Why did they hide behind General Enemark's smug, misleading assertion of "an active drug amnesty program," that "keeps no records on individual cases" and then punish Doug because there was no record that he sought help? He did try. He tried again and again to get the attention of doctors and psychiatrists. He willingly went to see the psychiatrist, who ignored him—very possibly the same one General Enemark cites as seeing Doug on July 9, 1970, and whose alleged findings he *paraphrases*, "Private Johnson spoke clearly and coherently with no evidence of a thinking disorder or other signs of psychosis," offering further the psychiatrist's alleged pronouncement that diagnosed Doug as "an immature personality influenced by drug abuse." After being ignored by that psychiatrist, Doug turned to Captain Kleinwachter to confide in. Paul left his own record of what Doug was like while under the influence, "frightening and pathetic," adding, "Due to his sickness he is no longer a vital functioning member of his unit." In that same letter "What Is To Be Done with Private Johnson" letter of

August 16, Paul adds that Doug "occasionally has been sent to the 17th Field Hospital to dry out his system." Does this not count as seeking help? When Doug was told he was to go into Cambodia (again), "In desperation I returned to the Battalion Doctor [Cantrell] and turned myself in for being strung out on speed." Is this not asking for help?

• • •

There is a very odd note in the file from Brigadier General Louis J. Prost to Senator Mansfield, who sent it to my parents. With regard to the denial of a Medical discharge, it reads:

25th February 1971

> This is in further reference to your inquiry in behalf of Mr. William J. Johnson regarding his request for a medical discharge in the case of his son, Douglas S. Johnson.
>
> Douglas was discharged under other than honorable conditions 25 August 1970 for the Good of the Service in lieu of trial by court martial (drug addiction).

In the margin, Mom uses an arrow and writes: "I found this letter in my file. Please note the signature, date and the fact that Army records indicated at that time (2nd paragraph) that the reason was 'drug addiction.'" When did my mother make this note? If it was in 1971, before Laird's amnesty, might Doug have come under the auspices of "Operation Awareness," then informally in place since 1970? If she noted this after May 1972, she was alerting Dad that Laird's canopy forgiveness might offer a new path.

Other than the possibility of the Laird amnesty, by May 1972 only two possibilities for exoneration remained: to file a civil suit (financially out of the question) or approach the Army Board for the Correction of Military Records. Though my father includes reference to the Laird amnesty as part of the materials he would assemble for this board in 1972, it was not the central tenet. Since drug addiction was not the *official* reason for the Undesirable, perhaps he feared this would be an excuse they would take to deny. But

I think it's also possible that placing drug addiction at the center of his argument would have tarnished Bill's foundational premise: that Doug Johnson was a fine human being. Drugs were an aberration. In Vietnam he turned to drugs out of soul-shriveling fear, feelings of utter desolation and acts incompatible with conscience. But for the extraordinary circumstances of combat in Vietnam, he never would have succumbed. "Here is a young man worthy of your assistance, his moral fiber, his attitude, his mental and physical strength are exemplary to youth today." And now that he was home, "Doug is complying with the highest standards of living and his actions and citizenship are above reproach. He is gainfully employed and has regained his health, mentally and physically." Bill insistently proclaimed that drugs were now behind Doug forever and ever! He was "a new man."

Doug three months after his return from Vietnam, December 1970. This photo accompanied the materials for the Army Discharge Review Board in 1971. Photo credit: William J. Johnson.

21. "A New Man"

<u>1970-1972</u>

Every Fourth of July Doug Johnson would wait out the holiday in a darkened room. My mom once sorrowfully told me that the shrieks and explosions tortured him. They must surely have sent him mentally back to the reek and remembrance of misery, to dangers unforgotten and traumas unsheathed, to acts "incompatible with his conscience." What did Doug Johnson carry in his head, his heart, his conscience? What did he tell his father as they sat on the lawn at Loma Linda Medical Center, Doug sobbing to recount his experience in Vietnam? Whatever Doug revealed of acts incompatible with conscience, Dad took it to the grave. If Dad learned of the actual circumstances that compelled Doug to take the sandal off a man he had just killed, to clutch that sandal, hold it, and bring it home with him, he never said. When I think of their conversations at Loma Linda, father and son, I keep hearing the lyrics to the poignant ballad from that summer, "Teach Your Children," reminding parents that their children's hell would surely go by and that love could still sustain.

On my brother's return, in addition to the collapse of his physical health and the disintegration of his mental health, there were the drugs to be reckoned with. Once home, Doug visibly confronted everyone with what Paul Kleinwachter termed "his misuse of drugs." If Paul, a young Army officer, looked at Doug and saw someone "frightening and pathetic," imagine what Doug looked like to his family, friends, and fiancée, to the ordinary people of Turrill Court. I don't think it's possible to overestimate the paralyzing shock the family experienced seeing a person who for more than a year had been "mainlining speed and opium seven or eight times a day." And then there is the corollary question: How did the family, the friends, the fiancée, the people of Turrill Court seem to Doug? Did the smiles on those white, well-known faces seem to him something from a bland dream while the nightmare raged inside?

Doug was released from Loma Linda Medical Center in September 1970 and did not have a job until December. During the day, he would have been home alone when our parents were at work and Brian was at middle school and Helen at the community college. Turrill Court was peaceful, a world away from the sounds, sights, and demands of Vietnam. Did he wander the house? Press the keys of the baby grand piano that had been purchased to reward his musical achievements? As a boy he had mastered difficult pieces, filled the house with music. After he returned from Nam, my sister has no recollection of him playing the piano at all.

My father's mild admission to Jerry Pettis that Doug's return home was "extremely difficult," and that "we all suffered with him" was surely an understatement. Veiled as the language is, it's all Dad ever committed to paper about the challenges of Doug's homecoming. Helen remembers some alarming incidents in those years, events that must have given my parents not merely pause, but big fat doses of shame and trepidation. Incidents of bizarre behavior occurred and accrued, the sorts of stories that profoundly shock and then, as time passes, tatter and wane because they're too painful to be given voice, to be recalled in detail, such as Doug's coming up the lawn waving a gun at Mom while Helen hid, crouching, in the hallway.

However, nothing could alter Dad's core belief in Doug's intrinsic worth. Once Doug was home, Bill's paeans had a new chapter and verse, never mind what he actually witnessed of his son's behavior. In Dad's correspondence beginning in the fall of 1970, Doug was doing so well! Regained his ideals, desires and goals! Returned to health! Working part-time! NO DRUGS! Had no wish to do drugs ever again! A college student pursuing his education in hopes of becoming a teacher! Doug was "a new man, physically and mentally, completely recovered." One can all but hear the palpable pride in my dad's narrative voice when he wrote in 1972, "[Doug] has brushed death in more ways than one and tonight he is at the college library studying Chaucer for a class in English Literature." What could be more beautiful, more distant from drug addiction than Middle English?

Hoping to get GI benefits for Doug's education, my father opened new communication with a Mr. Hansen at the local Veterans Administration office. Mr. Hansen made clear the inroads the Undesirable would make on Doug's future. Not only were no educational funds forthcoming, but "The V. A. informs me that Doug will not be allowed any civil service job," Bill wrote to Jerry Pettis, "nor will he be accepted at any teaching institution as a teacher."

Jerry Pettis, in fact, had intervened to get Doug accepted at San Bernardino State in the first place. Doug did not have the high-school grades to qualify for admission, nor sufficient credits from the community college to transfer, but Mr. Pettis prevailed on the university to give him credit for his military service. He wrote to Doug that he would need to present proof he'd been in the military for at least a year. He added, "I have been assured they are not interested in what type of discharge you received—only the amount of military service." Doug probably started at State in Fall 1971, majoring in English. Bill Johnson informed Senator Mansfield:

> He is presently preparing himself to teach secondary schools or college level. Douglas is a student in good standing at California State College; he has now met all academic requirements and he is active in student affairs. He is on the student election committee and has been asked to be associate editor of the school newspaper next fall. He is also working four hours a night part-time at St. Bernardine's Hospital as a janitor.

Some of this is wishful thinking or perhaps Doug's own inflation of his experience. He was never associate editor of the student newspaper and he might have done some electioneering for candidates, but he wasn't part of the student election committee.

Although the college was not far from Turrill Court, Doug moved into the dormitories. I think it's entirely possible that the parents wanted him out of the house. My sister says that they wanted him to have a fresh start. (The fiancée was gone within months. Her youthful love had sustained him while he was in Nam, but at twenty-one she wasn't equal to dealing with a traumatized veteran and drug addict.) When Helen transferred from Valley College to San Bernardino State in 1972 she found Doug socially established there, the center of a lively set, including the girl who would later become his second wife. He was also jumpy, agitated, angry, and still doing, possibly dealing, drugs.

An early part-time job after Doug came home was at a gas station owned by a friend of Dad's. At work Doug was apparently dealing or at least buying drugs from the other young guy who worked there—who happened to be a narc (police informant). One evening the station owner, Dad's friend, came to the Johnson house roaring drunk, very upset, tearful, and angry. Standing outside the house, he railed at Dad that Doug should not to come to work the next day, that the gas station was going to be raided. Because of this warning, Doug was spared arrest, but he remained on the San Bernardino police radar.

The family dentist himself told Helen about Doug's showing up at the office and asking for money—just a loan—and waiting for it. She was humiliated to hear this, even though she was touched when the dentist confessed to her that his daughter was also a drug addict. As for Doug's turning up at the home of my high-school friends to ask for money, I only learned of that in the 1990s.

In the summer of 1971, the parents sent Doug to Salt Lake City, Utah, to work for the family of Dad's aunt, who owned a prosperous construction company there. Their son was about Doug's age and he had gone with the Johnsons on a family vacation when both boys were in high school. These relatives even found a little apartment for Doug, though I'm sure his parents paid the rent. In any event, the Salt Lake City gig did not last long. Doug often didn't show up for work and when he did, he was high. He "borrowed" money, and he had such a crippling fear of heights that he swooned and almost fell off a roof. The construction firm fired him. These Utah relatives thought Doug was a loser and a liability. My parents thought the relatives had treated Doug unfairly. The rift between the families never mended.

Jobless, Doug hitchhiked over to Boulder, where some of my college friends now lived. I got a phone call from them at my house in Pennsylvania.

They informed me that Doug had shown up unexpectedly at their place, that he was weird as owl shit and wearing a long blond wig. I called my parents, who didn't know my brother was in Colorado or that he had taken to wearing a blond wig, though they knew he had been fired from the job in Salt Lake City. Within a few weeks Doug hitchhiked back to California and moved back in with his parents, his sister Helen, his little brother Brian, and the dog, a big Irish setter named Chief.

I feel certain that my parents saw these events, and no doubt others, as aberrations, that they believed when the Undesirable was changed to Honorable, Doug's outlook, attitude, his sense of self would improve dramatically. This conviction fueled their persistent struggles and filled up my parents' private prayers: *Please God, let him truly be and become a new man. Please help us defeat these demons.*

• • •

"We the unwilling, led by the unqualified to kill the unfortunate, die for the ungrateful." This sad aphorism (originally said to have been coined in the First World War) was resoundingly correct for those who fought in Vietnam. Vietnam vets were not embraced by a grateful nation as was Bill Johnson's generation. In the film *The Best Years of Our Lives* (1946) the veterans' reentry after World War II may be complex, but they are respected, revered as heroes. Doug Johnson and the Vietnam generation returned to a far grimmer reception and a society riven by dissent. The nation was increasingly bitterly divided over the war in Southeast Asia. Friendships were sundered; people quit speaking to each other and were rude in elevators. Families fractured as well. Secretary of Defense Melvin Laird's own son, John Laird, attended peace protests and came out vocally against the war. It's said that President Nixon and Henry Kissinger both told Laird he should muzzle his son; Laird, to his credit, refused. Conservatives believed that antiwar protesters were sex-crazed, drugged-up, disrespectful hippies who didn't love America. Opponents of the war believed that Americans were being lied to, that lives, American and Vietnamese, were being squandered in a war that had no just cause and no hope of conventional victory. This was later proved true.

Soldiers who served in Vietnam returned to an ungrateful nation. Society held no parades, offered no recognition of their sacrifices. The returning Vietnam vet was met with distrust, disgust, and anger, particularly as American casualties mounted and knowledge of the war's excesses spread (for instance, through press coverage of the court-martial of men charged in the My Lai massacre of 1968). Americans looked at returning vets as possible perpetrators of atrocities. Some writers of Vietnam memoirs recount alarming incidents on their return to civilian life: harrowing instances of being hassled, harassed, spat on, called baby-killers. In various documentaries about the Vietnam War, we see old men weeping to recount the harsh treatment they received once they were home. They suffered this abuse in addition to whatever toll their wounds and memories exacted from them. The plight of the returned Vietnam veteran is made visceral and dramatic in the 1989 film *Born on the Fourth of July*, based on a 1976 memoir by Ron Kovic. Contrast the scene in that film where the father is putting his paraplegic son to bed with the same moment so tenderly portrayed in *The Best Years of Our Lives*.

At the peace protests I attended on the East Coast there were always cadres of returned veterans carrying banners reading "Vietnam Veterans for Peace." These veterans were often on the stage with the main speakers and greeted with enthusiastic cheers, but in the hearts and minds of those cheering there lurked unspoken questions about acts committed that were incompatible with conscience. Some veterans wore the medals they had earned and there, before the crowds of protesters, they tore those medals off and flung them to the ground, scenically disavowing their part in the war, wishing, no doubt, that they could do the same with their memories.

Whatever these men suffered in Vietnam, their return and reintegration into American society was often harsh. This, too, affected Doug Johnson's return home, his relationship to his family, his fiancée, high-school friends, and the people he later met at San Bernardino State—in short, to anyone who did not go to Nam, who did not know what he knew. And though the university had an active group of Vietnam Veterans Against the War—men who knew what he knew—contemporaries of his at SBSU have no recollection of Doug taking any part in it. Perhaps he could not bear to speak of the war or his wartime experience in any context. And of course he had nothing to visibly, dramatically part with. The sandal was long gone.

22. The Armenian Connection

Summer 1972

The Army denied any kind of accountability for themselves. In asking Jerry Pettis to request the minutes of the Army Discharge Review Board meetings, my father tried to call them into account. He failed. There was no word (ever) on what happened at Walter Reed to make them deny the Medical discharge. Feeling dismal, if still defiant, in 1972, Bill flailed away, reflexively peppering Jerry Pettis with desperate possibilities:

> Thank you for your letter advising that no minutes were kept of the Board's action relative to the application for reversal of the discharge for Douglas. I am interested and wish to know the names and rank of the men who sat on the Board at which denial was made. (This will include the names of Board members who denied the medical discharge as well as the latest honorable discharge request.) This should be a matter of public record, and if not, perhaps you could ascertain this through your channels
>
> If the only way to reverse this decision is to seek out and personally ask for an appointment with Secretary Laird or President Nixon to review the case, we must initiate this now. If either one will study the facts of the case, Doug would surely be exonerated.
>
> Should I make up a cover letter, a new application and include correspondence, letters, statements which were made under oath etc.

to submit to the Defense Secretary or President Nixon? The Review Board must not be allowed to ruin Doug's life.

By mid-June, however, my father had plummeted into despair, writing candidly to Mr. Pettis:

> I cannot help but feel very disenchanted with the so-called fairness of the United States Army Review Board. It seems to me that the odds against "a grass roots citizen vs. the U. S. Army" are a million to one or none, of winning a fair and just decision. Both review boards missed entirely the whole point made in the request of a change in the nature of the discharge. The Board's decision is a mockery of justice . . .
>
> Under these circumstances I feel it would be a waste of time at this point to apply to the Board for Correction of Military Records.

But two weeks later, something had clearly changed. Bill Johnson, in a note utterly devoid of rhetorical flourish, is ready, once again, to fight:

July 3 1972

Dear Congressman Pettis: . . .

> I shall very shortly submit another request for reversal through a Washington DC attorney who has agreed to act as counsel. I will advise you when the application is submitted and certainly appreciate any assistance you may give him if and when he contacts you . . .

Enter Robert Mardian, first-generation Armenian American, former Assistant Attorney General of the United States, current counsel to the Committee to Re-Elect the President. Future defendant in the Watergate conspiracy trial.

• • •

On June 22, 1972, Bill Johnson cold-called Robert Mardian's home to ask him—probably to beg him—to intercede on my brother's behalf. He asked Mardian, in fact, to serve as Doug's attorney. What nerve. Or what balls. Or possibly how desperate or stupid could Bill have been? A week passed before he followed up in writing, on July 3 (the same day he wrote to Jerry Pettis citing "a Washington DC attorney who has agreed to act as counsel"). This assertion was on the slippery slope somewhere between bravado and delusion. But on that day, Bill's spirits, his conviction, his resolve were clearly at a high because his letter to Mardian begins with no apology for his nerve (or balls or desperation or stupidity, for that matter), but with a declaration:

July 3 1972
Mr. Robert Mardian
Committee to Re-Elect the President
1701 Pennsylvania Avenue
Washington, D. C.
<u>PERSONAL</u>

Dear Mr. Mardian:

> Out of sheer desperation, I boldly called your home a week ago Thursday night to ask you for your assistance. I called because you are Armenian and an outstanding attorney, and I hope you would help an Armenian young man who needs, and most important, deserves your help. My son is desperate. After two years of fighting this extreme injustice, you are his last hope. If Douglas were guilty as charged, I would not turn my hand to help, but he is not guilty and was not guilty, and I ask you as one Armenian to another to fight his cause. The fact is, had the officer in charge honored a medical officer's orders, this whole episode would have been averted.
>
> My wife, one of four girls, was born in Istanbul and came to Los Angeles with her parents in 1923 as an infant. We know injustice. My mother-in-law's life was spared only because of a series of events during the Armenian massacres. My wife is the former Peggy Kalpakian …
>
> I telephoned to ask you for a few hours of your time to study this presentation and to present this to the Army Board for Correction of

Military Records. I have outlined the case as closely as possible to save you time. I cannot afford to reimburse you for what your time and talents are actually worth. I will, however, make some financial remuneration; I am a salesman for Lederle Laboratories Division of American Cyanamid Company.

For the few hours you spend on his case, my son will have at least 50 years of peace of mind. It will bear heavily upon his success or failure in life in addition to having a direct effect on his own future family. As it is, the Veterans Administration informs me that he will be unable to follow his chosen work, for which he is now preparing himself, teaching in high school or college levels so long as he has the stigma of Undesirable Discharge. In addition, and probably more important, are drawbacks such as attitude and development avoidance-approach syndrome, judgment with his identity, his feeling of adequacy, etc. In addition, positions in any city, county, state or federal areas are closed to him, as well as most employment possibilities in private industry. Already the GI educational benefits and other veteran benefits have been denied. I am contesting the Undesirable Discharge because it is completely unjust, completely unfair, and completely morally wrong.

Let me assure you, Mr. Mardian, that Douglas is worthy of your efforts. [Descriptions of Doug's current studies, Eagle Scout status, etc.].

We have submitted two applications for reversal of discharge through our Congressman, Jerry L. Pettis. At the suggestion of two eminent private physicians (copies of their letters enclosed), [recounts attempt for the Medical discharge and the physical at Letterman Hospital in San Francisco on November 29, 1971, and that Walter Reed denied it].

We then submitted a second application requesting an Honorable; also denied. We are enclosing a copy of that file. Here you will find pertinent factual data which is also applicable to this new request for discharge reversal. We are submitting this (1) in accord with the May 12, 1972, order of Secretary Laird for reversal of discharges other than honorable due to drugs, and (2) we enclose new application to the Army Board of Correction of Military Records. Also enclosed are copies of pertinent letters as well as other applicable data . . .

Congressman Jerry Pettis advises us that there is but one avenue remaining, an appeal to the Army Board for Correction of Military Records, Department of the Army, Washington, D. C 20310, regulations enclosed. I am earnestly requesting that you present this application for discharge reversal and act as his counsel before the Army Board.

Thank you.
Sincerely yours,
William J. Johnson
Enclosures

When I first read the opening line, I thought: Holy shit! What was that conversation like? How long did it last? Why didn't Robert Mardian tell Bill Johnson to get off the phone and go to hell? But he didn't. He must have heard my father out regarding the Undesirable and why Doug had been unfairly, unjustly treated. Mardian must have asked for more information. Thus my father's long letter. Bill probably took a week to assemble the whole because he included the thirty-four-page single-spaced account, the "digest" of the case which would need to be typed again.

The Johnsons put it in the mail, and then, once again, they waited.

. . .

What my parents could not have known was this: In summer 1972 Robert Mardian was embroiled in what would be the cauldron, the crisis of his life, deep in events that would stain his name and reputation. He was mired in a situation that he himself would describe to the televised Senate Watergate committee in the summer of 1973 as "quicksand," and indeed, Robert Mardian was going down.

On June 17, 1972, just days before Bill's telephone call, several men botched the burglary of the Democratic National Committee's offices in the Watergate complex and were arrested. One of them was James McCord, security chief for the Committee to Re-Elect the President (CREEP). That day, Robert Mardian and top Republicans, including John Mitchell (former Attorney General of the United States, now the director of CREEP) were in the Los Angeles area spearheading a Republican rally for Ronald Reagan.

Word of this disaster reached them swiftly and frenzied phone calls ensued as well as furtive strategizing meetings. Mitchell, Mardian, and CREEP's other chief officers—all men with close ties to the White House—were suddenly caught in a flurry of obligations and evasions. Singly and collectively they tried to maintain power and reputation, and yet to stay out of culpable connections with activities that they knew were sordid at best, criminal at worst.

In his excellent book *The Watergate Conspiracy Conviction and Appeal of Assistant Attorney General Robert Mardian*, University of Baltimore Law School Professor Emeritus Arnold Rochvarg carefully lays out the dizzying chronology of events that resulted from the Watergate break-in. The criminal charges that would be brought against Mardian and others basically stemmed from questions of Who Knew What When and What Did They Do About It? Mr. Rochvarg was a lawyer on the team that represented Robert Mardian's successful appeal of his criminal conviction for conspiracy. His book states that Mardian's "alleged involvement in the conspiracy had lasted only thirty days, from mid-June to mid-July." Those thirty days were among the most crucial of Robert Mardian's life. He and his allies were engaged in a desperate dance of accountability and denial. In his televised testimony before the Senate Watergate Committee in 1973 (which can be viewed online) Robert Mardian described his role in CREEP as "Counsel to the committee, as a lawyer." He saw himself as "implicated in the conduct of others whom I was to serve."

The legal system saw it differently. A grand jury indicted the former Assistant Attorney General for internal security for conspiracy, along with former Attorney General John Mitchell, former Chief White House Assistant for Domestic Affairs John Ehrlichman, former White House Chief of Staff H. R. "Bob" Haldeman, and Kenneth Parkinson, a lawyer from a private firm. These men were tried together. By the time of the trial several other important people deep in the Watergate cover-up, including John Dean, counsel to the President, and Jeb Magruder, deputy director of CREEP, were witnesses for the prosecution. Mr. Rochvarg's book details the whole trial in clear, but dramatic detail. After three months, in January 1975, Robert Mardian was criminally convicted of one count of conspiracy. Kenneth Parkinson was found not guilty; the others were guilty of multiple counts. The *Washington Post* reported that after the guilty verdict Mardian "seemed stunned, devastated," and that he remained "in the courtroom until it was almost empty, apparently trying to compose himself."

I'm very much indebted to Arnold Rochvarg's book and to his personal recollections of Robert Mardian, whom he describes as "A very straight-arrow, very conservative guy, and something of an outsider in Washington politics." Mardian comes off less positively in the *Washington Post*'s description, as a "balding, gravel-voiced and dour-faced man." And his portrait is even more sour and angry in Jill Wine-Banks's 2020 book *The Watergate Girl.* Jill Volner, as she was known in 1972, was the only female on the prosecution's team; they chose her to cross-examine Mardian during the trial because he was "known to be a hot-tempered, nasty guy." During Ms. Volner's questioning, Mardian screamed at her, prompting Judge John Sirica to intervene and call a recess. Mr. Rochvarg, too, says that Mardian did not fare well with the woman attorney, that his aggressive demeanor made the jury hate him.

Given these unflattering contemporary accounts of Robert Mardian, he seems to me unlikely to have responded to the cry of a distraught father, an utter stranger who "boldly called your home," particularly in the midst of such intense moral upheaval, such personal and political turmoil. Why, under these fraught circumstances, would he so much as tiptoe into my brother's case? And yet, on July 13, just ten days after Bill's letter, and amid what was no doubt unbearable personal anxiety, Mardian wrote:

Dear Mr. Johnson:

> I have received your letter of July 3, 1972, and the enclosed file relating to your son, Douglas.
>
> Because of my present duties, I am unfortunately precluded from acting in your behalf on an official basis. I have, however, read the entire file and am most impressed by your presentation of the facts.
>
> Therefore, I have taken the liberty of forwarding the file to Mr. Kenneth BeLieu, Undersecretary of the Army for his review and comments. I will notify you as what he advises as soon as I hear from him.
>
> Sincerely yours,
> Robert C Mardian

Arnold Rochvarg thought that the Armenian connection was a powerful bond. Mr. Rochvarg offered as well the thought that, as Assistant Attorney General of the United States for internal security, Mardian had energetically prosecuted antiwar protesters, draft-dodgers, and the like, and here was a young man who had enlisted, gone to Vietnam, had fought, and was suffering for it. That, too, could have been a factor. For myself, I cannot help but think that amid these dire events from mid-June to mid-July, 1972, Robert Mardian, astute attorney that he was, knew that he himself was in real peril and perhaps he too might one day be in a situation where he needed help.

· · ·

So that Robert Mardian could "digest the case," my father included his thirty-four-page, single-spaced account, all the customary points he had made in previous presentations, including the nineteen items he had asked Jerry Pettis to take to the Army Review Board. Doug's written testimony (that Bill wrote) was included. Bill also enclosed a passionate letter speaking as a father, touting Doug's worth and great potential. But the materials my father created for Robert Mardian had a decidedly new tone, a thrust rehearsed in those two angry Inspector General rebuttals in 1971. He wasn't simply imploring the court to find mercy in its heart. He went on the offensive, excoriating the Army for their treatment of Doug. He railed at the military for continually referring to the 1969 court-martial as evidence of "instances of misconduct" that served as reason for denying Doug an Honorable discharge. He pointed out, correctly, that Doug fulfilled the terms of that 1969 punishment: the demotion, the pay cut, even confinement in Long Binh (until he was airlifted to the hospital in Japan). "Doug paid his debt and the Army accepted it." No more should be said of it, he wrote; otherwise, it would be "trying a man twice for the same crime."

Moreover, Bill slashed at the conduct of the 1969 trial itself, using the official "Record of Trial" that I found in the basement. He particularly condemned the misconduct of Doug's so-called defense counsel, as noted in chapter 7:

Defense counsel made no opening statement (page 29)

> Defense counsel did not offer any defense
>
> Defense counsel did not cause prosecution to prove guilt
>
> Defense counsel had nothing to present (page 27)
>
> Defense counsel made no arguments (page 30)
>
> Defense counsel hindered the defense by his statement (page 32)
>
> Defense counsel allowed the assistant defense counsel to be excused
> (Pages 19, 23)
>
> Defense counsel was unmindful and incomprehensibly blind to the
> physical condition of the accused at the time of the trial.
>
> Counsel was uninterested, incompetent, unreliable, unrealistic and
> uninformed. Trial lasted thirty five minutes.

Bill also called on Doug's medical records, which seem to have been found in summer 1972. (How or exactly when, I do not know.) These records chart persistent, recurring bouts of hepatitis, malaria, diarrhea, fevers, and the like, illnesses treated in hospitals or convalescent facilities. Bill Johnson had a BA in physiology and a Masters in public health and he could and did assess (in detail) what these lab results and other figures meant. He cited the physical toll these ailments and drug abuse took on the human body, symptoms that would have been—certainly should have been—evident to the professionals so often invoked in the Army's Bullshit Paragraph. Moreover, using the dates on those health records and the medical tests administered, Bill could point out that, shortly after that November 1969 trial, Doug was hospitalized for three weeks for hepatitis, and now he chided Major Charles D. Bryan, president of the court-martial, for failing to recognize how jaundiced Doug was.

Bill quoted great swaths of Doug's testimony at the Duddy hearing. He included Paul Kleinwachter's measured, reasoned letter requesting a general discharge that would have allowed "a sick, sick individual" to be treated. He cited (the correct) news reports about the two plane crashes that prohibited Doug from returning to his unit following his release from the hospital on December 18, 1969.

Bill lambasted the unnamed officer who in June 1970 assigned guard duty to Private Johnson, just returned from six days AWOL, who confessed to popping speed the whole time. "It was poor judgment on the part of the officer to assign a man to any job who, in reasonable judgment, could not accomplish that job," he wrote, adding that this officer had thus knowingly put his other men at risk and had acted out of malice just to add one more charge to Doug's crimes.

Robert Mardian—for whatever unknown reason lurking in his inscrutable heart—sent Bill Johnson's materials with his endorsement, on to Undersecretary of the Army Kenneth BeLieu.

On August 1, 1972, Mardian's assistant wrote to my father to say that "Mr. Mardian was out of the city and asked that I forward the enclosed letter to you":

July 28, 1972
Mr. Robert Mardian
Committee for the Re-election of the President
1701 Pennsylvania Avenue NW
Washington, DC 20006

Dear Bob:

This is in further reply to your letter concerning Douglas Scott Johnson.

A preliminary review of the file has been made and the application and the records which accompanied the letter are now in the hands of the Army Board for the Correction of Military Records. The Board has an extensive backlog; however I have asked that the Board act on the application as soon as circumstances permit. When the action is complete, the paper will be returned as you requested.

Douglas has the right either to appear personally before the Board when it hears the case, to be accompanied by the counsel of his choice, to be represented by counsel without appearing personally, or to have his case considered on the basis of records alone. In any event he can be assured he will be afforded every proper consideration.

You may want to inform Mr. Johnson that my Special Assistant, Mr. Francis X. Plant (telephone Laurnber AC 202 OX 79641, Room IE 520, Pentagon, Washington D.C., 20310), is available to provide information and assistance relative to the presentation of the case to the Board.

I am pleased to provide this information; if I can be of any further assistance, please let me know.

With highest regards,
Kenneth E. BeLieu
Undersecretary of the Army

Kenneth BeLieu (1914–2001) was a man of impeccable military and civilian distinction. He took part in the invasion of Normandy and the Battle of the Bulge during World War II. His actions were such that he was awarded, among other honors, the Silver Star and the Croix de Guerre. He also fought in the Korean War and lost his leg below the knee in combat. He had an equally distinguished career in politics. In 1961 President Kennedy named him Assistant Secretary of the Navy and he served there until 1965. On January 21, 1969, Richard Nixon appointed him Undersecretary of the Army, a position he would hold until 1973. For a man of this rank, indeed, this stature to oversee Doug's case before the Army Board for the Correction of Military Records, and at the behest of Robert Mardian, recently Assistant Attorney General of the United States, must have filled the parents' hearts with almost unspeakable joy. New hope, true hope beckoned. The Mormons had gotten Doug airlifted out of Long Binh jail. The Armenians might just get him lifted out of Undesirable hell.

23. The Fifteen-Point Silver Bullet

<u>Autumn 1972</u>

Bill Johnson immediately opened a vast correspondence (and no doubt many phone calls) with Kenneth BeLieu's special assistant, Mr. Francis Plant. In October, my parents learned that despite the "extensive backlog," the Army Board for Correction of Military Records would hear Douglas Johnson's case at 9 a.m. on Wednesday, November 8 in Room 11-517 at the Pentagon.

My father also had considerable correspondence with Mr. George Sowa, who put together the Army's case *against* reversing the Undesirable. When Mr. Sowa had completed his summary he sent it to my father on official Department of the Army stationery. On reading it, my parents must have grinned at one another, might well have gotten up and done a little dance for all I know because, although Bill made copious notes all over this document, they surely saw it for the silver bullet that it was. My father was so delighted that he wrote Mr. Sowa a thank you note, cc'ing Mr. Mardian.

October 15 1972

Dear Mr. Sowa

I wish to thank you for your courtesy and consideration in sending us a copy of the case summary of our application. I was impressed at the fairness of the summary in which you extracted pertinent data from the voluminous material we submitted.

Bill Johnson had every reason to be impressed at Sowa's extraction of the "pertinent data." His document was as unique for what it withheld as for what it offered. His October 5, 1972, Case Summary differed significantly from other Army descriptions of my brother's appeal. Many supporting documents were attached, but the case itself made fifteen points and it made them briskly and simply in four short pages.

Number 1, Applicant Requests stated plainly that Doug Johnson wanted an Honorable discharge.

In *Number 2, Applicant States*, Mr. Sowa drew readers' attention to the attached nineteen pages, which is to say, Bill Johnson's highly polished, carefully argued document extolling the worth of Douglas Johnson. By way of précis, Sowa continued that "after Basic and Advanced training the applicant had a fifteen day leave and on 10 June 1969 was sent to Vietnam where he was faced with pressures never experienced before and started using drugs." This was almost verbatim Doug's opening statement at the Duddy hearing (wording echoed in Bill's attached nineteen-page statement). And then, in a glorious 333-word run-on sentence, Mr. Sowa went on to hit all Bill Johnson's high notes, among them "Eagle Scout with 35 merit badges, Assistant Scout Master and now after being released from the hospital is not on any drugs prescription or otherwise, is gainfully employed and has regained his health and is a student at California State College." Sowa noted that Doug was "convicted by a Special Court-Martial for absence without leave, he had recurring hepatitis and was hospitalized in Japan for a month." There was no mention of Doug being jailed for another AWOL in December (much less of anyone contesting that planes crashed that day). There was no "alleged" or reference to an "unnamed person" in Sowa's assertion that Doug had a valid note from Dr. Cantrell, that Doug handed that valid note to a sergeant, and that thereafter, the note had vanished. Sowa included the diagnosis of the Loma Linda doctor who treated Doug on his return, including his listing of Doug's many physical afflictions (thus implicitly calling into question the Army's refusal to grant a Medical discharge in 1971, a finding he cited in point number 13).

Number 3 (all of page 2) was Doug's sorry military record: a chart of places and dates, including the many AWOLs and the punishment meted out by the November 1969 court-martial. It also noted "Awards: NDSM, VSM,

VCM" (National Defense Service Medal, Vietnam Service Medal, Vietnam Campaign Medal Ribbon (a note is added in my mother's careful hand, "never received by applicant"). It mentioned an incident on October 23, 1969, when Doug was caught in an "off limits area" and fined $30 for that month, something not otherwise alluded to in any of these documents.

Number 4 noted the charges against Doug in May and June of 1970 (two AWOLS and asleep on guard duty, with no mention of the drug Binoctal).

Number 5 was an odd note: "On 22 May 1970 the applicant's "Commanding Officer recommends that he be barred from reenlistment in the Regular Army in that he did not respond to rehabilitation and his conduct and efficiency evaluation indicated unsuitable and substandard performance." This was the first time I had read of this. It seems to me almost comically moot since there was certainly no chance in hell that Doug Johnson would reenlist. Doug's service record attested that after Basic Training he was consistently substandard, but I wonder what it means that "he did not respond to rehabilitation." What kind of rehabilitation was under discussion? Unclear. Does it refer to the rehabilitation assured in the Bullshit Paragraph? Does it refer to his having been confined in the stockade? Does this refer to drugs? Is this "Commanding Officer" the same man who noted how dirty and unhygienic he was? We don't know. Who requested it? Unknown. Under what circumstances was this document written? *Why would this have been written at all?* Perhaps it is somehow allied with what would have been standard procedure, that is, that Doug ought to have rotated out of Vietnam on June 9. (This date, May 22, 1970, it should be noted, also coincides with Doug's going AWOL until June 8.) There is no other reference to this information amid all the materials exhumed from the basement.

Number 6 stated verbatim the psychiatric evaluation that General Enemark used in the Inspector General's report, including his paraphrasing of the Army psychiatrist about an "immature personality influenced by drug abuse," but it added immediately after this "and <u>recommended separation under the provisions of Army Regulations 635-212</u>." In addition to the underlining there are notes in both my mother's and my father's handwriting: This is the very path that Paul Kleinwachter advised. This last bit clearly *did not appear* in any of General Enemark's or Colonel Hughett's assessments, not to Bill Johnson, not to Mansfield or Pettis or Blandford. Accordingly, here is the pertinent question: *Had this unnamed psychiatrist actually included this suggestion in his recommendations? Did General Enemark choose to ignore it? Is this why General Enemark paraphrased the unnamed psychiatrist rather than quoting him?*

If Enemark consciously deleted or omitted this suggestion, it raises another question: *why?* The answer I infer is that he and Hughett were covering for General Burke. Burke ignored Paul's request for "separation under the provisions of Army Regulations 635-212." Could Burke have ignored *this same request* if, additionally, it had come from an Army psychiatrist? Questionable. The General was within his rights, militarily, to opt for the Undesirable, but Doug's sorry military record ought to have sufficed. If the psychiatrist made this suggestion, and if Enemark and Hughett deleted or ignored it, were they also covering for the willful vindictiveness implied in this infamous addition? The General "observed the applicant on several occasions and had yet to see him clean or in proper uniform; that he refused to comply with the most basic of requirements and personal hygiene. . ."

Number 7 was a brief medical history apparently filled out by Doug on August 13, 1970, (about a week before he left Vietnam), with a long list of physical afflictions including "drug abuse per the patient's admission." Again, this implicitly calls into question the Army's refusal to grant a Medical discharge in 1971 or forgiveness under the Laird canopy. (My mother has noted this in the margin.) To my eye this also raises the question of why Doug should have been denied "the provisions of Army Regulations 635-212." He had admitted to drug abuse.

Number 8 was a nearly verbatim recap of Paul Kleinwachter's reasoned letter "What is to be done with Private Johnson," which Bill had included with his materials. It further substantiated Doug's drug addiction.

Number 9 noted that on 20 August 1970 Doug "requested the discharge for the good of the service in lieu of trial by court-martial under circumstances which could lead to a bad conduct or undesirable discharge" and that this was Doug's own choice.

Number 10: "On 20 August 1970 the Commanding officer recommended approval of the applicant's request for discharge for the good of the service, that he observed the applicant on several occasions and had yet to see him clean or in proper uniform; that he refused to comply with the most basic of requirements and personal hygiene and recommended an Undesirable Discharge."

I am astonished that Mr. Sowa included General Burke's infamous addendum, but there it is. Nowhere in the vast sea of paper from the Army—all the various brass and offices and officers who repeatedly fought my father, who denied his claims—does any other entity use this "dirty" description as to why Doug was given the Undesirable. Other than occasional references to drug addiction, they generally nail Doug simply with "his poor service record," or "instances of misconduct." I believe these other entities could see that this "dirty and disobedient" reasoning was so totally without any kind of military merit, that even men like General Enemark were loath to quote it. More to the point, with regard to Mr. Sowa's fifteen-point case assembled here, I think that is exactly *why* he quoted this remark: that is, to put before the Army Board for Correction of Military Records the petty, punitive vendetta this Commanding Officer visited on a troubled enlisted man. To me, from a distance of half a century: if Enemark, knowing that Burke had zapped Doug because he was insufficiently hygienic, purposely excluded the psychiatrist's recommendation for a drug-related release, then the institutional culpability is conspicuous and the cruelty explicit.

Number 11 simply noted that Doug was given the Undesirable and returned to the States and that it was issued on 25 August. In my mother's hand is the note: "two recommendations for 212 ignored." She clearly believed there was one other besides Paul's.

Number 12 noted that my father sought a Medical discharge and Doug had a physical at Letterman Hospital in San Francisco in November 1971.

Number 13 noted that the U.S. Army Physical Disability Agency reviewed this material and that medical discharge was denied.

Number 14 noted that the Army Discharge Review Board denied the reversal of the Undesirable in April 1972. Sowa added only that Doug had no representative present other than someone from the Red Cross. This bit of information was the only insight my parents ever had with regard to the deliberations of the Army Discharge Review Board, who claimed that "no minutes were kept of the Board's action."

Stunningly, Mr. Sowa made *no reference whatever* to the reports, the lengthy denials, the emphatic defeats that Colonel Hughett and General Enemark of the Inspector General's office inflicted on Doug Johnson. He makes no mention of the Duddy hearing, no mention the December 1969 AWOL or news reports of plane crashes. The registered Medical denial, yes. The Army Discharge Review Board denial, yes. But the Inspector General's Office? They were not mentioned by name, not mentioned at all. And yet it's abundantly clear that Mr. Sowa read General Enemark's Final Report. He quoted from it at length without citing the source, including words attributed to the psychiatrist: "Immature personality with drug abuse." This incredible omission, other than references to the psychiatrist (which now seems to support a discharge due to drug addiction) suggests to me that Sowa found the Inspector General's assessment spurious. Or Kenneth BeLieu found it spurious. Or Robert Mardian found it spurious. Someone in authority found it spurious.

Indeed, Sowa's very last point, *Number 15*, acknowledged that drug use lay at the root of Doug's problems, adding (just above his signature):

> That Army Regulation 635-212 applicable at the time of the applicant's separation, provided for an Undesirable Discharge when separation was for unfitness due to drug addiction or the unauthorized use or possession of habit forming drugs, marijuana, misconduct etc. etc.

Just below this my father has handwritten: "If the reg [ulation] applied for a 212, why didn't General Burke follow the rec [commendation] of JACG?" (Paul Kleinwachter's "What is to be done with Private Johnson?" letter). The wording of number 15 implies that the terms of "Operation Awareness," in effect in 1970, could have been invoked to secure a discharge other than Undesirable. However, the wording here could also be read to mean that at the time my brother left the Army, an Undesirable discharge was a possible outcome for "unfitness due to drug addiction." (This, remember, was not the official reason given.)

This, the Army's adversarial brief, echoed (sometimes verbatim) my father's longtime contentions in support of an Honorable discharge.

• • •

The top of the first page of Sowa's summary lists Doug's name and social security number, the place where the Army Board for Correction of Military Records will meet, Room 1E-517 in the Pentagon, the date of the review, 8 November 1972. And "Counsel: Mr. Robert Mardian."

I would have guessed that this last was Mr. Sowa's assumption because the request for review of the case had originated with Mardian. But it might not have been. On October 13, Bill, exuding both chutzpah and high-flown flattery, wrote:

Dear Mr. Mardian,

> We received a notice from the Army Board for Correction of Military Records of the case hearing for Douglas set for Wednesday, 9 a.m., November 8 in Room 11-517 at the Pentagon.
>
> On November 7th, President Nixon will have won the election and will have been re-elected to another term as President of the United States. Your Committee to Re-elect the President has done its job well. On November 8th, the Army Board for correction of Military Records will sit in judgment, of a request for reversal of discharge from Undesirable to Honorable. Douglas must also win.

Then, being my father—he cannot help himself—he heaps more clarifying information into the letter, concluding with:

> Everyone needs someone, sometime, Mr. Mardian, In this case, your presence at the hearing would be more than an act of gracious befriendment. Doug has literally lived in hell, or worse. He has brushed death in more ways than one, and tonight he is at the college library studying Chaucer for a class in English Literature. What I am pointing out is that Doug's Armenian heritage has given him guts, and he knows where he is going. Without real guts, which gave him the initiative, stamina, and desire to fight for his strength, all our love, medical help, and guidance would have been inconsequential. He would have been a tax burden instead of a taxpayer. Here is a young

man worthy of your assistance. Doug's moral fiber, his attitude, his mental and physical strength are exemplary to youth today.

Mr. Mardian, would it be possible for you to appear to represent Doug at 9 a.m. on November 8 at the Pentagon?

We have taken the liberty of advising the Board that Doug would be represented at the hearing. If for any reason you are unable to appear on that date, would you please so advise the Board? If you are unable to appear at all, would you please forward enclosed comments . . . ?

"Taken the liberty of advising the Board . . . " Really? My father must have dreamed of some sort of dramatic courtroom scene where—on behalf of the greatness yet to be redeemed in Douglas Johnson—the honorable Robert Mardian addressed the "Gentlemen of the Court." But instead, Bill was about to get his ears pinned back and a rap on the knuckles.

[Official stationary of the Committee for the Re-Election of the President]

October 18 1972

Dear Mr. Johnson,

I received the enclosed today. As I told you earlier, I am not in a position to get involved in this matter any further than transmitting to the Department of the Army the request relayed through you. I would suggest that you obtain counsel for your son and notify the appropriate Army Board of the fact that he will represent your son

Very truly yours,
Robert C. Mardian.

My father realized he had egregiously overstepped himself. His apology, quoted below, is probably the shortest letter Bill Johnson wrote in all the papers exhumed from the basement.

October 21, 1972
Mr. Robert C. Mardian
Committee for the Re-election of the President
1701 Pennsylvania Avenue, N. W. Washington, D. C, 20006

Dear Mr. Mardian:

I wish to apologize to you for any inconvenience the correspondence has caused you and for the volume precipitated by the crossing of mail. I am embarrassed at having misinterpreted your letter of July 13.

Please accept the sincere gratitude and thanks of our entire family, and our very good wishes to you. We shall let you know the outcome of the hearing.

Sincerely yours,
William J. Johnson

Bill must have spoken to Francis Plant on the telephone before the "crossing of mail." Plant probably also told him that Mardian would not act as Doug's attorney. On October 19, my father wrote to Mardian, "We feel it is only through your interest [that] the formal hearing is being held, and we are most grateful." He enclosed a copy of the October 19 letter he wrote to Mr. Plant acknowledging that the case would be heard on the basis of the documents alone, with no attorney present.

Even so, the Johnsons had new confidence in their case. Never mind that they had been defeated three times before. This time, the Army's own case *against Doug* held significant material supporting Bill's contentions. These documents arose from within the Pentagon itself. The case that my father had spent years developing was escorted to the meeting with the unspoken aegis of Undersecretary of the Army Kenneth E. BeLieu and brought before the Army Board for Correction of Military Records by Mr. BeLieu's special assistant, Mr. Francis Plant. Mr. Robert Mardian would not appear as attorney on Private Johnson's behalf, but—as those officers on the Board surely knew—the case came to them with the imprimatur of Robert Mardian, a man who had served at the very top echelons of the Nixon administration and who was serving now at the very top of the Committee to Re-Elect the President.

Historically—that is, in retrospect—we can also see that the timing could not have been more cosmically auspicious. The election held the day before the hearing resulted in a Nixon landslide, thus adding further luster to Mardian's reputation as counsel to CREEP.

On November 8, 1972, the morning after the election—and three years almost to the day from his court-martial in Vietnam—the case of Private Douglas Scott Johnson went before the Army Board for Correction of Military Records in the Pentagon's own Room 11-517. I picture perhaps six or eight middle-aged, maybe even elderly men, officers, clean-shaven, crew-cut, uniformed, decorated, facing each other at a polished oval table under fluorescent lights in a paneled conference room, shuffling through the dossier *Douglas Scott Johnson*, their hands literally holding the fate of a twenty-two-year-old veteran.

I picture Bill and Peggy Johnson on November 8 with their hands knotted, sitting at their kitchen table at Turrill Court. The coffee is going cold in their cups. Never mind that it is a Wednesday and they ought to be at work. They can't move. Too much is at stake for their beloved son for the rest of his life.

And Robert Mardian? I feel certain that on November 8 and every day after that for the rest of his life, he and all the Watergate conspirators—men later indicted, convicted, humiliated, some of them imprisoned, their reputations forever ruined, their names irrevocably tarnished—must have shaken their metaphoric fists at fate. Never mind the Watergate break-in, never mind civil unrest nationwide, never mind the increasingly unpopular Vietnam war: On November 7 Nixon swept that 1972 election like a hurricane through Florida Keys. He flattened his opponent, George McGovern, carrying all but two states on his rampage to victory. Given that sweeping victory, on November 8, the plot to bug the Democrats at the Watergate complex must surely have seemed an exercise in comic futility.

And though the implications of that break-in would unfurl over many months, I find it absolutely fitting that Nixon himself eventually paid the price for it, forced to resign in disgrace in August 1974, thus bringing his entire presidency and all his decades of public life to a deservedly ignominious close.

General Discharge

Under Honorable Conditions
from the Armed Forces of the United States of America

This is to certify that

DOUGLAS SCOTT JOHNSON   PRIVATE E-1   INF   REGULAR ARMY

was Discharged from the

United States Army

on the 25th *day of* August 1970 *under honorable conditions*

LOUIS J. PROST
BRIGADIER GENERAL   USA

DD FORM 257A
MAY 50

24. Victory—and Surrender

1973

Department of the Army
Office of the Under Secretary Washington DC 20310
18 December 1972

MEMORANDUM FOR THE ADJUTANT GENERAL

Having approved the findings, conclusions and recommendation of the Army Board for the Correction of Military Records, and under the provisions of 10 W. S. C. 1552, it is directed:

That all of the Department of the Army records of DOUGLAS S. JOHNSON be corrected to show that he was separated on a Certificate of General Discharge from the Army of the United States on 25 August 1970.

That the Department of the Army issue to DOUGLAS S. JOHNSON a Certificate of General Discharge from the Army of the United States, dated 25 August 1970 in lieu of the Undesirable Discharge of the same date now held by him.

(sgd) Kenneth E. BeLieu

Kenneth E. BeLieu

Under Secretary of the Army

There it was. Signed by the Undersecretary of the Army.

On December 19, the Executive Secretary for the Board for Correction of Military Records sent a similar note to the American Red Cross, cc'ing Douglas S. Johnson, Senator Mike Mansfield, and Congressman Jerry L. Pettis.

On December 19, Jerry Pettis sent a telegram to the director of the Veterans Administration Regional Office, Los Angeles, California, that read:

RE: CLAIM DOUGLAS S. JOHNSON [address], SECRETARY OF ARMY HAS CHANGED CHARCTER OF DISCHARGE TO GENERAL UNER HONORABLE CONDITIONS. AM SURE YOU WILL RECIVE OFFICIAL NOTIFCATION NEAR FUTURE AND WILL APPRECIATE YOUR FAVORABLE RECONSIDERATION OF HIS CLAIM AS SOON AS POSSIBLE. PLEASE ADVISE BY PHONE WHEN ACTION IS TAKEN.

Cc: Mr. William Johnson

Department of the Army
Office of the Under Secretary Washington DC 20310
29 January 1973
Mr. Douglas Scott Johnson
3246 Turrill Court
San Bernardino, California 92405

Dear Mr. Johnson:

The records have been corrected in accordance with the findings of the Army Board for Correction of Military Records. New separation documents are inclosed. [*sic*]

The Commander, US Army Finance Support Agency, Indianapolis, Indiana 46249 has been informed of the correction of the records.

Interested parties and your counsel have been furnished [with] a report of the action taken in your case.

Sincerely
Verne L. Bowers
Major General USA
The Adjutant General
Inclosures [sic]

The new "General Discharge Under Honorable Conditions from the Armed Forces of the United States of America" was enclosed, along with an official form noting that Doug had the Vietnam Service Medal with one Bronze Star, Republic of Vietnam Campaign Medal, Ribbon with device, and National Defense Service Medal. My parents made probably sixty copies of this document, which I found in the basement in its own big envelope. These slick, now-gray pages have retained a peculiar smell from the duplicating process. For my parents, that odor would have been the scent of victory. At last Doug's military service was acknowledged and his future was now assured; he would have health care, educational help, a path to home ownership, and he would not be excluded from teaching or any profession he chose. (If the medals listed were ever sent to my brother, there's no mention of them among the papers that came up from the basement.)

Christmas 1972 and early 1973 brought a rush of optimism and happiness to everyone at Turrill Court. In several of the many thank-you letters Bill wrote, he used the phrase, "If only you could have been here to share Doug's elated reaction, as well as ours, I'm certain you would have considered your efforts well worthwhile."

However, the General Discharge Under Honorable Conditions fell short of their hopes for an unambiguous, declarative Honorable. I suspect that the Army Board for Correction of Military Records opted for this rather than the Honorable because the General Discharge Under Honorable Circumstances provided the Army with an opportunity to right what was clearly a vindictive wrong inflicted on a vulnerable enlisted man, and yet not wholly acknowledge that an injustice had been done. In short, they could still save face.

· · ·

The next order of business for the Johnsons meant adhering to the rules of courtesy regarding the thank-you note. My mom was firm and unrelenting on this rule. When we were young, the Johnson children were not allowed to play with or enjoy any gift that came to us until we had written one.

My father wrote effusive, over-the-top letters of enormous, unstinting gratitude to everyone who had been supportive: Pettis, Mansfield, Mardian, and others, including Francis Plant, Ken BeLieu, and George Sowa. The letters looked back over the long struggle, the "problems that seemed unsurmountable," and particularly, in the case of Pettis and Mansfield, thanked both men for their years of support and contributions to the fight. All of these letters also looked forward to Doug's rosy future, when he would be "teaching and helping others," and stated that Doug's successes "on the highway of life may be due in part to your persistence in trying to right a wrong."

To Mr. Mardian, Bill wrote:

Mr. Mardian, Doug is totally indebted to you for his discharge reversal. Both our previous applications had never even reached a formal hearing stage, yet it was the same application with the same facts, the same problems, the same young man, and the same request.

In the opinion of historians, a man's stature is measured by his deeds. Even though historians will not record this event, to us, you are that man of stature and more, because you helped an unknown young man in a comparatively hopeless situation where for more than two years all avenues and approaches for reversal had been tried and were completely blocked, each with finality.

It is my fervent hope that you will please accept our deepest and sincere, heartfelt thanks. If in the annals of our lifetime, we ever owe a debt of gratitude to an individual, Doug and our family all owe you. It is also my hope that the day may come when we will be able in some way to satisfy this debt, regardless of time element. We all would welcome this opportunity.

In January and February 1973 there was a great flurry of stately replies from these men writing on official government letterhead. The note from Robert Mardian was from a quite different place:

Mardian Construction Company, Phoenix Arizona
February 1 1973
Mr. William J. Johnson and
Mr. Douglas Johnson
3246 Turrill Court
San Bernardino, California 92405

Dear Messrs. Johnson:

Your letters finally reached me circuitously and I appreciate them very much. By acknowledging your thanks, however, I would not like to leave the impression that it was I who was responsible for the action of the board and reversing the decision in Douglas' case. I simply asked the Secretary of the Army to insure that the matter was properly reviewed.

The important thing now is for Douglas to prove to himself, if to no one else, that the anguish all of you went through has not been in vain. I trust that it will not. As for the debt of gratitude you feel the family owes me, I would suggest that it could be discharged very simply by Douglas living up to the faith that his parents have in him. Thank you again for your thoughtfulness.

Warmest personal regards,
Robert C. Mardian

In the second paragraph of this dignified, touching note Robert Mardian, knowingly or unknowingly, stated plainly the hope that was closest to my parents' heart.

. . .

My father was not content to acknowledge simply with thank-you notes. To his principal allies in this struggle, he gifted marble-based pen sets. They each cost about seventy-five dollars, quite a lot in that era. (The invoice from a local stationary store is among the documents preserved in the basement safe.) Each was a pale amber marble slab base about eight inches long and six inches wide with notches for two ball point pens. I still have the one that sat on my mother's desk for decades. It was returned to my parents in 1973 because Francis Plant and George Sowa were prohibited from accepting gifts.

28 March 1973

Dear Mr. Johnson,

This is in reference to your letters to Mr. George Sowa and me, both dated March 19th 1973. The delay in writing concerning the pen desk sets has been solely mine. It has been occasioned by the need to consult with the General Counsel of the Department relative [to] our acceptance of these items. As I conjectured, we are prohibited by Departmental regulations from accepting. Mr. Sowa and I truly are most grateful for the thoughtfulness. However, you are assured that the relief in Douglas' case was predicated solely on the facts thereof and not upon any expectation that gratitude, much less, a gift, would result.

Under the foregoing circumstances we have no alternative but to return the sets to you. They are being forwarded under separate cover with a copy of this letter. . . .

With appreciation, I regret that you and Douglas have been inconvenienced and with regards and best wishes, I am

Sincerely,
Francis X Plant
Special Assistant

Two other people to whom Bill Johnson sent these pen sets could accept them, and did.

My dad sent one to Paul Kleinwachter early on, shortly after Doug had returned home, and even before he had requested Paul's help in finding Dr. Cantrell. Paul's response is handwritten and typically gracious:

6 October 1970
The Bill Johnson family
3246 Turrill Court
San Bernardino California 92405

Dear Johnsons,

I was completely overwhelmed yesterday to find that I had received a package from you and upon opening it, of course found the beautiful pen set. I couldn't have received a more beautiful and exquisite yet practical gift. It stands out as being the one "nice" possession that I have in Vietnam.

Of course as a lawyer and especially a lawyer in military service my greatest joy and satisfaction are derived from providing meaningful assistance to a client, however you have provided me with a tangible asset which will serve as a reminder of association with the Johnsons. If you ever come to the Seattle-Tacoma area of Washington our residence is open to you.

Once again I thank you and anticipate that I'll receive many years of use from the pen set. Before I leave Vietnam I may even demand a desk nice enough to accommodate it.

Sincerely

Paul

By the way the pens work fine as you can see by their example.

. . .

Robert Mardian also could accept. He was no longer in government. He resigned from CREEP immediately after the election and he did not return to the Department of Justice in the second Nixon administration. He moved to Phoenix, returning to DC only for the Watergate hearings, the Watergate conspiracy trial, and, later, for the appeal against his conviction. In 1976 prosecutors announced they would not re-try him on conspiracy charges; his appeal was granted. In Phoenix he joined his brothers in the Mardian Construction Company as a vice president. He also had a summer home in the Southern California beach town of San Clemente. He died there in 2006.

In the files brought up from the basement in an envelope with a Phoenix return address, I found this handwritten note from Mrs. Mardian:

Feb 12th

My husband received your lovely gift and really appreciated it. Unfortunately it arrived damaged—a piece of the marble base was broken off. Probably because the package had to be forwarded. Since it was insured I took it back to the post office and they filed a claim and said they would return it you so that the base could be replaced. I'm sorry to cause you this much trouble but I figured you would probably want to know about it.

Thank you very much

Yours truly
Dorothy Mardian (Mrs. Robert C)

And separately, this last letter from Robert himself:

Robert C. Mardian [letterhead]
February 14 1973

Dear Mr. Johnson

I just received the beautiful desk set that you sent me after it had traveled to about three addresses. It was totally unnecessary but your thoughtfulness is very much appreciated. I am deeply grateful.

I had not intended to mention that the marble portion of the desk set was chipped in transit. But in view of the fact that you had it insured, it would seem that if we can have the marble portion inspected by the Post Office Department here, it would be worthwhile to do so.

The Post Office Department indicated to my wife that it would have to be reported by you. You might inquire and if the matter could be adjusted here, fine, if not I will let the chipped portion serve as a reminder of your travails.

Warmest personal regards,
Robert C. Mardian

It seems to me metaphorically correct that the marble stand was damaged when it reached Robert Mardian in 1973. For myself, I like to think that in the grueling years that lay ahead for him and his family—years of anguish in which his name would be inextricably linked with those of arrogant criminals and inept clowns—he used the pen set with its chipped marble base. I like to think of it on his desk, and that he was reminded of the travails of the Johnson family, and I hope that he knew these were people who would be forever grateful for his assistance, who would always think of him as a generous spirit.

• • •

In spring 1973 my father petitioned the Army Board for Correction of Military Records for the General Discharge Under Honorable Circumstances to be amended simply to Honorable. Was this new request occasioned by fear or intuition, or even evidence that Doug still suffered from a sense of shame and disgrace? Or was it reflexive activism on his son's behalf? In any event, the same Major General Bowers who had written with the wonderful news of reversing the Undesirable denied this request. The letter, addressed to Doug, read in part:

April 18th 1973

The Army Discharge Review Board, after careful consideration of your military records and all other available evidence has determined that you were properly discharged. Accordingly the Secretary of the

Army has directed that you be advised that your request for a change in the type and nature of your discharge has been denied.

Interested parties and your counsel have been informed of the Board's decision.

Verne L. Bowers
Major General USA
The Adjutant General

This letter is interesting. There's no mention of the Army Board for the Correction of Military Records, the entity that had reversed the Undesirable and to whom my father had appealed. The request has gone back to—and the reply comes from—the Army Discharge Review Board, who in April 1972 had already denied Doug's appeal, asserting there were no minutes of their meetings during the year they required to deny. The wording here is *verbatim* their original denial. Also, as with the letter reversing the Undesirable, I cannot help but wonder who the "Interested parties" were. Jerry Pettis? Mike Mansfield? Possibly Kenneth BeLieu? "Your counsel . . . " Might that have been Robert Mardian, who had left Washington and had no role in the second Nixon administration? Were any Army men among the "interested parties"? These questions have no answers.

In any event, Bill Johnson did not contest this ruling. It was over. My parents put General Bowers's letter in its own envelope, packed up all these papers and letters and carbons and articles and telegrams, and shoved them into the bottom of the safe. And there everything stayed for over fifty years.

Except . . . in January 1974 Bill Johnson reached out one last time, approaching his ally, Francis Plant, assistant to Kenneth E. BeLieu. BeLieu had left his post as Undersecretary of the Army in 1973, so who knows where Francis Plant was, or if the letter ever reached him. When I opened the safe, I found a flimsy carbon copy just lying there, no envelope at all. I did not understand its orphaned significance until I had been many times through everything I took from the safe.

January 21 1974

Dear Mr. Plant:

I am writing to you for information relative to the final disposition of Douglas's Army discharge.

As you recall Douglas' Army undesirable discharge was reversed in 1972 to a general discharge. It is my understanding that after a period of six months or so, application may be made to the Army for a full, honorable discharge from the general. Douglas is a junior and a full time student at Cal-State in San Bernardino and will graduate next year and continue to graduate school for a secondary teaching credential.

If you would advise us of the procedures to follow for this Army discharge change, I would very much appreciate your assistance in this matter.

We all wish for you and yours the very best in the new year, 1974.

Sincerely yours,
William J. Johnson

That only this letter, of all the documents, was unhoused in an envelope suggests to me that when Francis Plant did not reply, at some point either my mother or my father opened the safe and tossed in the carbon. The door closed. The lock spun.

25. After

As of New Year's Day 1977, the Army ceased giving Undesirable discharges. The term itself was retired, though soldiers could still be released with a discharge that cited "other than honorable conditions." A tiny notice tucked at the bottom of page 64 of the New York *Times* on December 30, 1976, read, "More than 500,000 persons who have received undesirable discharges since 1948 will be eligible for a change in their status. About 173,000 of them were administratively discharged during the Vietnam war." Undesirable faded like a bad odor, a fart in the wind.

I do not know if my parents were even aware that Undesirable had been tossed onto the scrap heap of history. The San Bernardino *Sun Telegram* probably did not include such a small notice. Even if they knew, they would have been deterred from initiating new action by the devastating loss of Jerry Pettis who died in a private plane crash in February 1975. (Fittingly, the Veterans Hospital in San Bernardino County was renamed in Pettis's honor and remains so to this day.) Apart from that sadness, the late 1970s and early 1980s were good years for the Johnsons. Peggy escaped the portly Republican insurance agent and now worked as secretary to an orthopedic surgeon at County Hospital, a job with actual benefits and congenial coworkers where she was respected and admired. Bill's enormous energy was channeled into a new job. Lederle Laboratories had acquired Fisher Scientific, a firm that made diagnostic materials and medical tests. Bill transferred to Fisher and embraced new challenges, new colleagues. The family had weddings to celebrate, graduations. Best of all, Bear was born in 1979 and Brendan in 1983; the two boys lit up everyone's lives and their grandparents doted on them.

In 1987 my parents, both retired now, sold their San Bernardino home and moved to Washington to be near me and my sons. They were deeply immersed in our lives, as we were in theirs. They enjoyed good times and many satisfactions watching the boys grow up. They remained in Washington for the rest of their lives. They are buried here. A man who began life in St. Anthony, Idaho, surrounded by stubbled fields of sugar beets and a woman whose first cries echoed in the Armenian quarter of Istanbul lie together in a rural cemetery near the Canadian border, surrounded by rustling poplars.

• • •

By 1975 Doug had quit San Bernardino State University, so the struggle for educational benefits was moot. He would never be an English teacher. Perhaps he just lost interest in college, or possibly he flunked out. (SBSU did not reply to my inquiry regarding his records.) However, he was a homeowner. Thanks to his VA benefits, he bought a cheap, small nine-hundred-square-foot house, something of a comfy shack in an undeveloped area up near the university. It had a fenced yard, and he lived there with a cute little dog named Arrow after the dog in the song "The Point" and a lovely new girl-friend, a student at SBSU. Doug was unkind to animals and to people, and by 1976 she had left him and she took Arrow with her.

But he soon met an educator, a divorcée with a school-age son. She was attractive, articulate, had a good job as a school administrator in a town some thirty miles from San Bernardino where she owned a home. Doug went to live with her and rented out his own little place (Mom oversaw the rental). The parents liked this woman and had high hopes that she would bring out the best in Doug. In 1980 she and Doug were married.

The wife began pressuring Doug to sell his little San Bernardino house so they could finance construction of their custom dream home. My mom, very uneasy with this, tried to talk him out of it, to no avail. Sell it he did, and the money went into construction of their new house. Doug had various jobs, none of them lasting very long. He returned to his addictions. The marriage deteriorated. My mother was frantic and when the wife began divorce proceedings, Mom paid for a lawyer for Doug. However, Doug was agreeing to everything the wife wanted, including terminating his lawyer. I was teaching in Washington State, so when Mom called with this dire news, I sent her eight hundred dollars to rehire the lawyer. But finally it didn't matter. Doug capitulated to his wife's every demand and lost everything. As a family, we were pissed off—not that she should have divorced him, an understandable act when he relapsed into drug use—but that she should keep two houses and deprive him of the one place that might have sheltered him.

Doug drifted back to San Bernardino, homeless, jobless, impoverished, drug-addicted, struggling with alcohol, PTSD, and bouts of rage. He plunged downward into pathos and squalor. He crashed with friends and various women but sometimes he showed back up at Turrill Court broke, high, and hungry, where he clashed with Dad, who was retired and so often at home.

Moreover, Dad was unhappy, having been forcibly retired. The corporation pushed him out of the Fisher Scientific job, not for lack of performance, but because of his age, though he was only in his early sixties. He fell into an uncharacteristic slump, sitting at home, drinking more than he used to. In early summer of 1986 my father paid the deposit and the first month's rent on an apartment in San Bernardino, gave Doug some furniture, and told him to get out and stay out. Dad and Mom locked up their house and came to England for three months with my sons and me while I worked on a book. When they returned to San Bernardino in the fall, the apartment was empty. The landlord tried to get Dad to pay the damages Doug had left behind and the back rent he had run out on.

Forged in adversity, the deep bond between father and son ought to have endured, but it did not. In all his many letters my father had persistently warned that the next half century of Doug's life would be determined by what happened in 1969, 1970, 1971, and 1972. His prophecies proved sadly correct. Doug's life did not unfurl in the banner of fulfillment that Bill had promised every person he had beseeched on his son's behalf. My father's consummate faith in Doug's worth—faith that had sustained him through the entire battle from beginning to end—waned, eroded, leaving Dad with what, in my opinion, amounted to a small, hard, stubborn nub of bitterness. Surrendering his faith in Doug, Bill stepped back from the struggle. Father and son were not outright estranged, but a distinct chill grew between them, and they kept their distance.

Bill had fought a three-year battle on Doug's behalf, but he was not equal to what amounted to a thirty year siege. Peggy Johnson was in it for the siege. She would never wholly forgive my father for giving up on Doug. Acrimony and resentment bubbled beneath the surface of their long marriage and sometimes erupted.

. . .

At the very nadir of Doug's post-Nam life in the late 1980s, fate crossed his path with that of a woman he had known at Cal State San Bernardino when they were students. She had always adored him. She was by now a professional woman, living near the beach in Ventura County, and she lovingly plucked Doug out of misery and brought him to live with her. He gave her the tender nickname "Freen," short for friend, and she was indeed a friend to him. Freen paid for private rehab, for vast amounts of dental work (his teeth had rotted and/or fallen out from Agent Orange). For his fortieth birthday in 1990 Freen gave him a wetsuit and a custom surfboard; he loved surfing and he spent many happy hours riding the waves. He joined their Neighborhood Watch. To this day she remembers that Doug could be caring and playful and attentive, bringing her coffee in bed in the mornings, sharing a glass of wine on the beach at sunset. They had a sweet domestic idyll that Freen later likened to the contentment expressed in the lyrics of "Our House." They even had two cats in the yard.

Freen and Doug got engaged, though she did so with the caveat that if he relapsed into drug use, they would be finished. They married in late 1991. Doug's parents were delighted. Her well-to-do parents were dismayed. In the summer of 1992 she and Doug came to Washington and we had a party for them at my house. Doug seemed like his old bright, charming self. We all cherished hopes that Freen had restored him to the man he was meant to be.

Freen outfitted Doug with new clothes and a nice car so he could look for work. Veterans' preference helped him get a job with the postal service, where he processed letters on a conveyor belt, but the onrush of letters, the regimented demands were too much for him and he was fired. For a while he worked at Carl's Jr., a fast food chain in Southern California; he claimed he was in management training, but even if this were true, he didn't last long. Other jobs came and went. His last job was soliciting ads by telephone for a newspaper, work that suited his chatty personality. One day Freen called there only to be told he had been fired some time before. He had never told her.

Doug relapsed. His sense of scruples or obligation or decency became casualties of his addiction. He forged Freen's name on her checks, cleaning out her bank account. He ran up her credit cards at big-ticket stores, buying items that could be sold to pay off drug dealers. Strange, menacing people came around the little beach cottage they shared. Three years into the marriage, Freen got a formal financial separation. But before she divorced him altogether and moved away, she filled out all the bureaucratic paperwork to get him on Disability by virtue of PTSD, mental illness, and Agent Orange. This was a great kindness, and we were all grateful to her. She had his Disability checks sent to his mother in Washington and Mom mailed his room-rent to the landlady. Mom also sent him a weekly cash allowance from the Disability check. Doug lived in Ventura County for the rest of his life, but he never had a job after 1993.

Mom did the necessary paperwork so that Doug could join the class-action suit instigated by veterans for the suffering inflicted by Agent Orange. He was awarded something like a whopping $132. What is the phrase? Oh, yes. Thank you for your service.

• • •

In November 1995 my mother surreptitiously paid for a plane ticket for Doug to come to Washington for Christmas. That is, she kept it secret from my father. When she told me, I said, "Well, fine, let him come up here, but I won't be here." I told her flatly and without euphemism that I would not let my sons, Bear and Brendan, be anywhere near Doug, that he was toxic and dangerous. She was not happy to hear me say this, but neither did she contest it. The boys and I went to my sister's and had a memorable, joyful holiday season in Southern California. When we returned, my mother told me simply, yes, they had had a fine Christmas with Doug. My dad just shrugged and said nothing. Later, privately, he told me that Doug was continually high and bizarre, often drunk; Dad had wanted to leave, to go to my house and get away from Doug, but felt he had to stay to protect Mom.

By the early 2000s—thirty years after his return from Vietnam—Doug's life had calmed. He was no longer doing drugs, though I think he was on prescribed medications to keep him even-keeled. VA benefits had allowed him to be fitted with new dentures. The house where he rented a room had a vegetable garden that he tended happily. He had taken up benign activities, like writing poems in elegant calligraphy, colored inks on fine paper that he sent regularly to Mom, often in envelopes that were themselves hand-decorated with glitter and adorned with quips and lyrics. However, some of these hobbies were freaking weird, like scavenging bones from local restaurants, boiling them clean, and fashioning "jewelry" from them. He sent Mom and me each a pair of earrings he made from boiled bones. These were so creepy that I threw them in the trash immediately. (At her insistence, naturally, I wrote him a thank-you note.) Much as she adored him, I never saw her wear the pair he gave to her. Doug called Mom once or twice a week, greeting her always with, "Hello Mary Sunshine!" If Dad answered the phone, the two of them would chat pleasantly for a bit and then Dad handed the phone on to Mom.

Doug played a lot of guitar. He sent Mom cassette tapes of himself singing covers of classic rock songs and occasionally tunes he wrote himself. Sometimes he performed locally. In an especially poignant tape he sent her, he's playing in a coffeehouse, covering "Born Under a Bad Sign." When he finishes, he takes a deep breath, and the applause is scattered and wan. His music was the best of him.

In 2008 Doug married for the third time, to his widowed landlady. She took out a reverse mortgage on her house and Doug wanted to use some of the money to come to Washington to visit. My mom asked me if it was okay with me and I said yes. There was no need to fear for my sons, who were grown men, college grads, working musicians living in LA.

I collected Doug and his new wife at the airport and took them to their hotel. Then we went to the parents' house nearby. My mother had been cooking for days, Armenian specialties, and we all sat down to a sumptuous meal, the table set with her best china and crystal, candles, ironed napkins in silver rings. To see my mother gaze at Doug was to know the true meaning of the phrase *feast one's eyes*. My father, afflicted with dementia from a stroke two years before, recognized Doug, and was genuinely happy to see him, but kept asking me quietly, "Who is that woman?"

Doug's wife, who was probably older than he was, wore a cute hat and lacy little mitts on her hands. She kept saying, "God bless, God bless," to punctuate the conversation. She seemed very sweet, very much in love, and clearly content to smile in his shadow, to now and then chide him affectionately. On that five-day visit Doug, typically, took up more than his share of oxygen, but he had mellowed, and there was no talk of a chain of human ears, only boorish gaffes and crude lapses such as his table conversation about his really big dick.

That visit was the last time any of us in Washington saw him, though he continued to call Mom often with "Hello, Mary Sunshine" and send her letters, poems, and lyrics creatively embellished with elegant calligraphy. I later found them all when I cleaned out her house.

• • •

In 2018 Doug had a health crisis resulting in a series of major abdominal surgeries, and his recovery was long and difficult, requiring three months of care between the VA hospital and nursing homes. And yet he did recover. In October 2020 Doug telephoned my sister Helen and said he had been diagnosed with liver cancer and had six months to live. Bouts of hepatitis, decades of drug use and heavy drinking, to say nothing of the ravages of Agent Orange, had no doubt shredded his liver long before the cancer got to him. Still, this was a shocking revelation because physically, he was incredibly resilient.

When Helen telephoned me with this news she added: "You had better make your peace with him, if you're going to do it." A complex command I could evade for the moment because I had to drive to my widowed mother's house and tell her that Doug had terminal cancer.

Mom was ninety-nine and, amid the stress of the COVID pandemic and lockdown, her spirits had flagged and her stamina had faltered. For months now she had seldom gone out of the house, not even for short walks. She had quit cooking, so I brought her meals from my house and did the dishes. That day I sat her at the little table facing the front window and poured her a cup of tea from a freshly made pot. I took her hand and told her this heartbreaking news of her beloved son. I then telephoned him, using the speaker on my cell phone and putting it close to her ear. (She was by this time quite deaf.) I was grateful that Doug seemed upbeat with her, talking about treatments and so on. I do not know if what he said was the truth. I didn't even care. My immediate concern was my mother's health, her spirits, her well-being.

That autumn Helen, Brian, and I reached out to Doug with frequent phone calls. Though I recognized that cordial conversations were not the same thing as making my peace with him, still, when we spoke on the phone, I always thought: Why did it take decades and liver cancer to arrive at this, someone you could simply chat with? Mom and I spoke with Doug often. Invariably he pulled himself together to talk to her cheerfully. He truly loved her, and this was the best gift he could give her. I feel sure that he knew as much.

Doug did not have six months to live. In December 2020 he went into hospice. The program set up a hospital bed in his home and nurses came on a schedule. Given the demands of the raging pandemic, hospice services and personnel were stretched thin, and pain meds for Doug were not always delivered on time. My sister once called his house and could hear him bellowing in the background, *Get me out of here! Get me out of here!* Hospice also told my sister that he was not taking the meds at the times prescribed, but gulping them, that this behavior was common among drug addicts, or former drug addicts. Because Doug's elderly wife was herself unwell and undone by his illness, we, Helen, Brian, and I mostly dealt with her daughter, a nurse who lived near to them and checked in frequently.

On January 5, 2021, Brian tried to call Doug, only to learn that he had died earlier that morning. Brian tearfully phoned me. I would have to tell Mom.

For the women in my family, cooking is caring. I took food out of the freezer, supplies we always kept on hand from Mediterranean Specialties, a local Lebanese deli, and a bottle of wine and put all of it in the car. I had barely started down the street when Ennio Morricone's lush, gorgeous theme from *The Mission* came on my random music. This rich, cascading music seemed to me both fitting and ironic for my brother. Tears streamed down my face and I choked down sobs as I thought about Doug, about his many gifts, all wasted, and the American tragedy that was his squandered life. When the Morricone theme ended, random brought up my son Bear's haunting "Wander My Friends" and I began to blubber all over again, the simple, sad thrum of farewell, the wistful Gaelic lyrics throbbed with loss. In the driveway I collected myself, turned off the car and went inside to tell my mother that Doug was dead. It was the hardest thing I have ever done, the hardest words I have ever spoken. I feared that she would collapse, that the news, the loss might kill her on the spot.

She gazed at me sadly and said in a bewildered tone, "I thought he would beat it."

"Yes," I said, "well, he beat everything else, didn't he? No one ever thought he would live to be seventy, but he did."

Five days later, on the night of January 10, 2021, my mother fell and had a heart attack, or possibly she had a heart attack and fell. We never did know. As I followed the ambulance from her house to the emergency room, I thought to myself, *He's going to kill her after all, isn't he?*

COVID restrictions prohibited visitors even in the ER, but because she was ninety-nine I was allowed to stay with her until they placed her in a room that night. I did not see her again for the ten days she was hospitalized, though we spoke often on the phone and I did my best to soothe her escalating fears. I kept in frequent contact with the nurses and doctors as well. For her recovery, the hospital sent her to a nursing home.

Because of the pandemic, the nursing home placed her in complete isolated quarantine for thirty days. Daily I went there and stood among the rhododendron bushes by her window, talking to her on a cell phone. Even when the quarantine lifted, visitors were required to have their temperatures checked and recorded at reception, to be masked and wear hospital gowns. After months of physical therapy my mom nonetheless remained confined to a wheelchair. She never went home again.

She lived in a private room in the nursing home for nearly three more years. Her charm and cheer made her many friends, and she was well cared for and happy there for a long time. However, early 2023 saw a change. As that year progressed she was increasingly beset by multiple infections, accelerating heart disease, and deepening dementia that often took the form of bouts of rage. Alarmed and saddened, I did not want to see her life end in anger. I called in hospice and they were able to administer medication to help calm her when needed. In December 2023, on a Thursday evening, the nursing home called to say she had tested positive for COVID, and before dawn on Saturday morning, they telephoned to say she had died. She was a hundred and one.

• • •

The General Discharge under Honorable Circumstances would have allowed Doug Johnson the VA burial that had been given to my dad when he died in 2012: a paid-for headstone, a flag-draped coffin, an honor guard to fold that flag ceremoniously and give it to the widow. But in January 2021 COVID remained rampant and people were not congregating, not even for funerals. Doug's wife's family was none too fond of him, anyway, and the wife herself was in poor health. On the phone her daughter told me that they would have Doug cremated. Two or three weeks later she called again and asked if we wanted his ashes. I thanked her, but declined, thinking to myself: *My mom has had a heart attack; she is quarantined in a nursing home. What do you think the sight of an urn with her son's ashes would do to her?* I did not mention this call to my mother, figuring that when Mom felt strong enough, she would ask after his funeral.

Months passed. I braced and kept waiting for her to ask me what had become of Doug's remains. To inquire if there had been some sort of Christian service for him. But she never did. Not in three years. Not even as prayer and her Christian faith came to be increasingly important to her. She kept pictures of him and the third wife among the family photos in her room. She spoke of Doug lovingly. But she never did ask after his burial and I never did say that he was cremated or that, as far as I knew, there was no farewell of any sort and I had no idea what had happened to his ashes.

26. "A Scar in the Canyons of My Memory"

Thus, to my knowledge, nothing—other than this book—marks that Douglas Johnson once walked this earth. Writing this book has answered my sister's challenge to make my peace with Doug. Writing this book has restored my brother, allowed me to recognize, to see, to remember him with something of the glow reflected in my father's repeated praises. It has allowed me to feel for Doug a complex concoction of affection, anger, pity, regard, regret, and rage—not at him, but on his behalf, for what was denied him, taken from him. What was taken from his immediate family, taken from Freen and others who loved him, including the young, blue-eyed fiancée he so adored, taken as well from people who wanted to love him but who finally had to step away from him.

In his November 8, 1969, letter to his parents, just days before the court-martial, Doug wrote that the charges against him had "left a scar in the canyons of my memory." Reading, rereading all these hundreds of pages I brought up from the basement, that phrase kept coming back to me. It seemed to me to ripple out far beyond those immediate circumstances. One could truly say that Vietnam scarred his life for fifty years after he agreed to accept the Undesirable "for the good of the service." For fifty years the demons he met in Vietnam continued to haunt him. For fifty years he paid for having been "an immature personality influenced by drug abuse," as General Enemark so sourly pontificated. Doug lived to be seventy years old, but this book also bears witness that a part of my brother died before he was twenty-one, not his body—his name is not on the granite wall—but his life.

Certainly the life Doug might have had died in Vietnam, the life his parents envisioned for him, wanted for him, the life they believed they could somehow endow him with if only the Undesirable were reversed. If the Honorable were bestowed, Doug would have all those blessings of a healthy maturity that my father so often invoked; he would be a teacher enjoying the satisfactions of a happy, productive life. All that was irrevocably lost. And for what? What happened in those fourteen months to so completely alter Doug Johnson's life, before he was even old enough to vote? The crimes for which the Army punished him were not crimes he inflicted upon on screaming women and wailing children. This was no crazed GI turning his firepower on a bunch of villagers. No murder. No manslaughter. No rape. Doug did not betray his comrades to the enemy. The dead man's sandal he clutched? The chain of human ears? Are these talismans of acts incompatible with conscience? Do they tell us that my brother saved his life but parted with his humanity? Doug Johnson persistently went "on patrol with his platoon in situations of very great hazard and terror," a psychiatrist's way of saying he was constantly scared shitless. He went AWOL time and again, going God knows where, doing God knows what, with God knows whom. He slept on guard duty. He had marijuana and LSD and speed in his possession. He was dirty and disheveled and unhygienic. He had long hair. He was "an ineffective infantryman." He was "frightening and pathetic." He was a speed freak. He was an opium addict. He shot up continually, seven and eight times a day, until his arms were like pincushions. These are the crimes for which the Army condemned him to carry the Undesirable, for which they finally offered the sop of a General Discharge Under Honorable Circumstances—a sop for which his parents were grateful even if they were not totally satisfied.

In this struggle, my father maintained an unswerving commitment to his son. From the November 3, 1969, letter in which Bill forsook forever Sgt-Major-Kick-His-Butt's assumptions, my father was Doug's greatest champion. When Doug was in the military hospital in Japan, Dad tried desperately to have him transferred out of Vietnam, moved to some new post, even some new job that did not involve combat, where he could fulfill his military duties with a modicum of dignity. In this, Bill failed. And once the ravaged shell of Doug Johnson returned home from Vietnam and Dad sat with him on the lawn at Loma Linda Hospital, learning that Doug ought not to have been sent to Cambodia at all, my father was fueled with righteous wrath. The Undesirable was undeserved and utterly unjust. "The General was not aware . . ." My mother typed this October 16, 1970, letter over and over and over again; those words must have been seared into her brain. When Captain Cantrell corroborated Doug's account with a signed letter, the parents felt certain of victory. But this was not to be.

Denials. Declines. Failures. In the fall of 1970, all of 1971, and right up until November 8, 1972, my father hammered and refined and expanded and backed up his arguments. Why did the Army repeatedly deny the truths he set forward? Doug ought to have had the "AR 635-212 that authorizes a general discharge for alcoholics," that Paul recommended because Doug was "a sick, sick individual who is badly in need of treatment." The 212 might well have been the same recommendation offered by the unnamed Army psychiatrist that George Sowa included in his assessment—and that General Enemark may have elided, evaded, or outright repressed in his paraphrase of that psychiatrist's diagnosis. Given the battered twenty-year-old body that fetched up at Loma Linda Medical Center, that doctor believed that Doug ought to have had a Medical discharge. Doug ought to have come under the canopy forgiveness for drug addicts announced in May 1972.

When the Inspector General's office read the transcript of Doug's testimony from the Duddy hearing, when they had Captain Cantrell's supporting letter in hand, why did they *allow* that Captain Cantrell wrote the note, but only *allege* that Doug had given it—as ordered—to some nameless sergeant major who then handed it to some equally nameless yahoo who could never be found again? Perhaps this nameless yahoo put a match to Cantrell's letter and lit a joint with it, since the Army acknowledges in *U.S. Army Psychiatry in the Vietnam War* that drugs were an epidemic among enlisted men in Vietnam, and that by 1970 these soldiers were moving rapidly from marijuana into heroin. When the Inspector General's Interim and Final reports conceded that Doug, stricken time and again with malaria and hepatitis, was "malnourished and dependent on drugs" and thus "an ineffective infantryman," why would the Army not acknowledge that his health had been shattered by the summer of 1970? Under what unknown criteria did the Central

Physical Evaluation Board at Walter Reed Army Hospital deny the Medical discharge that had had been at least informally agreed to at Letterman Hospital in San Francisco (following the actual physical)? Why, when Senator Mansfield inquired after that denial, did General Prost inform him that Doug's Undesirable was due to drug addiction? If that was so, why was my brother not offered the general forgiveness for drug addicts announced publicly in May 1972 by the Secretary of Defense? (An amnesty that they—Walter Reed and the Army Discharge Review Board—surely knew was already nominally in place from August 1970 with "Operation Awareness," to respond to the epidemic of heroin use.) Did the Army Discharge Review Board truly require a year to make their decision, a year in which they allegedly took no notes, no minutes of their deliberations, kept no records? Was their failure to document something on the same order as General Enemark's reference to "an active drug amnesty program [that] . . . precluded the keeping of formal records"? Why—despite Doug's open admissions of drug use, his confessions of being "strung out," and pleas for help throughout the Duddy hearing—did Colonel Hughett and General Enemark tepidly state they could not be absolutely certain that he had asked for help?

I have asked these and other questions of the past revealed in the papers from the basement safe. Many remain unanswered. Except, possibly to observe that the Army is an institution. Institutions defend themselves. These military men, all of them, melted back into their entities, into their officialdom, their acronyms, their titles, their offices adorned with flags, their crisp uniforms adorned with medals and ribbons; they remained allied to the institution, shackled to it, indistinguishable from it, and committed to their own correctness. They became, in the apt phrase of Pink Floyd, just "Another Brick in the Wall." The Army met my father's assertions with a solid brick wall of defeat.

Then, in November 1972, with George Sowa's fifteen-point silver bullet document and a raft of supporting documents before them, the Army Board for the Correction of Military Records granted a General Discharge Under Honorable Circumstances. That is as far as they would go. When Bill Johnson again pressed for an unambiguous Honorable in April 1973, the Army declined. Major General Verne Bowers informed Doug that the Army Discharge Review Board had "determined that you were properly discharged" based on "careful consideration of your military records and all other available evidence." Really? *All the other available evidence?* In fact, *all the other available evidence* suggests that the Army covered for General Burke's egregious reasoning that Doug was—and should for the rest of his life continue to be—Undesirable because he (the General) "observed the applicant on several occasions and had yet to see him clean or in proper uniform; that he refused to comply with the most basic of requirements and personal hygiene." Were there other sloppy, stinking, long-haired, drugged-up, fucked-up young infantrymen who were also filthy, ineffective, and undesirable? Was my brother alone in this?

Indeed, *all the other evidence* suggests that my brother was not alone in the muck and dirty mire that was America's failure in Vietnam, and not merely military failure, though God knows there was enough of that to go around. The military also failed its own men. Let us consult *U.S. Army Psychiatry in the Vietnam War* and ask ourselves what the military would do with the wracked and bloody wounded—men who stepped on booby traps or who were blinded, gouged, or felled by enemy fire, who had a leg blown off like the young soldier on November 14, 1969, who bled into foreign soil—what happens to them if all the hospital beds were taken by drug addicts? That book tells us that during Doug's time in Vietnam soldiers "threatened with prosecution for drug possession demanded hospitalization (for both detoxification and isolation from drug suppliers)." Demanded detox *and* isolation from drug suppliers? Whoa! That's a tall order! Doug Johnson told Colonel Duddy: "I was using ever since I got into Vietnam. From the time I got introduced to opium, I was mainlining." And the Army's response? "They gave me a bed for the night and then threw me out." *U.S. Army Psychiatry in the Vietnam War*, chapter 9 tells us why: "The incidence of heroin use became so high, that if inpatient hospital-level service was provided for all users . . . the hospitals could be overtaxed." Doug Johnson was one of those drugged-up, ineffective infantrymen, on point, leading a bunch of other, equally drugged-up men through the jungles, where "late at night you have to hang on to the guy in front of you because you can't see. If you let go, you have to stop because of the intensity of the dark." How deep was that terrible darkness? And yet they kept walking, these young men. Some of them kept walking until they died, some until they had a leg blown off. If, in these forays, men were wounded, at least there were hospital beds available. Or not. Doug testified in the case of both wounds he received that he was given a shot of morphine and sent back into the fray. Colonel Hughett and General Enemark denied the truth of his wounds because he wasn't sent to a hospital. So . . . maybe there weren't beds available after all. In short, *all the other evidence* gathered in these pages suggests something quite to the contrary of what Major General Verne Bowers offered.

The Army saw Doug Johnson—and Ed from Wisconsin and that bedraggled dude you see at the freeway interchange with his scrawny dog, his dirty backpack, his sign *Vietnam Vet, Anything Helps*—as troubled men, needy men, men bedeviled by drugs, men committing acts incompatible with conscience, grunts who were unreliable infantrymen. They were, in fact, the unwilling led by the unqualified to kill the unfortunate, and they came home to the profoundly ungrateful, returned to a society that distrusted and despised them. Douglas Johnson, E-1, lowest of the low, gruntiest of the grunts, was one of them. As I have put together this book, based on these letters and documents, the inescapable conclusion I see is that that to General Enemark, to Colonel Duddy, to Colonel Ralph H. Hughett, and to Major General Karl Gustafson and Colonel W. H. Brandenburg and Colonel W. K. Wittwer who vomited up stale, pale chunks of uninformative prose (all three of these latter officers replying on behalf of Richard Nixon, President of the United States) to Lieutenant Colonel Robert Serra, Adjutant General, who reported that Doug's battalion had "undergone a change in commanders. The previous commander . . . is no longer available for comment," to Major General John A. Goshorn who opined that at the time Doug was airlifted from Long Binh jail to a military hospital in Japan, he "was in no severe distress," to Mack M. Dugger, Administrative Officer, replying on behalf of the "Commanding Officer" (who finished his letter with the usual Bullshit Paragraph), to Kenneth Hodson, Major General USA The Judge Advocate General, replying in July 1970 on behalf of the elusive Mr. Finch of the White House that he had no information whatever on Doug though he vowed to "write again" (and offered not another word, ever), to Major General William A. Becker, Chief of Legislative Liaison, Department of the Army, who also never replied to Jerry Pettis's plea ("I would sincerely appreciate any advice you might be able to offer providing

Private Douglas S. Johnson the opportunity to complete his enlisted service in an honorable fashion"), to LTC McKee, the commanding officer of the 3rd Battalion, 12th Infantry, who would recommend that Doug's request for discharge be disapproved and the court-martial should proceed, to the E-5 who lost Doug's records somewhere between Vietnam and Fort Lewis, to Doug's so-called counsel at the November 1969 court-martial who offered eighteen words into the trial record (and those not even on behalf of his client), to the S1 who greeted Doug after he'd been AWOL for eight days in December 1969, who asked if Doug had anything to say and when Doug replied yes, said, "I don't want to hear it" and who then ordered him arrested and escorted under armed guard to the hell known as Long Binh Jail, to the unnamed sergeant major "who seemed to me very much against me due to my rank as an E1 and the fact that I had long hair," who (not allegedly but for real) took Dr. Cantrell's letter and gave it to an equally unnamed Sergeant E-7 who "may have returned the profile to the Sgt. Major" or who may have simply lost it or wiped his butt with it for all we know, to the Captain who assigned the confessedly drug-addled, fucked-up Doug Johnson to guard duty and returned to find him asleep (and who, gloating, added this grisly crime to his already heinous offenses), to the various chaplains and social workers and doctors and nurses and "members of the correctional staff available" so lovingly described in the Army's Bullshit Paragraph who could "help solve any problems," including those prison guards who stood by and watched Doug being beaten by gangs and watched while a bunch of other no-name prisoners came to his aid, to the Army psychiatrists who didn't listen to his pleas, to whoever it was at Walter Reed who decided that the "malnourished and dependent on drugs" Doug Johnson was physically fit and totally fine for fighting duty in the summer of 1970, to Brigadier General Louis J. Prost, who informed Senator Mansfield, parenthetically, that Doug had been rendered Undesirable for "drug addiction," to the never-named officers of the Army Discharge Review Board who (so they said) took no minutes of their meetings, thus escaping any accountability for denying the reversal of the Undesirable after a year's "consideration," to General Bowers, who in April 1973, deferring to this same Army Review Board (which did not take a year this time around), denied the request to change the General Discharge Under Honorable Circumstances to an Honorable discharge, to the commanding officer, General Burke of the 3rd Battalion, 12th Infantry (who ignored Paul Kleinwachter's reasoned recommendations for the kind of discharge routinely handed out to alcoholics, and who may also have ignored a psychiatrist's similar recommendation), who, according to his own statement, had seen and reprimanded this filthy, disobedient kid—to these men, twenty-year-old Douglas Johnson was nothing but cannon fodder in a fight meant—in the words of the President of the United States—to do nothing more than "Buy Time."

And there he is, Doug Johnson, along with others, their faces grainy in the pages of *Time* magazine. "At an airstrip in South Viet Nam Central Highlands, US 4th Infantry troopers await helilift to join Operation Pacify One aimed at rooting North Vietnamese troops out of a rugged base area in NE Cambodia." Yeah, Doug Johnson, the guy, second from left, the one with the head covering and the big grin, flashing the peace sign in that single instant when his life intersected with the camera of an Italian photographer. The Army didn't give a shit if this grunt was strung out on heroin, buzzing on speed, blithering about a note from a doctor. Adios, asshole! Put a weapon in that fucker's hands, put his butt on a chopper, and up he goes! Roll up your sleeve, find a nice fat vein, close your eyes, shoot some speed, chase it with a little heroin, drop yourself another little candy-colored tab and there you go, man! You're ready! Hello Cambodia! Jump out into the jungle, prime your weapon and kill the Cong! You're on point! Your helmet strapped tight, your bayonet poking through other people's jungles, and of course, you're scared shitless! If it looks like you're fixing to die, guess what? Whoopee! You are! But what the hell, man! You'll never know what hit you, you'll think it's just a great fucking trip, and—hey, who knows—maybe it is! Someone's got to do it! Right? So bend over and kiss your ass goodbye. If the Cong don't kill you, then the opium will.

Coda: Peggy and Bill

One letter that went out on my brother's behalf is not among the documents unearthed from the safe. I know about this letter because my mother told me that she, personally, had written to Bob Hope, the comedian and entertainer. Hope had been doing USO tours as far back as the Second World War, and in the Vietnam era he brought an array of musicians, singers, and show folk to entertain the troops. He was renowned and beloved for raising soldiers' spirits in faraway military outposts. Peggy Johnson wrote to Bob Hope touting the talents of her wonderfully musical, piano-prodigy son, imploring him to take Doug out of the 4th Infantry and include him with the musicians of the USO tours. She waited for months for a reply, but none ever came.

As a result, my mother developed an intransigent animosity against Bob Hope. For the rest of her life, if Bob Hope came on the television, she would leave the room. Moreover, she passed this prejudice on to the rest of us. Though my own inherited grievance against him slowly waned, to this day whenever I see Bob Hope or read a reference to him, I reflexively think: *My brother went through hell and my mother's heart was broken.*

Peggy Johnson hovers over this book like a ghost, present because she saved everything, present because she typed everything (except that one carefully handwritten note to Jerry Pettis), but it's my father's insistent, oratorical voice that rises from the pages while she remains unheard. Those few documents that have her handwriting on them are mere organizational notes, occasionally bringing something to Dad's attention; they indicate nothing about how she actually felt. In his desperate letters of summer 1970, Bill wrote to Mendel Rivers, "My wife is on the verge of a complete nervous breakdown." It's the only insight he gives us as to Peggy's pain or her way of handling it.

In general, Peggy Johnson handled pain, hurt, and anger by concealing these emotions under politeness. How she truly felt could not always be discerned. Until the last year of her life when dementia unleashed her, she kept things locked up or picketed with euphemisms.

For her one hundredth birthday in 2022, I arranged to have privately printed a book of her memoirs. She wrote about the years 1969 to 1972, brutal, demanding as they were, in two paragraphs:

I can truthfully state that 1969 was the worst year of my life. To begin with, there was a terrible flood in Southern California that year, an ominous beginning. Doug, my oldest son was sent to Vietnam in the US Army, 4th Infantry, and my daughter, Helen, a teenager was very seriously ill with Crohn's Disease and had several surgeries. It was day-and-night worry. After going to bed at night, I would wake up in three or four hours, lie awake wondering if I had awakened because something awful was happening to my son. Hard getting back to sleep. My daytime life was seeing my beautiful, sweet daughter suffer surgeries—with no guarantees of her eventual health. To lighten this tense era, one day Bill brought me a small gift of an Authentic Worry Stone—a 2-inch long, 1/4-inch high onyx stone with a smooth round dip in the middle. On the back it said something like, "For best results, depress thumb slowly in round area." I still smile when I see this little worry stone on my desk. My prayers were answered and both of them survived. I will leave it there, but I prefer not to refer to 1969 again. Too painful.

However, I feel that a brief summary of that year should perhaps be mentioned. In Vietnam Doug used drugs to help him do the required jungle hand-to-hand fighting with long knives; he walked point in dense, enemy infested jungles. In Vietnam, he was hospitalized for malaria. They sent him home to us at age twenty-one—a drug addict with an undesirable discharge—no veterans' benefits.

In putting her book together for the printer, I read right past "undesirable discharge." I thought "undesirable discharge" was a euphemism. That's how little I knew of what had really gone down. Her paragraph continues (italics are hers):

PTSD is very real. We gave him medical, mental and rehab care over long periods of time. Bill was so outraged at the discharge he started writing letters to the US Army in Washington, DC requesting that the discharge be changed. They refused. He did not give up, just kept refuting their allegations as if he were a trained attorney, with evidence of newspaper clippings and even a photo of Doug and his unit in Time Magazine. (Doug was in the front row.) After three years of letter writing, the discharge was reversed—with full veterans' benefits. *It was Bill's shining hour. He did what everyone said was impossible.* With these veteran's benefits, Doug was finally able to recover from the drugs and PTSD.

No mention that it took thirty years.

. . .

My parents bore these burdens together, but otherwise alone. When they sought character references for Doug in the summer of 1970 before the second court-martial they would have been obliged to say something of Doug's circumstances, *why* they were requesting letters to be sent to Doug's attorney, Captain Paul Kleinwachter. Other than that, I can't imagine either of them actually explaining to a friend or neighbor in San Bernardino the depth, the extent of their son's troubles. Indeed, my dad's October 12, 1970, thank-you note to those who wrote character references is carefully worded. It conveys *a* truth about Doug's final months in Vietnam, if not *the* truth. "Thanks mainly to the good character references, all charges were dropped . . . and he was cleared. He has now completed his Army enlistment. He plans to work until next semester and then register for school."

Bill Johnson might have boldly written of "shame and trepidation" in his letters, but these are not emotions of which he would have willingly spoken. Not to anyone. Sharing emotions was not his strong suit. In San Bernardino, Bill had a wide array of professional associates, but no one with whom he might have confided the true nature of his son's travails. In these years, he was probably closer, more open with Jerry Pettis than anyone other than his wife. My father had no family in Southern California. They were all scattered across the Northwest and, anyway, his contact with them was minimal.

As it turned out, my mother was equally bereft. Although the Kalpakians—her widowed mother, her three sisters, and their families—all lived in Southern California, they proved no support or ballast for her.

When my Kalpakian grandparents arrived in America in 1923, they resolutely closed the door on the past, never referring to the losses or trials they had endured in Turkey during the Great War or the Armenian Genocide. The only element of their past to escape this erasure was Armenian food. Settling in Los Angeles, they resolved to speak only English in the home so that their children could more quickly prosper in school. (This vow was the more remarkable given that my grandfather spoke no English at all.) My grandparents became actual US citizens in 1931, but they became American with all possible haste. Eager to adopt cheerful American attitudes, they seldom alluded to sadness, sorrow, bad judgment, or even bad taste. Or perhaps their reluctance to acknowledge anything amiss was a reflex learned in their early lives as Armenians living in Turkish cities where, ideally, one remained inconspicuous. In any event, it's an instinct my sister and I dubbed How Nice Dear and they passed this mindset down the Kalpakian genetic IV drip and into new generations.

After Doug's return, as his problems (physical and psychiatric) became known to the extended family, my grandmother asked my mother if Doug was on drugs. Peggy broke down and wept and the whole tale came tumbling out. My grandmother's only response was something along the lines of "Ah." No offer of solace or empathy. Just "Ah." A drug addict in this American family? Absolutely outside the perimeters of the possible.

My mother told me this story. Sadly, she felt the sting of this shame, this humiliation, for the rest of her life. Of my mother's three sisters, only the youngest reached out to her amid this suffering, offering a loan. My mother thanked her, but declined. Ever after, among the extended Kalpakian family, it was generally agreed upon that no one asked after Doug. And no one did. Peggy Johnson felt always that she had failed where her parents and her sisters had succeeded. They all had successful children, fine, tidy lives, unplundered incomes. But the Johnsons? Their finances were devastated by medical and psychiatric bills. Their son was ravaged by drugs and tortured by searing memories of war; he had unpredictable rages and mental breakdowns sometimes requiring hospitalization.

But Peggy Johnson was not wholly alone through this ordeal. Helen's home tutor had her reading some John Steinbeck, books my sister liked. Helen asked Mom if she liked Steinbeck and Mom, who grew up in Depression-era Los Angeles, confessed to an urban prejudice against his work. (Steinbeck was, of course, associated with the Okies pouring into California during the Depression). But she agreed with Helen that this was an ancient, unthinking prejudice and so she read *Cannery Row*. From that and the equally charming *Sweet Thursday*, she moved to the great, the enduring tomes: *The Grapes of Wrath*, *Of Mice and Men*, *In Dubious Battle*, *East of Eden*. As she waded further and deeper into Steinbeck's work and life, she quit getting the books from the library. She bought them all. Bought multiple paperback copies. Pressed these books into the hands of unbelievers, or even the merely indifferent, saying, *Steinbeck is a wonderful writer. Here is a book you will love. Read.* She sent them to Doug in Vietnam. She sent them to me in Delaware.

But her conversion was not an altogether literary experience. Into the daily vortex of anxiety, dread, her daughter's unexplained illness, the possibility of her son's death in a distant jungle, in 1969 and 1970 there came into my mother's life the austere presence of John Steinbeck. Steinbeck's rolling prose became for her a kind of Holy Writ. He knew struggle; he recognized sorrow. In these years my mother found herself like Steinbeck's beleaguered Okies, overwhelmed by forces she did not understand and could not control. When she read that Steinbeck's son had been in Vietnam, she knew that he understood. In some strange way, John Steinbeck stood at her side. A grizzled ghost.

Books by and about John Steinbeck always had their own shelf in any house Peggy Johnson lived in, including her room in the nursing home. She was always a dedicated reader, and in old age her failing vision was a source of anguish. For two years I would go nearly every afternoon to the nursing home and read to her; this was a pleasure and connection for both of us.

But in 2023, the last year of Peggy Johnson's life, dementia advanced in frightening leaps. She sank into troughs of sadness and rose on great waves of anger. As her ability to process information diminished, she gave up watching TV, even her favorite MSNBC, because she couldn't understand what was being said. She concocted vast, weird conspiracies that she could not be talked out of. Peggy Johnson—the most polite person on the planet—would lash out at the nursing home staff or other residents. In the midst of this decline, she asked me to read Steinbeck. She did not ask for *The Grapes of Wrath*, but for lighter fare, *Tortilla Flat* (a book I, frankly, detested). Finishing that, we moved on to his 1961 travelogue of his cross-country journey with his dog, *Travels with Charley*. As her dementia deepened, I read to her very slowly so that she could process the words, the info. Sometimes she asked me to reread whole paragraphs, whole chapters again and again. For *Travels with Charley*, that was fine; the book is tinged with Steinbeck's melancholia, but it's benign. But then we moved on to the sunlit California stories in *The Long Valley*. This was a book I had not read. When I came to *The Red Pony*, the penultimate story, I did not know the gruesome animal cruelties that abound throughout, scenes all the more appalling because Steinbeck is such a vivid writer. Especially horrific was death of the pony where the boy fights off an attack of swarming buzzards plucking at its eyes. I could not bring myself to inflict these awful images on my mom, who was already given to inexplicable, intense bouts of fury or sadness. I elided some of the worst of these, but she insisted that I read the same grisly passages over and over. By the time I came to the end of *The Red Pony*, she had worked herself into a froth, claiming that I had changed the ending. Finally I just said flatly that I wasn't going to read it again, and if she had a problem with *The Red Pony*, she should take it up with Steinbeck. And I left.

I returned the next day to find her still angry. She announced she had found someone else to read to her, to read *The Red Pony* properly. I asked who that person might be and she said, "I'm not telling you." So perhaps the curmudgeonly, solemn loner, John Steinbeck, once again came to her, brought her solace in her hour of need. After that she refused my every offer to read to her again, even so much as an article from *Time* magazine, and our visits became shorter and more strained.

. . .

My father's dementia took a different route. He had double-bypass heart surgery in his eighties. It took him a year to recover and, shortly after that, he had a stroke. It wasn't totally debilitating, but he was never the same. After 2006 he had diminished mobility and deepening dementia. Mom looked after him for five years, at the cost of her own health and well-being.

In those years my dad was alternately very cranky and very easy to please, as a child is easy to please. The nicest thing anyone could do for him—the thing that made him beam—was to bring him a stack of yellow legal pads, a batch of ballpoint pens, and bottles of Wite-Out, which he used on everything (including the furniture), because he once again began writing. He wrote long, loopy "poems" (lacking meter, but not heart), "An Ode to _____," extolling the merits of his grandsons and others, long odes about "The Quest for Knowledge," and other inscrutable undertakings. His most famous poem, "Why," includes the line, "Why do I have 17 billion miles of DNA? I could probably get by fine with three . . ." These lines cracked us up. Bear and Brendan set these immortal lyrics to music, and performed the song for him. My mother dutifully entered various drafts of these poems into the computer, printed them and made copies. He would autograph these and dole them out repeatedly and advise my mother to mail them to various and sundry, along with long nonsensical letters he continually wrote.

As his vision faded, he gave up pens and wrote with markers. He scrawled on the legal pads, often writing the same thing over and over and over, particularly certain phrases he was fond of. His favorite, repeated wistfully, was "The drama of a dream." He also liked big, important words like "perspicacious," and he would use a magnifying glass to look them up in the dictionary and the markers to write the definitions on lampshades or walls or the pillowcases.

In summer 2011, at age ninety-three, he grew very weak and would not eat; he could not get out of his chair without falling. Mom and I called in hospice. They were wonderful to us, kind, considerate, filling out forms in two hours that would have taken me two weeks to understand. That very day, hospice moved him to a nursing home. We believed him to be within days of death, but with the care he got at the nursing home he lived for another fourteen months. The staff called him the Comeback Kid. I made CDs for him of his favorite trumpet pieces, music he had played as a boy. Music and ice cream made him happy. My mom went nearly every day to see him, usually at lunchtime, often feeding him.

He died peacefully early one morning on Labor Day weekend in 2012 at age ninety-four. The nursing home called me. It was not a surprise; he had seemed unresponsive the day before. With my younger son, Brendan, who was visiting, I went to my mom's house with this news. She paled, but she did not cry.

Brendan and I were making breakfast when Doug telephoned, chirping out, "Hello, Mary Sunshine!" mistaking my voice for hers. I corrected him, but I did not say why I was there on a Sunday morning. Mom took the phone and went into the bedroom. When she came out, she had been crying.

The following weekend we were a small group gathered at a country graveyard in the September sunshine, shaded by towering poplars. Doug and his third wife were not with us. My mother might have been willing to max out her credit cards on Doug's behalf, but she was ninety years old, bone-exhausted from years of caretaking, and she knew she did not have the strength to deal with Dad's death and with Doug. Nor did any of the rest of us.

Bill Johnson's coffin was carried to the graveside by my brother Brian, my sons, Bear and Brendan, and Brendan's best friends, Sean and Tyler. We sat on folding chairs, my mom on one side of me, my sister Helen on the other, Brian beside Mom. We faced the grave, where the coffin was covered with an American flag. Bill Johnson's Navy service in the Pacific Theater in World War II meant that the Veterans Administration sent an honor guard to his funeral: three young people, two men and a woman, uniformed, stoic, serene, expressionless. They stood at attention. An anodyne pastor offered Christian words of comfort. I gave the eulogy, speaking of my dad's frontier Idaho youth, the values he placed on education and family, what we, his children and grandchildren, admired about him and had learned from him. I spoke, too, of his finest hour—using that very phrase—his fight to get Doug's discharge changed from a General to an Honorable. After I finished and sat down, one of the uniformed soldiers took up a trumpet and played "Taps." I got all misty and choked back tears. With practiced precision, the other two soldiers took the flag from the coffin, folded it ceremonially, and gave it to my mother with a salute.

Twice a year, Memorial Day and Veterans Day, the staff at this cemetery place a small American flag by my father's headstone, as they do for all veterans buried there. The Veterans Administration paid for his headstone. It notes William Jess Johnson's name, his birth date (March 1, 1918), his death date (September 2, 2012), his rank in the Navy during World War II, pharmacist's mate. The VA told us we could put one short last line on the marker. We chose:

Hero To Family

Timeline

1969

January 17: Douglas Scott Johnson (DSJ, born January 19, 1950) enlists in
the Army.

January to May: Basic Training, Fort Ord, California.

May and early June: Fifteen days' leave at home, San Bernardino,
California.

June 10: DSJ arrives in Vietnam.

June 23 to July 15: Absent Without Leave (AWOL).

July 31 to August 8: AWOL.

August 8 to September 30: Hospitalized for malaria and hepatitis.

September 30 to October 6: AWOL.

October 10: Apprehended on suspicion of possession of marijuana.

October 13 to October 25: Hospitalized.

October 23: Found in an off-limits area. Fined $30 deduction from his
pay.

November 14: Court-martial at which DSJ's rank is reduced and pay cut.
Five months hard labor suspended.

November 26 to December 18: Hospitalized at Nha Trang.

[December 12: DSJ and girlfriend become engaged.]

December 19 to December 25: AWOL after plane crash disrupts
communications and travel.

December 26: Returns to unit and is arrested.

December 26: Shrieking letter.

December 27: Armed guard escort to Long Binh Jail. Put into solitary, "the box."

1970

January 3: Removed from solitary confinement into general prison population.

January 19: Airlifted from Long Binh to hospital in Japan for hepatitis.

February 17 to February 28: "In Transit Assigned to 4th AG Replacement."

February 28 to March 23: Assigned to the 12th Infantry.

April 16 to April 18: AWOL.

April 17 (approximately): Dr. Cantrell handwrites note medically exempting DSJ from combat.

April 18 to April 21: AWOL [on DSJ service records, these are listed as separate infractions].

[April 30 Nixon goes on television to announce invasion of Cambodia]

May 10 to May 15: AWOL (after going into Cambodia).

May 16: Returned to unit. Asleep on guard duty charge added to court-martial offenses.

May 22: CO "recommends that [Doug] be barred from reenlistment in the Regular Army."

May 22 to June 8: AWOL.

[May 25: *Time* magazine article detailing "Operation Pacify One" a.k.a. "Operation Buy Time."]

[June 9: DSJ scheduled to rotate out of VN after serving there for a year.]

June 15 (approximately): Imprisoned.

June 18: William J. Johnson begins his impassioned siege of letters seeking information on DSJ (continues all summer).

July 1 (approximately): DSJ released from LBJ and sent back to his unit at Camp Radcliff.

Early July: Paul Kleinwachter assigned as DSJ's attorney.

July 12: Paul Kleinwachter reaches out to WJJ.

July 19: WJJ replies to Paul Kleinwachter.

July 25: WJJ's long, pleading letter to the court. (Also my letter to Paul on DSJ behalf.)

August 3 to 5: DSJ AWOL.

August 16: Paul Kleinwachter writes to Battalion Commander suggesting a "202" for DSJ.

August 16 to 19: DSJ AWOL (unable to be found for processing-out procedures).

August 20: DSJ's Commanding Officer recommends approval of the applicant's request for discharge (including hygiene comments) "for the good of the service."

August 20: DSJ signs for Undesirable discharge.

August 22: DSJ departs 4th Infantry in Vietnam.

August 23: DSJ arrives McChord Air Force Base, Washington State. WJJ there to meet him.

August 24: Processing out at Fort Lewis.

August 25: Served with Undesirable "for the good of the service" and released from the Army.

POST-ARMY

August 30: DSJ admitted to Loma Linda University Hospital by his parents, stays ten days.

October 16: WJJ writes his multi-recipient letter "The General was not aware . . ."

[Autumn: Inspector General's hearing arranged through Congressman Jerry Pettis.]

October 26: WJJ writes to Paul Kleinwachter seeking whereabouts of Dr. Cantrell.

November: Paul replies with information about Cantrell.

November 29: WJJ writes to Dr. Cantrell via his sister.

December 4: Inspector General's hearing with Colonel Duddy at Fort MacArthur, Los Angeles.

December 8: Dr. Cantrell replies, substantiating DSJ's claims that medically he should never have been sent into Cambodia. WJJ sends on to Inspector General's office, believing the matter to be settled.

December 10: DSJ and WJJ return to Inspector General's office at Fort MacArthur to give follow-up testimony that Doug did not serve under a Captain Hughes.

1971

January: Interim Inspector General's Report (Colonel Hughett): Denied.

February 19: WJJ sends an outraged letter rebutting the Interim denial.

March: Final Inspector General's Report (General Enemark): Denied.

April 19: WJJ sends an even more outraged letter rebutting the Final denial.

April: WJJ creates and sends to the Army Discharge Review Board an elaborate package requesting a change to Honorable.

November 19: DSJ physical at Fort Letterman, San Francisco, pursuant to a Medical discharge. WJJ and DSJ leave convinced that Medical discharge will be granted.

1972

February: Medical discharge denied by Central Physical Evaluation Board of Walter Reed Army Hospital in Washington, DC.

April: Army Discharge Review Board denies request for change to Honorable.

May: Secretary of Defense announces forgiveness for GIs with drug problems.

[June 17: Watergate break-in and arrest of CREEP employees and others.]

June 22: WJJ cold-calls Robert Mardian at his home.

July 3: WJJ sends Robert Mardian a package with thirty-four pages of notes and information.

July 13: Robert Mardian "impressed" and replies that he will forward WJJ's files to K. E. BeLieu.

July 28: Kenneth E. BeLieu, Undersecretary of the Army, will undertake

to get a hearing before the Army Board for Correction of Military
Records. Francis Plant to assist WJJ.

October 5: George Sowa sends his case against reversal to WJJ.

October 13: WJJ asks Robert Mardian to appear personally as lawyer for
DSJ.

October 18: Mardian's peremptory decline.

October 21: WJJ apologizes to Mardian.

[November 7: Presidential election, won by Richard Nixon in a
landslide.]

November 8: Hearing before the Army Board for Correction of Military
Records.

December 18: General Discharge Under Honorable Circumstances
granted.

1973

January and February: WJJ writes thank-you notes to one and all and
sends marble-base pen sets to several.

April: WJJ applies to the Army Board for Correction of Military
Records for an Honorable discharge.

April 18: Army Discharge Review Board denies request.

1974

January 21: WJJ writes to Francis Plant requesting a "a full, honorable
discharge." No reply.

1977

January 1: US Army discontinues Undesirable discharge.

Acknowledgments

The author works alone, but seeing a book into print is a collective enterprise. As part of that collective, especially for this book, I am indebted to my sister Helen and my brother Brian. Thank you, too, Judi Jones for her recollections, her time and care. Affectionate recognition is due to the late Eddie Fenn who was a good friend to Doug for decades. Connie Mann Eggers and Margaret Ann Marchioli contributed SBHS and SBSU info.

Especial gratitude to my agent Pamela Malpas who has supported this project from the beginning. She read several versions and brought her excellent skills, insights and suggestions to the work. I rely on her, and she does not disappoint.

Thank you to Arnold Rochvarg for his thoughts and suggestions and for his book *The Watergate Conspiracy, Conviction and Appeal of Assistant Attorney General Robert Mardian* (2017), which brings clarity to the byzantine complexity of Watergate. Robert Mardian Junior has been generous with his memories of his father and his Armenian family.

Although my parents knew that Paul Kleinwachter lived in Washington, they made no move to contact him after they moved here. Clearly, they could not bear to revisit these painful events. When I began reading the files brought up from the basement and realized Paul's crucial role I reached out to him with an actual letter. My letter went awry, and yet somehow still found him. He replied and has stayed in touch with me over the course of writing this book. I am grateful for his generosity, sharing photos and memories of Camp Radcliff. When I read my father's first letter to Paul, July 1970,

I felt as though he was talking to me from the grave. Hence, the dedication. My dad would have been pleased to see his promise fulfilled.

I have been fortunate in my readers as this work was in progress. Paul Kleinwachter and Arnold Rochvarg both read early versions. Andrea Gabriel, Pam Helberg, Helen Johnson, and Brendan McCreary read near-final drafts and gave me invaluable insights.

The Scribbling Women offered welcome responses on early chapters: Victoria Doerper, Connie Feutz, Frances Howard-Snyder, Carol McMillan, Cami Ostman, Nancy Taylor, Brenda Wilbee.

I am also grateful for the skills, attention, and resources of the University of New Mexico Press in bringing this book to fruition: Elise McHugh, editor, Stephen Hull, director, James Ayers, editorial, design, and production manager, Felicia Cedillos, designer, Anna Pohlod, editor, Don Redpath, sales and marketing manager, Sarena Ulibarri, publicist, Anne Steen, senior marketing associate. Also for the time and care of Katherine Harper, copyeditor, and the two peer review readers who offered welcome thoughts.

Thank you to Kelly at Applied Digital Imaging who gave me the first glimmer of hope that these fragile, fifty-year-old documents could become a book.

About the Author

Laura Kalpakian is the author of five collections of award-winning short fiction and thirteen novels under her own name, published internationally. Her work has been recognized with a National Endowment for the Arts Fellowship in Fiction, a Pushcart Prize, and other honors. She has taught creative writing (fiction and memoir) at University of Washington and Western Washington University. A native Angeleno, she has a BA in history from the University of California, Riverside, and an MA in history from University of Delaware. *Undesirable* is her third work of nonfiction, following *Memory into Memoir: A Handbook for Writers* and *The Unruly Past: Memoirs*. She lives in the Pacific Northwest. Follow her work at laurakalpakian.com.